Science, Politics, and Controversy

Other Titles in This Series

Technological Innovation: The Experimental R&D Incentives Program, edited by Donald E. Cunningham, John R. Craig, and Theodore W. Schlie

Federal Funding of Civilian Research and Development, edited by Michael Michaelis

Ceramic Microstructures '76: With Emphasis on Energy Related Application: Proceedings of the Sixth International Materials Symposium, edited by Richard M. Fulrath and Joseph A. Pask

The State of Science and Research: Some New Indicators, edited by Nestor E. Terleckyj

Flavor: Its Chemical, Behavioral, and Commercial Aspects: Proceedings of the Arthur D. Little Flavor Symposium, April 1977, edited by Charles M. Apt

Technology Transfer to Cities: Processes of Choice at the Local Level, W. Henry Lambright

Valuing Life: Public Policy Dilemmas, edited by Steven E. Rhoads

Westview Special Studies in Science, Technology, and Public Policy

Science, Politics, and Controversy: Civilian Nuclear Power in the United States 1946-1974
Steven L. Del Sesto

This book traces the evolution of civilian nuclear power in the United States between 1946 and 1974, describing and analyzing the commercialization of nuclear energy and surveying pivotal events in the dissension that has recently accompanied its large-scale application. Professor Del Sesto views these events in terms of three themes: federal regulation of advanced technology, the gradual entrance of more diverse interest groups into the political arena, and the problems created by the conflicting claims of experts. He concludes that the lessons of the nuclear debate are most important for their implications for the expanding use of scientific and theoretical knowledge in democratic social orders. More broadly, he writes of the confrontation between knowledge and power that lies at the heart of the growing number of technological controversies that mark late twentieth century industrialized societies throughout the world.

Steven L. Del Sesto, currently assistant professor of science, technology, and society at Cornell University, has taught sociology at the University of Southwestern Louisiana, the Rhode Island School of Design, and the University of Rhode Island.

Science, Politics, and Controversy: Civilian Nuclear Power in the United States, 1946-1974

Steven L. Del Sesto

Routledge
Taylor & Francis Group
LONDON AND NEW YORK

First published 1979 by Westview Press

Published 2019 by Routledge
52 Vanderbilt Avenue, New York, NY 10017
2 Park Square, Milton Park, Abingdon, Oxon OX14 4RN

Routledge is an imprint of the Taylor & Francis Group, an informa business

Library of Congress Catalog Card Number: 79-5227

ISBN 13: 978-0-367-28672-9(hbk)
ISBN 13: 978-0-367-30218-4(pbk)

To Angelo Del Sesto

Contents

Preface

As of June 1977, the United States had some 232 nuclear power plants either planned or in operation, with a generating capacity estimated at about 321 million kilowatts. To date, the industrial world has spent over $200 billion in order to produce useful energy from nuclear fission. By all odds, civilian nuclear power is one of the largest technological ventures in history. To many, this massive effort is completely justified: No other single technology offers as much promise for satisfying world energy needs in the years ahead--particularly as fossil fuels dwindle and climb drastically in price. Yet to others, there is no single technology which raises such serious questions of risk to public health and safety.

Given the world energy situation, it is unlikely that nuclear power development can or will be halted in the near future. Many countries, without the resources of the United States, simply have few adequate alternatives to nuclear power generation, and they will likely push ahead with the nuclear option irrespective of what the United States does. Barring significant technological breakthroughs, there appears little choice but to deal with nuclear power as a fact of life in the remainder of this century. The task, therefore, is not simply deciding how to abolish nuclear power, but rather, deciding how to manage its use in the best interests of humanity. Hopefully, by tracing the story of nuclear power development and its accompanying controversy in the United States, this book will contribute to the realization of that task.

A word also should be mentioned about the time period covered in this study. The 1974 date was selected as a cut-off point for two reasons. The principle reason was that in 1974 the passage of the Energy Reorganization Act--which abolished the Atomic Energy Commission and created the Nuclear Regulatory Commission and the Energy Research and Development Administration--signaled a basic shift in government policy toward nuclear energy regulation and control. While many skeptics believe nothing really changed except the names and the number of agencies involved, the break-up of the AEC's monopoly nevertheless indicated a more pluralistic assessment of nuclear energy development was in the offing. So in a sense, a new "era" of nuclear policy actually began in 1974.

Second, and perhaps more realistically, is that significant spade work with primary source material--such as the work assembled in the "official" nuclear energy histories prepared under the direction of the Department of Energy's chief historian, Richard G. Hewlett--still needs to be done for the post-1974 period. This would be a major study in itself and is clearly beyond the scope of the present work. Thus, much of the story of nuclear energy development in America remains to be written, since the post-1974 period will undoubtedly prove crucial to this story.

Naturally, I have accumulated many debts in the course of writing this book, since no book is an individual effort but a cooperative enterprise. Many people have contributed to the project in one form or another at several points along the way, and though doubtless insufficient considering the value of their contributions, I would like to take this opportunity to acknowledge their help and advice.

Much of the material herein was drawn directly from my doctoral dissertation completed between 1976 and 1978 at Brown University. In the initial stages of the study, I profited a great deal from the many discussions and contributions of my Brown colleagues. Particularly useful and valuable was the insight and advice of A. Hunter Dupree, whose vast knowledge of science policy in the federal government lent great utility in establishing an adequate historical framework in which to view the development of nuclear energy. Dietrich Rueschemeyer also deserves special acknowledgement for his penetrating criticisms of earlier drafts of the manuscript and for his insistence on analytical and organizational clarity. Martin U. Martel and J. Allen Whitt, through careful critical reading various chapters, also provided valuable assistance and advice which influenced the shape and direction of the book, and I am indebted to them for their important contributions. Other Brown colleagues provided various forms of support and encouragement and I would especially like to thank Basil G. Zimmer, Frances Kobrin, and Barbara Anderson. Mark Shields also deserves special thanks for arranging convenient access to the nuclear energy library at Oak Ridge National Laboratory, a resource of obvious value to this work. Finally, without the generous financial support of Brown University during the years 1974-1977, this book would not have been possible.

I would also like to extend thanks to several of my colleagues in the Program on Science, Technology, and Society at Cornell University who have read and commented on various parts of the manuscript. Especially useful were the comments of Ronald Brickman, Michael Pollak, Brendan Gillespie, and Dorothy Nelkin. In addition, I am grateful for the Program's assistance with typing the manuscript and special thanks goes out to Marlene Reitz, Mary Gallagher, and Marilyn White who typed these pages expertly and cheerfully. Amy Fishelson also deserves special acknowledgement for proofreading the manuscript and for making many useful editorial suggestions. Finally, Lis Thorn organized and facilitated the typing and editorial chores, and I am grateful for her help and assistance with these tasks.

The initial research for this project was facilitated by former United States Senator from Rhode Island and Chairman of the Joint Committee on Atomic Energy, John O. Pastore. Senator Pastore and his staff supplied me with several crucial and hard-to-get government reports and documents, including a copy of the hearings on *The Status of Nuclear Reactor Safety* that forms the basis of Chapter Seven, and many other materials which have enriched the study considerably. I am grateful for his help and support in this venture. Also, Rita Campbell and Wayne Range of the Office of Public Affairs of the United States Energy Research and Development Administration directed me toward important survey materials on public acceptance of nuclear power in the United States; and John A. Harris of the Office of Public Affairs of the United States Nuclear Regulatory Commission provided useful information regarding studies of the social effects of nuclear power plants. The study probably would not have progressed beyond the incubation stage without the basic source materials supplied by these people.

Many others have provided various forms of support for this project and I would like to thank my family, Lorne Levinson, Tom and Carol Randall, Janet Zimmer, Judy Perrolle, Mark Elchardus, Bill Mosher, Ian Rockett, Barbara Entwisle, Anneliesse Greenier, Jane Wilkinson, Sue Perry, and Norma MacDonald for their encouragement.

Finally, all the interpretations and views expressed in these pages are my own, and I bear the sole responsibility for any errors and opinions expressed herein.

Steven L. Del Sesto
Ithaca, New York
May 25, 1979

Science, Politics, and Controversy

1
Science, Politics, and Controversy: Introduction and Statement of Purpose

> If the radiance of a thousand suns were to burst at once into the sky, that would be like the splendor of the Mighty One ... I am become death, the destroyer of Worlds.
>
> -J. Robert Oppenheimer

INTRODUCTION

On Tuesday morning at 10 A.M., January 22, 1946, in Room 424B of the Senate Office Building, Brien McMahon, the Freshman Senator from Connecticut, called to order a meeting of a special United States Senate Committee on Atomic Energy. Present were Senators Johnson, Austin, Millikin, Hickenlooper, and Hart. Also present were Dr. Edward U. Condon, science advisor, special counsel James R. Newman, and staff director Christopher T. Boland.[1] After gavelling the meeting to order, Chairman McMahon asked that bill S. 1717, a bill for the development and control of atomic energy in post-War America, be inserted into the record. S. 1717 was the result of nearly a year of intense discussion and debate concerning official United States policy on the future development and control of atomic energy, a policy that was likely to have as much impact on the rest of the world as it would have on the United States.

In this book we are concerned with basically one element of that policy: the events surrounding the development of civilian nuclear power by the United States Government and private industry between the years 1946 and 1974. By viewing these events in terms of three broad dimensions or themes--federal regulation of high-technology, the gradual entrance of more diverse interest groups into the political arena, and the shift of debate from scientific and technical questions to political and ideological issues--we hope to show how the deployment of nuclear reactors became embroiled in bitter controversy by the middle 1970s.

While the lessons of the nuclear controversy are important for their own sake, in a very real sense they are perhaps more important for their implications regarding the expanding use and application of scientific and theoretical knowledge in democratic social orders. Thus the present study is also concerned, broadly speaking, with the relationships between science and politics in the late-twentieth century, as evidenced by the growing number of technical controversies such as the nuclear power debate.[2]

ORGANIZATION AND PLAN OF THE BOOK

The book is divided into three main sections. In the immediately following chapter the events surrounding the formation of the atom's regulatory "subsystem"--the Atomic Energy Commission (AEC) and the Joint Committee on Atomic Energy--are discussed in detail.[3] Chapter Two examines how the quest for what observers called "government control" of nuclear energy culminated in the Atomic Energy Act of 1946, as well as the formation of the AEC and the Joint Committee. For all practical purposes, the 1946 Act provided the rules and policies for nuclear energy development and control, while the AEC and the Joint Committee were seen as the primary administrative and political instruments for achieving these policies. The discussion, in addition, covers some of the policies and programs set forth by the Act, as well as the statutory duties and responsibilities of the AEC and the Joint Committee. Finally, the chapter discusses what "government control" of the atom meant for the future of nuclear energy policy in the United States immediately following the War.

Chapters Three and Four make up the second part of the book, and focus on the development and commercialization of civilian nuclear power in America between the years 1946-1974. Chapter Two examines the 1946-1960 period, the period during which the essential outlines of the present-day reactor programs were institutionalized. The chapter discusses the main features of the AEC's Reactor Development Program, the Five-Year Power

Program and its various Power Reactor Demonstration Programs, and the Ten-Year Civilian Power Reactor Program. The basic thrust is to show how a government-industry "partnership" in nuclear energy resulted from the AEC and Joint Committee's policies of civilian nuclear power development. Finally, some outcomes and consequences of this partnership are discussed.

Chapter Four focuses on the commercialization of civilian nuclear power during the years 1960-1974, the time during which nuclear power was believed to have achieved economic competitiveness with conventional generating technologies. In accomplishing this task, the chapter discusses the AEC's continuing invitiations to industry via the Modified Third Round Power Reactor Demonstration Program and some of the policies which contributed to further industry involvement in nuclear energy development and eventual commercialization. Included here are discussions of the Private Ownership of Special Nuclear Fuels Act of 1963 and the so-called fixed price or "turnkey" plants offered to utilities by General Electric and Westinghouse at bargain prices, hoping to arouse the utilities' interest in the possibilities of nuclear power. The economics of the turnkey plants are evaluated and their impact on the great order surge for nuclear power during 1966-1967 is discussed. In addition, considerable attention is given to the fossil fuel picture in the late 1960s and the early 1960s and the effect rising prices had on the commercial acceptance of nuclear power during this time. Finally, some of the growing problems of licensing and regulating nuclear power are considered, particularly the AEC's safety research program and the problems with gaining external credibility and public confidence.

The third section of the book is comprised of Chapters Five through Seven and discusses the extension of the nuclear debate into what we call the "macropolitical sector," such that groups formerly outside the rather narrowly drawn government-industry structure became increasingly involved in policy-making.[4] Chapter Five begins with the AEC's official public participation procedures in the complex review process as it stood in 1974. The major aim is to show that although the licensing process solicited participation from a diverse number of groups from the macropolitical sector, it framed such participation in terms of devices (i.e., the public hearing) which were responsive primarily to the smooth functioning of policy formation at the regulatory subsystem level. The process not only left citizens with bitter experiences, but suggested an inherent weakness in the regulatory process which appeared preoccupied with promotional efforts.

The evolution of opposition and expansion of groups and issues involved in the debate is chronicled in detail in Chapter Six. It begins with the first interveners in nuclear power cases, the labor unions, and traces the development of conflict through the radiation controversy, the conflict over the disposal of high-level radioactive waste, the enforcement of the requirements of the National Environmental Policy Act of 1969 on to the nuclear power programs, and the criticism of independent scientists evaluating the breeder reactor program and the AEC's Interim Criteria for Emergency Core-Cooling Systems, to name a few highlights.[5] The chapter traces the evolution of concern up to about 1971-1972, when the Joint Committee announced its intentions to reevaluate the entire civilian nuclear program and the status of nuclear reactor safety, the latter representing the subject of the Joint Committee's open public safety hearings held in 1973-1974.

Finally, Chapter Seven uses pro- and anti-nuclear testimony found in the 1973-1974 Congressional hearings--the *Status of Nuclear Reactor Safety*--to show that the expansion of debate into the macropolitical sector by the middle 1970s inevitably expanded the issues far beyond any simplistic conflict. Rather, what was at stake was not simply the deployment of nuclear power reactors, but of two diametrically opposed ideological systems which defined the implementation, significance, and ultimate meaning of nuclear technology within society. Thus we suggest that the nuclear debate had become a political battleground for two opposing views of the "good life": one that favored growth, centralization, and economic independence as the way, and the other which advocated decentralization, moral commitment to future generations, and greater political accountability, among other things.

We conclude the book by suggesting that the current debate appears to rest on a number of factors unique to the development and implementation of nuclear technology; specifically, those factors tied to the problems of federal regulation and rapid commercialization of nuclear power, the limits of subsystem procedures in an expanding political environment, and the shift from scientific and technical questions to political and ideological issues as the controversy broadened across society. The last factor is particularly important because it implies that the meaning and use of nuclear power, by solidifying within more encompassing ideological systems which ultimately define its implementation, is likely to remain a key political issue in the future. In short, the most intense days of the nuclear debate probably are not behind us, but remain to be faced.

NOTES

1. United States Congress, Hearings before the Special Committee on Atomic Energy, *A Bill for the Development and Control of Atomic Energy*, 79th Congress, 2nd Session, 1946 (Washington, D.C.: U.S. Government Printing Office, 1946), p. 1.

2. For some comparative materials, the reader may consult Samuel A. Lawrence, *The Battery Additive Controversy* (Montgomery, Alabama: University of Alabama Press, 1962); Allan Mazur, "Disputes Between Experts," *Minerva* 11 (April 1973): 243-62; Allan Mazur, "Opposition to Technological Innovation," *Minerva* 13 (Spring 1975): 58-81; Dorothy Nelkin, "The Political Impact of Technical Expertise," *Social Studies of Science* 5 (January 1975): 34-54; Paul A. Doty, "Can Investigations Improve Scientific Advice?: The Case of the ABM,"*Minerva* 10 (April 1972): 280-94; and Ian D. Clark, "Expert Advice in the Controversy About Supersonic Transport in the United States," *Minerva* 12 (October 1974): 416-32.

3. Broadly speaking, we use the term "regulation" in the following sense. Regulation of any activity, including nuclear power, attempts to identify and maximize certain "benefits," while at the same time identifying and minimizing anticipated "costs" or harmful side-effects. We usually think of the former as "development," and the latter as "control." Regulation is successful if benefits are maximized with negligible costs; and it is unsuccessful if costs are allowed to outweigh benefits. For a discussion of these points, see Marver Bernstein, *Regulating Business by Independent Commission* (Princeton: Princeton University Press, 1955). See also Allyn D. Strickland, *Regulation: A Case Approach* (New York: McGraw-Hill, 1976).

As for the notion of "regulatory subsystem," it should be pointed out that the politics of regulation are ordinarily rather compact, and consist of the regulated activity, the agency which regulates that activity, the Congressional committee(s) to which the agency is (are) responsible, and the interest groups most directly affected by regulation. Under such an arrangement, policy making is for the most part confined to this political "subsystem" of immediately involved "actors," which claim to represent the broadest possible range of "public" interest. However, the closeness and intimacy of actors in subsystem politics generally produces an overarching consensus which can result in a narrowness and rigidity of policy. Interests outside the subsystem (which the subsystem presumably also represents) become represented only indirectly, promotional efforts often outpace safety and control programs, and the regulatory agencies and Congressional committees which oversee regulatory programs tend to identify their own goals with those of the very parties they are supposed to regulate. These problems, as will be shown in detail below, clearly applied to the regulation of nuclear energy in America. For a discussion of the subsystem concept, see Emmette S. Redford, *Democracy in the Administrative State* (New York: Oxford University Press, 1969). For an earlier attempt to articulate this concept see J. Leiper Freeman, *The Political Process: Executive-Bureau-Legislative Committee Relations* (New York: Doubleday, 1955). For relevant discussions see also W. Henry Lambright, *Governing Science and Technology* (New York: Oxford University Press, 1976) and George Eads and Richard R. Nelson, "Governmental Support of Civilian Technology: Power Reactors and the Supersonic Transport," *Public Policy* 19 (Summer 1971): 405-27. The conflict-of-interest problem is discussed in an insightful article on the railroads and the Interstate Commerce Commission. See Samuel P. Huntington, "The Marasmus of the ICC: The Commission, the Railroads, and the Public Interest," *Yale Law Journal* 62 (December 1952): 171-225.

4. While the sophisticated and esoteric nature of high-technologies such as nuclear power generally confine decision-making to the subsystem level of politics, the ultimate deployment and wide-spread implementation of a given technology always spreads its effects throughout society, affecting a diverse number of individuals and groups. As implementation proceeds, more and more interest groups are affected and attempt to influence decisions through the basic policy machinery of government. The situation then moves away from simple subsystem politics to what Redford calls "macropolitics," where the increased involvement of additional political groups and subsystems eventually forces a shift to "national" policy-making. In such instances, a diversity of political leaders and agencies throughout government as a whole, including courts, state and local government agencies and political representatives from any number of interest groups become increasingly vocal. See Redford, *Democracy and the*

Administrative State, pp. 107-31.

5. For a good discussion of the role of experts in technical controversies see Mazur, "Disputes Between Experts," and Nelkin, "The Political Impact of Technical Expertise."

2

Government Control of the Atom: Defining the Political and Administrative Subsystem of Nuclear Energy Regulation

> Mr. Chairman, and members of the committee, most of the previous witnesses before this special committee have discussed the scientific and technical aspects of the development and control of atomic energy. A knowledge of nuclear physics and engineering alone, however, cannot solve the problem that faces the Nation and the world. At the moment, our national safety and welfare depend more immediately on our legislative and administrative knowledge. It is the administrative aspects of this problem ... that I would like to discuss today ... We must now consider, as your committee is considering, how we may organize the Government in order to control such a force through democratic processes. Only by such control can we protect our safety and enhance our welfare without destroying the freedom of thought and speech which is the foundation of our constitutional system.
>
> -Harold D. Smith

THE CHALLENGE OF THE ATOM: A QUEST FOR GOVERNMENT CONTROL

The Legislative Battle

August 6, 1945:[1]

> Immediately after the bomb was dropped from 31,600 feet, the plane began its getaway maneuver. The flash was seen during this turn and fifty seconds after the drop, the shock waves hit the plane ... five minutes

> after the release a dark gray cloud of some three miles in diameter hung over the center of Hiroshima. Out of the center of this grew a column of white smoke which rose to a height of 35,000 feet.... Four hours after the strike ... most of the city was still obscured by the smoke cloud, although fires could be seen around its edges ... 60 percent of the city was destroyed ... the area devastated at Hiroshima was 1.7 square miles ... the Japanese authorities estimated the casualties at 71,000 dead and missing and 68,000 injured.
>
> August 8, 1945:[2]
>
> The Nagasaki bomb was dropped from an altitude of 29,000 feet ... 44 percent of the city was destroyed ... the greatest area of destruction (was) 2.3 miles (north-south axis) by 1.9 miles (east-west axis). The United States Strategic Bombing Survey later estimated the casualties at 35,000 killed and 68,000 injured.

The two atomic bombs, dropped three days apart, had thus devastated two Japanese cities, killing some 106,000 people and injuring 136,000 others. There could be little question that the atomic bomb was the most lethal weapon ever devised by man. Robert Redfield, the Dean of the Social Sciences at the University of Chicago, ably summed up the potential consequences of this new weapon on January 25, 1946 at the Hearings of the Senate's Special Committee on Atomic Energy:[3] "For the first time in history the necessity to prevent another war is absolute because we can no longer look forward to both war and the preservation of civilization ... now a great war will not leave even the victorious nation with enough to enable it to go forward with the work of civilization." While Redfield seemed to have drawn an overly gloomy picture, he was wholly correct in stressing these potential dangers. The question, however, was not simply describing the awesome power of nuclear energy, but rather, determining how it would be used and controlled in the service and not the destruction of mankind.

Some form of immediate national and international control seemed imperative, for by September 1945, Princeton University Press had already published Dr. Henry D. Smyth's *Atomic Energy for Military Purposes.*[4] The report systematically outlined and made public for the first time the general development of the atomic bomb by the United States Manhattan Engineering District. While the report didn't exactly provide enough scientific and technical information to jeopardize United States military secrets, it nevertheless outlined the basic scientific knowledge used in developing the bomb. As much as anything, though, the release of the report seemed to signify both a growing awareness of the deepening moral responsibility of science in world affairs, and a painful recognition that the United States would not long remain the world's sole producer of atomic weapons. And while Louis Ridenour was busy writing about how an all-out nuclear war could easily be triggered by simple human error,[5] international pressures had already resulted in the creation of the United Nations Atomic Energy Commission, founded in January of 1946.[6] It was apparent, therefore, that nuclear energy's awesome power mandated immediate, if not radical, regulation and control measures by the major powers.

Although there was little question that nuclear energy would require the most extensive technological regulation ever imposed, there seemed little consensus on exactly how it should be done. Indeed, in late-1945 and early-1946, the United States Congress had already been debating several competing regulatory strategies. In its initial stages, the debate focused on whether regulatory powers should be centered in the Congress, in the Executive, in the military, or in a civilian regulatory agency.[7] However, insofar as any consensus existed at all, most spokesmen seemed to agree that the military and international significance of atomic energy mandated some kind of what informed observers called "government control." Dr. Robert M. Hutchins, the Chancellor of the University of Chicago, where a good deal of original experimental work on nuclear energy had been done, aptly summarized this position in January 1946 before McMahon's Special Committee on Atomic Energy:[8]

> ...any legislation in the field of atomic energy *must contemplate an unusual degree of governmental control.* The Government must know all about the developments at all times, because of the international ramifications of any development at any time. This discovery is the most important since the discovery of fire. Its social, economic, military, and

political consequences cannot now be foreseen ... the people of the United States must plan to develop this discovery for the benefit of the world; they must plan to protect the world against it. *This matter is too serious to be left to the casual activities of individual enterprisers.*

A little later in the hearings, Dr. John von Neumann, a mathematical physicist and former consultant to the Los Alamos Laboratory, out of which the first bomb was tested, drew perhaps an even bolder picture for Senator McMahon and his colleagues by suggesting that atomic energy necessitated government control of science itself:[9]

It is for the first time that science has produced results which require an immediate intervention of the Government. Of course, science has produced many results before which were of great importance to society, directly or indirectly. And there have been before scientific processes which required some minor policy measures by the Government. But it is for the first time that a vast area of research, right in the central part of the physical sciences, impinges on a broad front on the vital zone of society, and clearly requires rapid and general regulation. It is now that physical science has become "important" in that painful and dangerous sense which causes the state to intervene... The legislation on atomic energy represents the first attempt in history to regulate science in this sense. In the past wartime and peacetime emergencies, governments did influence various phases of the social effort, including science, in order to promote military or economic ends. However, such efforts were always limited in time and in scope, and directed toward some ulterior, independent purpose. It is only now that science as such and for its own sake has to be regulated, that science has outgrown the age of its independence from society.

Yet exactly what Hutchins and von Neumann meant by the term "government control" was far from clear. As the situation stood in 1945-1946, government control meant authority vested primarily in the Executive branch of the government. To be sure, this arrangement would have to be altered, since in an area pervaded with inflexible concerns of national security and a high degree of secrecy, the normal democratic processes of discussion, debate, and open investigation would be hampered. Thus, the nature and meaning of government control had to be spelled out clearly by the Legislative branch of the government.

The members of the United States Congress were not oblivious to these concerns; in fact, there were already several legislative strategies afoot in Congess shortly after the successful strikes at Hiroshima and Nagasaki in August. On September 6, 1945, Senators McMahon of Connecticut and Vandenberg of Michigan, perhaps coincidently, both introduced measures in the Senate dealing with atomic energy regulation. McMahon's bill, if it could be called that, was little more than a slapdash effort which proposed creation of an atomic energy control board comprised mainly of Cabinet members and other federal officials. Vandenberg's measure, on the other hand, called for establishing a joint Congressional investigative committee.[10] Meanwhile, the War Department, at the urgings of Secretary of War, Henry L. Stimson, had already drafted a detailed bill outlining its own proposals and recommendations. It was unclear, however, whether the measure--known as the Royal-Marbury Bill--would gain a favorable reception in Congress, and its sponsors contacted Congressional leaders concerning the most efficient means of introducing it to the nation's lawmakers.[11]

Senator Alben W. Barkley and Speaker of the House Sam Rayburn suggested that the bill's proponents contact the ranking member of the Military Affairs Committee in the Senate, Senator Edward C. Johnson, as well as Representative Andrew J. May, Chairman of the House committee. This the proponents did, and on October 3 Representative May introduced the War Department's measure in the House, with the bill being promptly referred to his committee by Speaker Rayburn. The next day, Senator Johnson introduced the resolution in the Senate, but was prevented from committee referral on the objection of Senator Vandenberg. Vandenberg insisted that before the Senate consider the War Departments bill--now called the May-Johnson Bill--the House should first act on his pending legislation calling for a joint Congressional committee on atomic energy, a resolution which the Senate had already passed on September 27.[12]

While Vandenberg's parliamentary maneuvering had succeeded in killing the May-Johnson Bill for immediate consideration in the Senate, May-Johnson did seem to be moving smoothly through the House. Indeed, by the middle of the committee hearings on the bill, Representative May anticipated little difficulty in reporting it back to the House at the end of the first week. Yet beneath the seemingly smooth flow of events loomed some rather important considerations. For one thing, it had become apparent that May-Johnson placed heavy emphasis on military control of atomic energy, a move that would certainly not appear consistent with the United States international pledges to develop the atom for peaceful purposes and to restrain and eliminate its military uses. In addition, the bill seemed overly preoccupied with security and placed heavy restrictions on scientific research, a provision which had been annoying scientists since the Manhattan Project and General Groves' iron-handed security restrictions. Many angered scientists subsequently organized their efforts against the May-Johnson Bill and turned out to be effective lobbyists in later defeating the proposal. Thus, the mounting criticism during the last few weeks in October indicated that a long and arduous debate was in store.[13]

With the proceedings all but hopelessly deadlocked in both the Senate and House of Representatives, Senator McMahon's October 4 suggestion of establishing a special Senate committee became more promising, and by October 23, his resolution was adopted. The committee would consist of eleven members, with McMahon as its chairman. Initially, its purpose would be primarily educational: the committee would make a thorough study of atomic energy and consider all resolutions and bills related to it. In the months ahead, McMahon's special committee would devote detailed discussion and study to nearly all conceivable aspects of atomic energy. Innumerable consultations would be made with scientists, engineers, high-ranking military officials, and with key members of President Truman's staff and cabinet.[14]

However, the most important considerations facing McMahon's committee during the last days of 1945 seemed to be organizational ones: what administrative methods should be used to control the atom? Morgan Thomas organizes these considerations into five broad categories:[15] (1) whether the control agency should be predominantly civilian or military; (2) whether the agency should be allowed extreme independence or possess departmental status directly subservient to the President; (3) whether to adopt a commission-form of control agency or a single administrator; (4) what should be the role of laymen versus specialists, i.e., atomic scientists, engineers, and technicians; and (5) whether a Congressional committee system roughly comparable to the ordinary pattern or special committee arrangements ought to be established.

Meanwhile, by December 1945 it seemed clear that "the combined forces of senators, scientists, and members of the President's official family had succeeded in blocking the Army's attempt to ram the May-Johnson Bill through Congress."[16] The opponents of May-Johnson had expressed several misgivings about the bill, but James R. Newman, special counsel to the McMahon Committee and later instrumental in drafting what was to become the Atomic Energy Act of 1946, perhaps best summed up the general tenor of criticism. He pointed out that May-Johnson over-emphasized the military uses of atomic energy while slighting its potentially more valuable civilian applications. He felt the civilian applications should be more heavily emphasized and that they would buoy a more realistic United States policy. As he expressed it:[17]

> This new force offers enormous possibilities for improving public welfare, for revamping our industrial methods and for increasing the standard of living. Properly developed and harnessed, atomic energy can achieve improvement in our lot equalling and perhaps exceeding the tremendous accomplishments made possible through the discovery and use of electricity.

At the same time, scientists all over America had interpreted the May-Johnson Bill as a stumbling block to independent research and free inquiry. The scientists' outrage had not been helped any when General MacArthur's forces seized three cyclotrons from Japanese universities and dumped the valuable research instruments into the Pacific Ocean on November 25. As indeed it must have appeared to the scientists, the Army apparently intended to monitor atomic energy research with the same firm hold which the Manhattan Project had exercised throughout the War. It was perhaps these kinds of actions that prompted physicist Harold Urey to remark the month before at Columbia University that the May-Johnson Bill was the "first totalitarian bill ever written by the Congress ... You can call it either a Communist bill or a Nazi bill, whichever you think is worse."[18]

Thus, by mid-December the May-Johnson proposal seemed inextricably mired in Congress when McMahon finally introduced for consideration in the Senate his Committee's candidate for the new nuclear energy legislation: Bill S. 1717, "A Bill for the Development and Control of Atomic Energy." However, it would take more than eight highly charged months of debate, discussion, and revision in both the Senate and House of Representatives before S. 1717 would become law as the Atomic Energy Act of 1946.

Perhaps the major point of disagreement during this eight month period concerned the role of the military. As far as the opponents of the McMahon Bill were concerned, the military had not been given enough authority by the measure. After all, they argued, so far the only proven application of nuclear energy had been as a military weapon. On what grounds, therefore, could the measure provide the military only a minor role in the nuclear energy field?

Critics were also openly concerned with the handling of patents and the dissemination of scientific and technical information. The patent issue was subjected to especially heavy attack in the House, with opponents claiming the bill would transform the free-enterprise system into a socialist or communist regime. Representative Forest A. Harness, for example, criticized the bill for placing "in the hands of a five-man commission complete and absolute authority over American industry and the lives of the entire population." He claimed that the compulsory licensing of patents would destroy "one of the fundamentals of the free-enterprise system under a free government." Still another Representative, Clare Booth Luce, characterized the patents section of S. 1717 as "politically revolutionary," and that it "might have been written by the most ardent Soviet Commisar."[19]

Finally, critics of the bill questioned the sections dealing with control of information. While most spokesmen seemed to support the idea of the freedom of scientific information, they were not in favor of removing all security provisions and criminal penalties. As the bill stood, there seemed no adequate measures to prevent revealing secrets whose disclosure might prove inimical to the national security. Decidedly overstating his case, Representative J. Parnell Thomas nevertheless declared:[20] "If you want to get the cue of who is pushing hard for the passage of this bill, read the Daily Worker. . . or read, in the New York papers of last week, the suggestion of the Russian delegate Andrei H. Gromyko."

Despite these criticisms and several amendments offered by members of the House, the main issues in contention were ultimately negotiated and compromised in the House and Senate throughout the spring and early summer of 1946, and on July 26, 1946 both houses accepted a compromised version of the original McMahon Bill. Six days later on August 1, President Truman signed the measure into law as the Atomic Energy Act of 1946.[21] Thus began the first systematic effort by the United States Government to develop and control atomic energy. Indeed, it looked as if a new era in science-government relations had arrived.

THE ATOMIC ENERGY ACT OF 1946 AND THE REGULATORY SUBSYSTEM OF THE ATOM

Purposes and Policies of Atomic Energy Development and Control: The Statutory Delineations

Now that the legislative battle had been waged, the Atomic Energy Act of 1946 laid out the United States first domestic national policy of nuclear energy development and control. Its essence may be extracted from the first few lines of the Act, "FINDINGS AND DECLARATION:"[23]

> Section 1. (a) FINDINGS AND DECLARATION.--Research and experimentation in the field of nuclear fission have attained the stage at which the release of atomic energy on a large scale is practical. The significance of the atom bomb for military purposes is evident. The effect of the use of atomic energy for civilian purposes upon the social, economic, and political structures of today cannot now be determined. It is reasonable to anticipate, however, that tapping this new source of energy will cause profound changes in our

present way of life. Accordingly, it is hereby declared to be the policy of the people of the United States that the development and utilization of atomic energy shall be directed toward improving the public welfare, increasing the standard of living, strengthening free competition among private enterprises so far as practicable, and cementing world peace.

Having made this declaration of policy, the Act proposed in its next section, "PURPOSE OF ACT," six major programs to "effectuate these policies:"[24]

> (b) PURPOSE OF ACT.--It is the purpose of this Act to effectuate these policies by providing, among others, for the following major programs:
> (1) A program of assisting and fostering private research and development on a truly independent basis to encourage maximum scientific progress;
> (2) A program for the free dissemination of basic scientific information and for maximum technical information;
> (3) A program of federally conducted research to assure the Government of adequate scientific and technical accomplishment;
> (4) A program for Government control of the production, ownership, and use of fissionable materials to protect the national security and to insure the broadest possible exploitation of the field;
> (5) A program for simultaneous study of the social, political, and economic effects of the utilization of atomic energy; and
> (6) A program of administration which will be consistent with international agreements made by the United States, and which will enable the Congress to be currently informed so as to take further legislative action as may hereafter be appropriate.

In additon to its specification of these policies and programs, the Act contained sixteen other sections which set forth provisions for the creation of the Atomic Energy Commission (AEC) and the Joint Committee on Atomic Energy; guidelines for research and development; requirements for the production of fissionable materials and their control; provisions for military applications of atomic energy; the requirements necessary to own and operate atomic energy devices; guidelines for patents and dissemination of basic scientific and technical information; specifications of the authority, general organizational subdivisions, and property of the AEC and conditions of enforcement, reporting, and financial support for carrying out the provisions of the Act.[25]

Besides stipulating this declaration of policy, the Act also established the major administrative and political elements--or what we have called the regulatory subsystem--of nuclear energy regulation in the form of the AEC and the Joint Committee on Atomic Energy. We turn now to a brief discussion of the purposes and functions of these administrative and legislative bodies.

The Civilian Regulatory Arm: The Atomic Energy Commission

To oversee and supervise these new atomic energy policies, the 1946 Act made provisions for a civilian body in the form of the Atomic Energy Commission, one of the primary elements of government control of the atom.[26] The framers of the Act had decided that a five-man commission would be better suited than a single administrator to the basic processes of policy formulation in nuclear energy regulation, since in an area so important in national defense and security the perspective of a single administrator would be too limited. Moreover, commission regulation was more likely to result in greater presentation of alternative viewpoints, more wide-ranging and specialized expertise, and increased impartiality and insulation from the cumbersome machinery of interest group politics.[27]

Yet with several programs already in progress, including the immense activities of the Manhattan Engineering District, there was an undeniable need for coordination and managerial skills. The Act therefore created the Office of General Manager, appointed by the President, to coordinate the AEC's various programs: military and national security programs, biomedical research and development, civilian power programs, production of fissionable materials, physical research programs, and others.[28] Each of these programs had its own director, all of whom were responsible for reporting directly to the General Manager, as well as to the appropriate military officials when developments in their areas seemed to have military significance. Since contact was often on a personal basis and communication direct, general operations decisions and policies could be made informally.29 While the General Manager and the Commission as a whole of course had the final authority, the program directors were generally quite autonomous, and paper directives from above were rare.

Besides the program divisions, the Act created several management officials to supervise management policies and staff work. These offices included security and intelligence, budgets, general council, public and technical information service, administrative operations, organization and personnel, and comptroller.[30] Similar to the program directors, management directors were free to communicate between themselves in establishing directives by more or less informal means but nevertheless remained under the direct authority of the General Manager and Commission.

As for the supervision of the AEC's on-going operations, this responsibility was delegated to the managers of the field offices, organized on a functional basis. Niehoff describes their duties as follows:[31]

> They are responsible for the supervision of the AEC field organizations which negotiate contracts and provide policy direction, control, and assistance within the broad framework of commission policy to research, engineering, production, construction, and other contractors who do almost all of the actual operational work of the commission.

In addition, the field managers possessed nearly full authority in personnel appointment, and where appropriate, they were permitted to issue licenses and take other administrative actions necessary in dispensing their functions.[32] Hence, they played a central role in helping formulate overall Commission policy even though they worked out of decentralized offices.

The General Manager, the program directors, the management directors, and the field managers, usually working together in some combination, were therefore essential components in the program and policy-making function of the Commission. Depending on the nature of the agenda, several of the above would meet in bi-weekly (or more) sessions to discuss and formulate policy and programs, which were then submitted to the entire five-man Commission for review.[33] More often than not, the Commission approved these staff recommendations, indicating its confidence in the staff's general procedures and suggestions.[34]

The Act also created several important advisory bodies to assist the AEC with specialized problems, particularly those of scientific and technical nature. To a greater extent than most rapidly developing technologies, nuclear energy was fraught with many highly complicated scientific, technical, and engineering problems that a civilian commission could never handle alone. In order to relieve this situation, the Act created a body known as the General Advisory Committee (GAC) to provide the AEC with scientific and technical guidance and advice, which allowed the Commission increased flexibility and greater opportunity to concentrate on basic policy matters. The function of the GAC was spelled out in the Act this way:[35]

> There shall be a General Advisory Committee to advise the Commission on scientific and technical matters relating to materials, production, and research and development, to be composed of nine members, who shall be appointed from civilian life by the President.

Furthermore, the 1946 Act recognized the extent and complexity of the Commission's military programs, perhaps the AEC's most pressing responsibilities at that time. Provisions were made for a Military Liaison Committee (MLC) as an advisory body to the Commission to help with the AEC's extensive military duties. The status of the MLC was clearly specified by the Act:[36]

> There shall be a Military Liaison Committee consisting of representatives of the Department of War and Navy ... The Commission shall advise and consent with the Committee on all atomic energy matters which the Committee deems to relate to military applications, including the development, manufacture, use, and storage of bombs, the allocation of fissionable materials for military research, and the control of information relating to the manufacture or utilization of atomic weapons. The Commission shall keep the Committee fully informed of all such matters before it, and the Committee shall keep the Commission informed of all atomic activities of the War and Navy Departments. The Committee shall have the authority to make written recommendations to the Commission on matters relating to military applications from time

to time as it may deem appropriate.

By creating the MLC as an advisory body within the AEC, the framers of the Act attempted to have their cake and eat it too; that is, the military aspects of atomic energy were incorporated into the atomic energy programs without divesting the AEC of civilian control.[37]

Finally, the Commission established several of its own advisory committees to assist in the more complex and highly specialized areas encompassed by its activities. These included:[38]

1) The Advisory Committee for Biology and Medicine
2) The Advisory Committee for Exploration and Mining
3) The Patent Administration and Patent Advisory Panel
4) The Industrial Advisory Group
5) The Safety and Industrial Advisory Board
6) The Advisory Board on the Relationships of the Atomic Energy Commission with Its Contractors
7) The Committee on Scientific Personnel
8) The Committee on Isotope Distribution

Having briefly outlined the AEC's administrative and organizational machinery, we turn now to a consideration of its duties in the nuclear energy field as stipulated by the 1946 Act. Probably the most notable point was that the AEC was given almost a total monopoly in atomic energy development: it was authorized to make whatever arrangements it deemed appropriate to insure the continuance of basic research and development in the nuclear energy field; it was to be the exclusive producer of fissionable material of any sort; all research and development activities associated with the production of fissionable materials had to be reported to the Commission; the Commission was given the authority to inspect any facility where fissionable materials were being produced; and the Act specified that "no person may ... possess or operate facilities for the production of fissionable materials in quantities or at a rate sufficient to construct a bomb or any other military weapon unless all such facilities are the property of and subject to the control of the Commission."[39]

The Act also required all atomic energy devices to come under AEC license, with the Commission being required to report to Congress "whenever in its opinion industrial, commercial, or other uses of fissionable materials have been sufficiently developed to be of practical value..."[40] Similarly, all property and facilities associated with atomic energy were to be turned over to the AEC. According to the Act:[41]

> all fissionable materials; all bombs and bomb parts; all plants, facilities, equipment, and materials for the processing or production of fissionable materials, bombs, and parts; all processes and technical information of any kind, and the source thereof (including data, drawings, specifications, patents, applications and other sources, relating to the refining or production of fissionable materials); and all contracts, agreements, leases, patents, applications for patents, inventions and discoveries (whether patented or unpatented), and other rights of any kind concerning such items (shall become the property of the Commission).

Lastly, the Commission was responsible for controlling and disseminating both "basic scientific information" and "related technical information;" for supervising the licensing of patents for atomic energy devices; and for submitting:[42]

> reports to the President, to the Senate, and to the House of Representatives... (which) shall summarize and appraise the activities of the Commission and of each division and board thereof, and specifically shall contain financial statements; lists of licenses issued, or property acquired, of research contracts and arrangements entered into, and of the amounts of fissionable material and the persons to whom allocated; the Commission's program for the following quarter including lists of research contracts and arrangements proposed to be entered into; conclusions drawn from the study of the social, political, and economic effects of the release of atomic energy; and such recommendations for additional legislation as the Commission may deem necessary or desirable.

In sum, it was evident that nuclear energy had been subjected to near total regulation and control by the AEC. Never before had the surveillance of a technology been established by statute in this fashion. Indeed, it was rare in the history of science and technology that man had attempted in statutory fashion to control so throughly the forces of a technology *prior* to its implementation.[43] Perhaps most noteworthy in this regard was the substantial authority given the AEC at the conceptualization stage of nuclear energy development, most strongly established by placing basic research and development responsibility with the Commission, as well as control of all fundamental scientific and technical information. As a major component of government control, it was clear that the AEC had been given substantial powers. Together with the powers granted to the Joint Committee on Atomic Energy, the subject of the next section, the outlines of nuclear energy regulation in post-War America had begun to emerge.

The Congressional Regulatory Arm: The Joint Committee on Atomic Energy

The Atomic Energy Act of 1946 did not leave regulatory powers solely in the hands of the AEC; it further specified the nature of government control by creating the Joint Committee on Atomic Energy. Since the original McMahon Bill (S. 1717) contained no provisions for a Congressional regulatory body, the House and Senate were required to spend several weeks after the bill was first introduced debating and discussing what should be its own role in atomic energy development. Basically, the question was how to provide the Congress an effective position *vis-a-vis* the executive branch of the government, as well as a position that would insure it the greatest possible surveillance powers over the AEC and its demonstration programs. And in light of nuclear energy's anticipated importance in national defense, security, and foreign policy, these concerns naturally received considerable attention from a Congress eager to furnish itself a pivotal role in these important areas.[44] To be sure, it was no accident that Senator Johnson and others had forcefully pressed this point throughout the hearings on the McMahon Bill in 1945 and 1946.[45]

Yet considerable administrative difficulties seemed to stand in the way. The traditional committee system was likely to be cumbersome, especially considering the military and international importance of atomic energy and the enormous volume of administrative work the atom was likely to generate. Clearly, no existing Congressional committee could handle the job as they were presently set up, and the over-extension of any currently operating committee was likely to hamper the strong control and regulation Senator Johnson and others felt atomic energy required. It was evident, therefore, that some sort of "legislative innovation" was required.[46]

By July 29, 1946, and after considerable debate and discussion in the House and Senate, a solution was finally reached. The bill sent to President Truman for signature provided for a Joint Committee on Atomic Energy comprised of eighteen members, nine each from the House and Senate, with not more than five members from either body belonging to the same political party.[47] The bill also clearly specified the general authority and powers of the Joint Committee as follows:[48]

> The joint committee shall make continuing studies of the Atomic Energy Commission and of the problems relating to the development, use, and control of atomic energy. *The Commission shall keep the joint committee fully and currently informed with respect to the Commission's activities.* All bills, resolutions, and other matters in the Senate or House of Representatives relating primarily to the Commission or to the development, use, or control of atomic energy shall be referred to the joint committee... The joint committee or any duly authorized subcommittee thereof, is authorized to hold such hearings, to sit and act at such places and times, to require by subpoena or otherwise, the attendance of such books, papers, and documents, to administer such oaths, to take such testimony, to produce such printing and binding, and to make such expenditures as it deems advisable... The joint committee is (further) empowered to appoint and fix the compensation of such experts, consultants, (and) technicians ... as it deems necessary and advisable ... (and) is authorized to utilize the services, information, facilities, and the personnel of the departments and establishments of the Government.

Thus when President Truman signed the bill. into law as the Atomic Energy Act of 1946 on August 1, Congress had provided itself with substantial jurisdiction in nuclear energy regulation. The entire atomic energy program, directed by the Atomic Energy Commission, was now fully accountable to the legislative branch of the government as well.[49]

In addition to providing the Joint Committee with these never before granted powers of surveillance over technological development, the Committee was accorded the status of a regular standing committee in Congress, with all matters relating to atomic energy being turned over to it. The result, of course, was the Joint Committee would eventually stockpile a vast amount of specialized scientific and technical knowledge, every addition of which strengthened its power and legislative clout within the Congress as a whole. Seldom had a single Congressional committee possessed legislative and political power of this magnitude.[50] As will be shown below, these extensive powers allowed the Joint Committee to more or less exercise a free hand in formulating policy, and they became the source of consternation among critics of the nuclear energy programs in the United States.

As for the major functions of the Joint Committee, they may be grouped into four broad categories.[51] Its primary function, of course, was legislative. As discussed above, the Joint Committee's legislative functions were complete--"*all* bills, resolutions, and other matters in the Senate or House of Representative relating primarily to the Commission or the development, use, and control of atomic energy shall be referred to the joint committee" (emphasis added).

Second, the Joint Committee was seen as having important "watchdog functions," especially crucial in an area shrouded by secrecy and concerned with the security and well-being of the country. In all matters of nuclear energy utilization and application, the Joint Committee was expected to receive frequent reports from both the Department of Defense and the AEC:[52]

> The AEC is required by law to keep the Joint Committee fully and currently informed with respect to all of the Commission's activities. The Department of Defense is required to keep the committee fully and currently informed with respect to all matters within the Depart-

ment relating to the development, utilization, or application of atomic energy. All other Government agencies are required to furnish any information requested by the committee with respect to the activities or responsibilities of those agencies in the field of atomic energy. In accordance with the latter requirements the Joint Committee receives briefings from other agencies and departments of the Government, including the Department of State and the Central Intelligence Agency.

Third, the Joint Committee was to exercise extensive policy and review functions, having the final authority in all such matters. At first the Joint Committee was rather passive in the policy arena, but in 1949 this role shifted markedly. As Green and Rosenthal demonstrate,[53] after 1949 the Joint Committee assumed a major leadership role at all levels of nuclear energy policy. For example, it created the major impetus for the naval nuclear propulsion program, the development of the hydrogen bomb, the establishment of the International Atomic Energy Agency, the creation of the aircraft nuclear propulsion program, the utilization of atomic energy in food preservation and space application, and the acceleration of the civilian power reactor programs, to name a few.[54]

The fourth major function of the Joint Committee may be considered informational. For the most part, the nature and extent of the public record on atomic energy has been generated by the reams of Committee documents, reports, memorandums, and especially by transcripts of the Joint Committee's public hearings. The Joint Committee also required the AEC to make appropriate documents and reports public, as well as provide libraries, universities, industry, and others with pertinent information about nuclear energy. As the Joint Committee undoubtedly realized, providing information to the public was an important task for gaining support of the civilian power programs.

From this one may conclude that the Joint Committee was imbued with broad powers in nuclear energy use, development, and control. Never before had a new technology been subjected to near total scrutiny and evaluation by public agents. In large measure, this was a significant new relationship between technological innovation and government. By adding phrases such as "the Commission shall keep the joint committee fully and currently informed with respect to the Commission's activities;" "the joint committee shall make continuing studies of the Atomic Energy Commission and of the problems relating to the development, use, and control of atomic energy;" the joint committee is "empowered to appoint and fix the compensation of experts, consultants (and) technicians;" and the joint committee "is authorized to utilize the services, information, facilities, and personnel of the departments and establishments of the Government;" a vast new sweep had been made that boldly redefined the nature of governmental responsibility in matters of technological innovation.

SUMMARY AND CONCLUSIONS

As World War Two drew to a close, mankind had reached a new era in scientific and technological achievement. However, the sobering experiences of Hiroshima and Nagasaki were grim reminders that these achievements also had unleashed a terrible new destructive force upon the world in the form of atomic weapons. When Robert Hutchins and John von Neumann suggested that the government should move immediately to control nuclear energy in January of 1946, they appeared to echo the sentiments expressed by the United States Congress, which was already debating the exact mode this control should assume, finally achieving consensus with the signing of the Atomic Energy Act of 1946 on August 1. While the 1946 Act had defined what we have called the "political subsystem of the atom" and interpreted government control in a number of ways, the basic instrument of this control would be lodged in a civilian administrative agency, the Atomic Energy Commission, whose activities would be directly accountable to the government. Such accountability would be achieved primarily by means of a Congressional Joint Committee on Atomic Energy, which had been given wide-ranging watchdog and surveillance privileges over the AEC, as well as broad political powers over all aspects of nuclear energy policy in the United States. In short, the 1946 Act had established a political regulatory body whose reign over nuclear policy would approach the absolute. Seldom had such encompassing political controls been instituted.

Yet despite the creation of the AEC and the Joint Committee, themselves innovative agencies of technology regulation, the most important innovation promulgated by the Atomic Energy Act of 1946 was not an organizational or administrative one, *per se*, but rather, the Act specified an entirely new *approach* or philosophy of technology assessment. The Atomic Energy Commission and the Joint Committee, therefore, actually represented only one part of a broad attempt to set policy and rationally evaluate the costs and benefits of a major technology *before* rather than *after* substantial amounts of operating experience had been accumulated. As Thomas Keating summarizes it:[55]

> The question... is whether the benefits to be gained from the implementation of nuclear energy (would) outweigh the costs to be incurred. In the normal course of a technology, this question is of no great public concern, and in fact remains unanswered until well after the particular technology has gained widespread implementation. Nuclear energy may represent perhaps for the first time in regard to a major technology that this situation was reversed in the case of public policy regulating the implementation of nuclear energy.

By actually specifying public policy objectives from the very beginning, the Act preempted a task that is usually left to a host of normal societal pressures, including market conditions, legal restraints, value choices, and the workings of diverse political interest groups--those social and political processes which ordinarily mesh together to determine the direction and objectives of public policy regarding technological innovation. The Act thereby created a unique, unrestrained, and fertile developmental environment for the nuclear energy projects. In this way, the peaceful uses of the atom might grow and flourish, thus serving notice to the world that the atom could be used for something other than making bombs and ravaging civilization.

Yet in stipulating policy and organizational directives in this fashion, the Act also created a number of accompanying dilemmas. Somehow the government would have to maintain a tight grip on the applications of nuclear energy while at the same time "fostering private research and development on a truly independent basis," thereby ostensibly "strengthening free competition among private enterprises so far as practicable."

Moreover, the idea of a commission-type regulatory agency was deemed desirable for the usual reason which commission regulation is invoked: because commission experts could be insulated and protected from the potentially devastating influences of partisan political pressure; because more rational and objective policy making could be undertaken; and because commission regulation would promote a more fertile and conducive environment for the rapid development of the peaceful applications of nuclear energy.[56] But at the same time, it was not clear whether the Atomic Energy Commission could fulfill the intended advantages of commission regulation while being subjected to the continuing direction and scrutiny by the Joint Committee on Atomic Energy, as the 1946 Act required. That is, could--and should--nuclear energy development and control, as seen in the context of commission regulation *really* be freed of political pressure exerted by the spectre of government "control"? And wouldn't the ultimate implementation of the peaceful atom eventually subject it to increased political activity and controversy by the groups most directly affected, groups that could charge the AEC and the Joint Committee with conflict-of-interests?

But in the early days of 1946, answers to these questions could not have been known. To be sure, more important was to get on with the serious business of devising some workable plan for government control, for it seemed that science had indeed "outgrown the age of its independence from society" as John von Neumann had suggested at the McMahon hearings. Hence, when in 1945 atomic energy burst upon man's consciousness, it was surely no accident that the very scientists who had worked feverishly on the bomb throughout the War had also stressed the significance of careful surveillance of all levels of operation of every nuclear energy device, military or otherwise.[57] While nuclear energy ushered in a magnificent new era of technological innovation and promise, they realized that its very nature also demanded radical new social institutions, agencies, laws, and administrative strategies to cope with its use. Mankind had progressed to the threshold of a vast new technological era, replete with immense areas of uncharted terrain. Nuclear energy had introduced a staggering array of new questions and concerns, questions such as for what purposes should the atom be used? How could mankind avoid the catastrophic consequences of human frailty and error? How could the proliferation of nuclear weapons be halted? What were the most promising ways to employ the atom for peaceful purposes? And how would this vastly powerful new energy source be controlled and regulated in mankind's best interests? These are a few of the questions probably already running through the minds of the B-29 crew, as they saw the incredible flash over Hiroshima and the first shock waves began hitting the plane on August 6, 1945. Nuclear energy had arrived, and with it, so had a new era in the relationships between science, technology, and society.

NOTES

1. Leslie R. Groves, *Now It Can Be Told; The Story of the Manhattan Project* (New York: Harper and Brothers, 1962), pp. 318-19.

2. Ibid. p. 346.

3. United States Congress, Hearings before the Special Committee on Atomic Energy, *A Bill for the Development and Control of Atomic Energy*, 79th Congress, 2nd Session, 1946 (Washington, D.C.: U.S. Government Printing Office, 1947), p. 103. Hereinafter referred to as Hearings, 1946.

4. Henry D. Smyth, *Atomic Energy for Military Purposes: The Official Report on the Development of the Atomic Bomb under the Auspices of the United States Government, 1940-1945* (Princeton: Princeton University Press, 1945).

5 Louis Ridenour, "Pilot Lights of the Apocalypse," reprinted in Morton Gordzins and Eugene Rabinowitz (eds.), *The Atomic Age: Scientists in National and World Affairs* (New York: Basic Books, 1963), pp. 47-52.

6 For a comprehensive treatment of the drive for international control, see Richard G. Hewlett and Oscar E. Anderson, Jr., *The New World, 1939/1946; Volume One of the History of the United States Atomic Energy Commission* (University Park: Pennsylvania State University Press, 1962), pp. 531-79. See also J. Robert Oppenheimer, "International Control of Atomic Energy," in Grodzins and Rabinowitz, *The Atomic Age*, pp. 53-63.

7. For a discussion of this debate see Harold P. Green and Alan Rosenthal, *Government of the Atom: The Integration of Powers* (New York: Atherton Press, 1963), p. 2; Hewlett and Anderson, *The New World*, pp. 435 ff.; and Morgan Thomas, *Atomic Energy and Congress* (Ann Arbor: University of Michigan Press, 1956), pp. 16 ff.

8. Hearings, 1946, p. 102; emphasis added.

9. Ibid., p. 206.

10. Green and Rosenthal, *Government of the Atom*, p. 2.

11. Hewlett and Anderson, *The New World*, pp. 434-35. See also Alice Kimball Smith, *A Peril and A Hope* (University of Chicago Press, 1965), pp. 128-200 and 365-436. For related materials see Arthur Steiner, "Scientists, Statesmen, and Politicians: The Compelling Influences on American Atomic Energy Policy, 1945-1946," *Minerva* 12 (October 1974): 498-99.

12. Hewlett and Anderson, *The New World,* p. 429.

13. Ibid., pp. 431-33. See also Donald Strickland, *Scientists in Politics* (Lafayette, Indiana: Purdue University Press, 1968), p. 105. Regarding scientists' opposition to the May-Johnson Bill, Steiner has written: "It provoked more interest among the scientific community than any other of the subsequent developments in domestic legislation, and the opposition was near unanimous." See "Scientists,Statesmen, and Politicians," p. 499.

14. See Hewlett and Anderson, *The New World,* pp. 436 ff.

15. Thomas, *Atomic Energy and Congress,* p. 4.

16. Cited in Hewlett and Anderson, *The New World,* p. 482.

17. Ibid., p. 427.

18. *The New York Times,* October 31, 1945. Cited in Ibid., p. 445. For a good discussion of scientists' opposition to the May-Johnson proposal, see also James R. Newman and Byron S. Miller, *The Control of Atomic Energy; A Study of Its Social, Economic, and Political Implications* (New York: McGraw-Hill, 1948), pp. 10-11 and Claire M. Nader, *American Natural Scientists in the Policy Process: Three Atomic Energy Issues and Their Foreign Policy Implications* (New York: Unpublished Doctoral Dissertation, Columbia University, 1964).

19. Both quotations from Hewlett and Anderson, *The New World,* p. 523. For additional information on the anticipated effects of the new atomic energy legislation on the free enterprise system see Newman and Miller, *The Control of Atomic Energy.* As they remarked about the 1946 Act: "The Act creates a government monopoly of the sources of atomic energy and buttresses this position with a variety of broad governmental powers and prohibitions on private activity. The field of atomic energy is an island of socialism in the midst of a free enterprise economy" p. 4. For a related analysis of interest see Harold Orlans, *Contracting for Atoms* (Washington, D.C.: The Brookings Institution, 1967).

20. Hewlett and Anderson, *The New World,* p. 524.

21. Ibid., p. 530.

22. For a good discussion of the political subsystem concept see Emmette S. Redford, *Democracy and the Administrative State* (New York: Oxford University Press, 1969), pp. 96-102.

23. See Public Law 585, "The Atomic Energy Act of 1946," in *United States Statutes at Large,* V. 60, Part 1 (Washington, D.C.: U.S. Government

Printing Office, 1947), p. 757. For a good analysis and discussion of the new Act see Byron S. Miller, "A Law is Passed--The Atomic Energy Act of 1946," *University of Chicago Law Review* 15 (Summer 1948): 799 ff.

24. Ibid.

25. Public Law 585, "The Atomic Energy Act of 1946," pp. 758 ff. For a related discussion see Frank G. Dawson, *Nuclear Power: Development and Management of a Technology* (Seattle: University of Washington Press, 1976), pp. 20 ff.

26. A good discussion and description of the AEC's duties is found in Newman and Miller. See their *Control of Atomic Energy*.

27. See Thomas, *Atomic Energy and Congress*, pp. 6-7. And Dawson, *Nuclear Power*, pp. 22-24.

28. See Public Law 585, "The Atomic Energy Act of 1946", p. 757. See also Richard O. Neihoff, "Organization and Administration of the United States Atomic Energy Commission," *Public Administration Review* 8 (Spring 1948): 95-96; Thomas, *Atomic Energy and Congress*, pp. 6-7; and Newman and Miller, *The Control of Atomic Energy*, pp. 26-47.

29. Niehoff, "Organization and Administration of the United States Atomic Energy Commission," p. 96. and Newman and Miller, *The Control of Atomic Energy*, pp. 26-47.

30. Ibid.

31. Niehoff, "Organization and Adminstration of the United States Atomic Energy Commission," p. 97.

32. Ibid.

33. Ibid., p. 99 and Corbin Allardice and Edward R. Trapnell, *The Atomic Energy Commission*, (New York: Praeger Publishers, 1974), p. 65. See also United States Atomic Energy Commission, *Semi-Annual Report to Congress July-December 1946* Washington, D. C.: U.S. Government Printing Office, 1947).

34. Allardice and Trapnell, *The Atomic Energy Commission*, p. 65.

35. Public Law 585, "The Atomic Energy Act of 1946", p. 757.

36. Ibid., pp. 757-58.

37. Thomas, *Atomic Energy and Congress*, p. 14; and Niehoff, "Organization and Administration of the United States Atomic Energy Commission," pp. 92-93. It is also worth noting at this point that as the Commission's licensing and regulation duties multiplied, an office called the Director of Regulation was created. The Director's position was akin to that of General Manager but concerned

only licensing and regulatory matters. There were three additional offices under the Director of Regulation's general authority; Directorate of Licensing, Directorate of Regulatory Standards, and Directorate of Regulatory Operations. The Directorate of Licensing also supervised three Deputy Directors concerned with reactor projects, technical review, and fuels and materials while the Directorate of Regulatory Operations supervised the Deputy Director of Field Operations and the five Field Offices. Allardice and Trapnell, *The Atomic Energy Commission*, p. 52.

38. Niehoff, "Organization and Administration of the United States Atomic Energy Commission," p. 101.

39. Hearings, 1946, p. 3.

40. Ibid., p. 5.

41. Ibid.

42. Ibid., p. 8.

43. See Newman and Miller, *The Control of Atomic Energy*, pp. 3-5. A similar position is taken by Harold P. Green. See his excellent articles: Harold P. Green, "The Strange Case of Nuclear Power," *Federal Bar Journal* 17 (April-June 1957): 100 and Harold P. Green, "Nuclear Technology and the Fabric of Government," *The George Washington Law Review* 33 (October 1964): 160.

44. Thomas, *Atomic Energy and Congress*, p. 16; Harold P. Green and Alan Rosenthal, *The Joint Committee on Atomic Energy: A Study in the Fusion of Government Power* (Washington, D.C.: George Washington University, 1961); and Dawson, *Nuclear Power*, pp. 32-36.

45. See for example, Hearings, 1946, p. 39.

46. Green and Rosenthal, *Government of the Atom* pp. 1-5.

47. See Public Law 585, "The Atomic Energy Act of 1946," p. 772.

48. Ibid., pp. 772-773; emphasis added.

49. For a relevant discussion see Thomas, *Atomic Energy and Congress*, pp. 13 ff. and Dawson, *Nuclear Power*, pp. 32-36.

50. Thomas, *Atomic Energy and Congress*, p. 19. See also Green and Rosenthal, *Government of the Atom*, and Green and Rosenthal, *The Joint Committee on Atomic Energy*.

51. Allardice and Trapnell, *The Atomic Energy Commission*, pp. 166-68 and Green and Rosenthal, *Government of the Atom*.

52. Cited in Allardice and Trapnell, *The Atomic Energy Commission*, pp. 166-67.

53. Green and Rosenthal, *Government of the Atom* p. 5.

54. See Ibid., pp. 233-65 and Allardice and Trapnell, *The Atomic Energy Commission*, p. 167. See also United States Congress, Joint Committee on Atomic Energy, *Current Membership of the Joint Committee on Atomic Energy* 92nd Congress, 2nd Session, 1973 (Washington, D.C.: U.S. Government Printing Office, Joint Committee Print, 1973), p. 4, which pointed out that the Joint Committee had "expedited and supported the naval nuclear propulsion program, the hydrogen bomb project, an expanded atomic power program, the preservation of food through irradiation, the utilization of atomic energy for space applications, and the liquid metal fast breeder reactor program." Cited in Dawson, *Nuclear Power*, p. 33.

55. Thomas W. Keating, "Politics, Energy and the Environment: The Role of Technology Assessment," *American Behavioral Scientist* 19 (September-October 1975): 46. See also John Gorham Palfrey, "Atomic Energy: A New Experiment in Government-Industry Relations," *Columbia Law Review* 56 (1956): 373 ff. and James R. Newman, "The Atomic Energy Industry," *Yale Law Journal* 60 (December 1951): 1263-1394.

56. Hewlett and Anderson, *The New World*, p. 412.

57. See for example, Steiner, "Scientists, Statesmen and Politicians."

3
The Government-Industry Partnership in the Development of Civilian Nuclear Power in the United States, 1946-1960

> The AEC acted as a promoter of the Promethian gift and was also responsible for regulating its use in the public interest ... (However) in the regulation of nuclear power, the identification between the AEC and the industry, together with its satellite trade associations, amounted to a commonality of interest and purpose. It is not surprising, therefore, that in the late 1950s there evolved a joint government-industry power structure with common goals and with access to money and political power to achieve them.
>
> -Richard S. Lewis

INTRODUCTION

In the previous chapter we discussed the establishment of "government control" of the atom as it was envisioned in late-1945 and early-1946, culminating with the Atomic Energy Act of 1946 which erected the major policies, programs, and agencies of nuclear energy development control. In the following chapters we turn our attention to the commercial development of civilian nuclear power in the United States, achieved primarily by means of a joint effort between the federal government and the nuclear power industry.

The present chapter seeks to accomplish two primary goals. Our first task consists in tracing the complex, often entangled, development and general outlines of the civilian reactor programs in the United States from 1946 to around 1960. Our major questions include: What was the nature and content of these programs? How and when were they implemented? And which parties were involved? Second, as we examine the civilian power programs we shall attempt to show that while they were at first largely dominated by the federal government, its monopoly in nuclear energy eventually gave way to a government-industry "partnership" in the development efforts. The partnership was nurtured in a number of ways, including government financial subsidies, research and development assistance, financial underwriting of industry liability by the federal government, and direct invitations from the Atomic Energy Commission which provided substantial incentives to these private industries involved in the nuclear energy business, to name a few.

To achieve these goals, the following text is divided into four sections. Section two discusses the events leading up to the country's first civilian power reactor development program, the Reactor Development Program (RDP), which the AEC announced in 1948. Part of the discussion focuses on how the AEC took charge of the programs and activities of the Manhattan Engineering District; the extent of its involvement in the military applications of atomic energy; its problems with secrecy and information declassification; and its efforts to develop civilian nuclear power programs in which private industry would share a major role. The latter was especially important since under the Atomic Energy Act of 1946 it was the Commission's duty to "strengthen free competition among private enterprises as far as practicable."

Sections three, four, and five, respectively, discuss the RDP as well as other nuclear energy programs subsequently announced by the AEC: The Five-Year Power Program and its three "Rounds" called the Power Reactor Demonstration Programs (PRDP) implemented in 1954, the Ten-Year Civilian Power Reactor Program announced in 1960, and the various non-government projects. Since the Five-Year Power Program and its three PRDPs represented the basic core of the civilian power programs and policies in the United States, most of the discussion is focused on them. Throughout, our concern lies with indicating how industry was slowly brought into the reactor programs by the AEC and, thus, how the government-industry partnership was formed and eventually consolidated. Because the partership by 1960 had already been institutionalized, and since the Ten-Year Program was essentially the same in structure and operation to previous developmental programs, our treatment of it here is brief. Finally, the sections also mention some of the legislative measures enacted by the Joint Committee on Atomic Energy to facilitate industry involvement in nuclear energy development; namely, the newly revised Atomic Energy Act of 1954, the Gore-Holifield Bill, and the Price-Anderson Act.

THE REACTOR DEVELOPMENT PROGRAM: THE FIRST YEARS

Since the peaceful application of nuclear energy was a major goal promulgated by the Atomic Energy Act of 1946, one of the first tasks of the AEC was to initiate a program that promised rapid commercial applicability. As the complex interaction of events began to unfold, it was apparent that the primary peaceful application of the atom would be the generation of electrical power from nuclear chain reaction.

Even though the goal of civilian nuclear power was foremost among the Commission's objectives, the initial atomic energy programs were in reality little more than an extension of the War Department's military programs, formerly conducted under the auspices of the Manhattan Engineering District. Green and Rosenthal have remarked that in its early years "the AEC was almost exclusively an operating agency carrying on research, development, and production activities, most of which were in direct furtherance of the national defense effort."[1] Similarly, Lee C. Nehrt reports that in 1948 over eighty percent of all funds spent on atomic energy went to military programs.[2] And since these programs involved serious considerations of national security, most of the AEC's activities were forced to meet stringent secrecy standards.

In compiling these facts, the inescapable conclusion was that the first atomic energy programs (pre-1950) had made little headway either in disseminating basic scientific and technical information or in fostering private industry and business participation in atomic energy development. As long as this situation persisted, the civilian application of nuclear energy would remain dormant in the pages of the 1946 Act.

Despite this situation, however, the AEC's first Chairman and former Director of the Tennessee Valley Authority, David Lilienthal, was accutely aware of the importance of making more information about atomic energy available to industry and the public. In a speech before the New England Council at Boston in 1948, he called for, among other things, greater public accountability and criticism of the AEC and its programs.[3] Under Lilienthal's leadership the AEC had already established in the previous year an Industrial Advisory Group to study ways to increase private industry participation in atomic energy research and development. Reporting their findings in 1948, the Group outlined the existing role of industry in nuclear energy development; stressed the need for greater industry participation; summarized the major obstacles thereto; suggested approaching industry with direct invitations; and recommended the establishment of permanent industrial advisory committees.[4] But more than anything else, the Group's report stressed two main goals: (1) the AEC should undertake to establish a well-planned out and organized atomic reactor developmental program; and (2) private industry and business should be given adequate opportunity to participate more fully in nuclear energy development, for then they "had no way of knowing whether opportunities existed."[5] Heeding these recommendations, the Commission set about organizing a solid reactor development program geared toward recruiting large-scale participation by private industry in late-1948.

Yet in 1948 it seemed that the utilization of nuclear energy for civilian application was not so easily attained as the 1946 Act had so enthusiastically implied. Indeed, as Lilienthal had said some years before, there were now recognized "a whole mass of involved, difficult, scientific, technical, and industrial engineering problems."[6] But perhaps most important were the administrative and organizational measures that would be necessary to realize the peaceful atom. Harold D. Smith, Director of the Bureau of the Budget, harped on these administrative measures throughout the special hearings in 1946,[7] and Lilienthal, himself a competent administrator, was not unaware of these concerns. Thus, when the AEC announced the Reactor Development Program (RDP) in late-1948,[8] essentially the nation's first domestic plan aimed at bringing about the systematic organization and control of atomic energy for peaceful application, the main question was what kind of program would emerge to pursue a massive civilian effort.

THE REACTOR DEVELOPMENT PROGRAM: PHASE ONE

Pre-Program Reactors

Even though the Reactor Development Program was the first domestic organizational strategy employed for meeting the goals of the 1946 Act, it was not as if the AEC and its industrial contractors were without large amounts of accumulated experience in reactor design and testing. To be sure, the Manhattan Project had experimented with several reactor types and designs, as well as with several methods of producing plutonium and other fissionable products suitable for use in a bomb.[9] Since most of the research and development work of the AEC had its origin in the Manhattan activities related to the military applications of atomic energy, a brief summary of the reactor types in service before the formulation of the Reactor Development Program is in order.

According to Nehrt,[10] there were at least six different plutonium production reactors and test reactors in existence before 1948. Some produced power, others did not.

The first reactor to produce power (200 watts) was built in Chicago in 1942 under the direction of Enrico Fermi. The reactor, a pile type, was a huge structure that housed six tons of uranium metal, fifty tons of uranium oxide, and almost four-hundred tons of graphite.[11] While the reactor did not produce usable power, the massive structure housed under the stadium at the University of Chicago's Stagg Field proved that a sustainable, controlled nuclear chain reaction was possible. In 1943 the reactor was replaced by a similar uranium-graphite reactor, Chicago Pile Number 2, designed to operate at higher power levels (12,000 watts). The Chicago Pile Number 2 was quite useful in a number of subsequent experiments conducted by Chicago nuclear physicists for many years after its construction.[12]

A second reactor was the Oak Ridge Graphite Reactor built in 1943. While this reactor was designed to operate at substantially higher power levels (2,000 kilowatts) than the Chicago Pile reactors, it was similar in design, also employing graphite and natural uranium. This reactor was a prototype of the large plutonium production reactors on the drawing boards of the Manhattan District.[13]

Modeled on the Oak Ridge prototype were

several plutonium production reactors built at Hanford, Washington in 1943-1944. Utilizing graphite and natural uranium, the purpose of these reactors was to produce the fissionable materials used in atomic bombs. The reactors were of such high power and produced so much heat that it was necessary to take in cooling water from the nearby Columbia River.[14] Later, these plants would be essential for producing much of the fissionable materials used in the first atomic bombs, exploded at the Alamogordo test site in New Mexico and later at Hiroshima and Nagasaki.

The fourth reactor built under the direction and auspices of the Manhattan District was different from the preceding reactors in that it used heavy-water and enriched uranium-235 instead of graphite and the usual natural uranium. This reactor was also built in Chicago and was utilized as a test reactor for examining the effects of using different materials. It was, however, much smaller than the Hanford and Oak Ridge reactors, being rated at a power level of only 300 kilowatts.[15]

A fifth reactor was built at the Los Alamos Laboratories in New Mexico in May 1944, and was known as "Water Boiler." In this reactor uranium was not employed in the normal manner, in the form of metallic fuel elements--rods, slugs, etc.--but was used in the form of a solution called uranyl sulphate. This reactor was employed purely for test purposes at the lab, with several crucial experiments leading directly to the design of the first atomic bombs being facilitated by it.[16]

Finally, a sixth reactor was installed at Los Alamos in 1946. Known as "Clementine," this reactor was different from the others in that pure plutonium instead of uranium was used as fuel, and the cooling system was a solution of liquid metal rather than water or air. In addition, the reactor had no graphite moderator, meaning that Clementine was the world's first "fast reactor."[17] Together with the other five reactor projects, Clementine demonstrated the underlying philosophy behind the government's very first research and development efforts which later carried over to the AEC's philosophy: experiment with not one or two different concepts, but with a diversity of designs and power ratings. This would permit evaluation of reactor types on a more meaningful comparative basis, as well as insure that if one or another of the different fuel cycles proved unworkable, then the entire program would not have to be scrapped but could still go forward.

The Reactor Development Program, Five Sub-Programs

For all practical purposes, then, the AEC had at its disposal the research experience accumulated from these six projects, the framework on which all subsequent reactor work would be based. Thus when the Reactor Development Program was announced by the AEC in 1948, one of the first tasks encompassed by the Program was a continuance of the materials testing reactor project begun at Oak Ridge in 1943-1944.[18] The Commission placed administrative responsibility for the project with the Argonne National Laboratory in Chicago, but the actual experimental and technological work was carried on jointly between Argonne and Oak Ridge.

As for the Program's second project, the Commission decided, at the urgings of the Joint Committee, to cancel the Daniels Pile Project begun at Argonne in 1948 and to proceed with a land-based prototype reactor suitable for use in a submarine. Oak Ridge had already begun work on this reactor in the fall of 1947 at the request of the Navy.[19] To help Argonne with design and construction of the reactor, the Commission brought in an industrial partner, the Westinghouse Electric Company. Along with General Electric, Westinghouse became the second large industrial firm to become involved in the design and construction of nuclear power reactors, and would later be instrumental in developing the world's first atomic-powered submarine, the *Nautilus*, launched in 1954 from the Electric Boat Yard in Groton, Connecticut.[20]

In addition to these two projects, the Commission authorized funds for three other programs. Two of these programs called for experimental work on a breeder reactor capable of producing high grade steam for central power station application. Argonne, which had been working on the breeder concept since 1945, and the Knolls Atomic Power Laboratory, a newly created division of General Electric, were given the go-ahead by the AEC to design land-based prototypes of the breeder. As for the third project, bringing the total number of projects under the initial Reactor Development Program to five, the AEC asked Oak Ridge to begin work on what was called the "Homogeneous Reactor Experiment," a reactor that would produce high temperature steam capable of turning large electrical turbines for the commercial production of electricity.[21]

The land-based prototype reactors--submarine and materials testing reactors--were all located at a remote 400,000 acre test site in a sparsely populated area of Idaho, known as the National Reactor Testing Station. For the General Electric reactor work, the site was at Knolls Atomic Power Laboratory's West Milton, New York facility. Both locations came under the direction of the newly created AEC office of the Division of Reactor Development, headed by the former director of the Johns Hopkins University Applied Physics Laboratory, Dr. Lawrence R. Hafstad, who served as the AEC director until 1954.[22]

In general outline, then, these five programs comprised the nation's first atomic Reactor Development Program as it was envisioned in 1948. It is evident that the United States had opted to experiment with a variety of reactor designs and types, to be used for different applications and purposes. In terms of design, all reactors had been developed to use enriched natural uranium as a fuel. The materials testing and submarine prototype reactors used water as both moderator and coolant, while the General Electric and breeder reactors used liquid as coolant, with the breeder, of course, needing no moderator since it utilized pure uranium-235 as a fuel.[23] Such a diversity of reactor types and designs, it was argued, would allow the United States far greater flexibility and efficiency in producing suitable reactors for any particular purpose. But perhaps most important to note is that all the projects under the Reactor Development Program were primarily AEC projects; industry participation was largely indirect and on a contractual basis, funded almost entirely by AEC monies.

Some Results of the Reactor Development Program[24]

The design and development of the materials testing reactor continued until the spring of 1950, when ground was broken and construction begun at Idaho's National Reactor Testing Station. Construction was completed in March 1952 with a total price tag of around $18 million. The reactor was brought critical and has been in successful operation ever since.

As for the Westinghouse submarine prototype reactor, construction also commenced at the Idaho Testing Station in 1950. Full power operation was achieved by the spring of 1953, and the reactor continues to operate today. The cost to the taxpayer was around $30 million. In addition, a modified version of this reactor was installed in the world's first atomic submarine, the *Nautilus*, in 1954. The *Nautilus* not only operated successfully for over two years before having its reactor core removed for refueling, but has remained in the United States' fleet, revolutionizing submarine warfare if not naval warfare in general.[25] In terms of practical application, the submarine prototype reactor built by Westinghouse may be considered among the most successful of the United States nuclear reactors. In fact, it was so successful that the first commercial nuclear stations which began coming on-line in the late 1950s and early 1960s have utilized essentially similar versions of the smaller light-water reactors first installed in the nation's nuclear submarine fleet. We shall have more to say about this important point later.

As for the experimental breeder reactor, construction also began in 1950 at the Idaho test site. Under the direction of the Argonne Laboratory, this reactor produced the world's first electric power generated from atomic energy on December 20, 1951. Even though only 100 kilowatts of power was produced, enough to run plant equipment and lights, the successful operation of the breeder reactor proved the technical feasibility of generating electricity from atomic energy. In 1955 the reactor underwent a series of tests for "simulated accidents,"[26] whereby the reactor was allowed to operate with disengaged safety controls. The reactor's uranium core promptly melted from the intense heat. The core was subsequently replaced and the reactor put back into operation.[27]

As for the General Electric project, in early 1950 it requested permission from the AEC to begin construction of a liquid-metal cooled breeder reactor at the West Milton, New York site. The Commission, however, felt the project was not sufficiently well developed to warrant issuing a construction permit. Furthermore, new discoveries of uranium ore had made materials procurement much easier, causing the breeder to lose some of its earlier appeal. In light of these circumstances, program director Hafstad announced the indefinite postponement of the breeder and requested the Knolls Laboratory to help Hanford with some thorny technical problems, and whether the reactor originally designed at Knolls could be considered for a submarine prototype instead.[28] General Electric responded to Hafstad's request and started work immediately in 1952 on a land-based prototype at the Idaho site, completing the project in early 1955 at an estimated total cost of $27 million. This reactor used enriched uranium for fuel, employed a beryllium moderator, and used liquid sodium as coolant. General Electric not only added a turbine to produce electricity but later modified the reactor to fit the Navy's second atomic powered submarine, *Seawolf*, which put to sea in early-1957. But because of the danger of leaks and the violent reaction of sodium with water, *Seawolf* was temporarily removed from service until a new reactor type could be installed, but not before *Seawolf* had completed a record submerged voyage of 60 days and 13,761 miles in October of 1958.[29] The Navy's removal of *Seawolf* from service, however, sealed the fate of sodium-cooled reactors for use in naval vessels and the original prototype was subsequently dismantled.

Lastly, as mentioned above, the Reactor Development Program was enlarged with the addition of the Homogeneous Reactor Experiment at Oak Ridge in 1947. This reactor was modeled after the original "Water Boiler," constructed at Los Alamos during the Manhattan days. By now (1948) Union Carbide and Carbon Company, under AEC contract, had assumed operation of the Oak Ridge facility from Monsanto Chemical Company and had already proposed a plan for producing steam from such a reactor for the purpose of generating electricity. In early 1950 Union Carbide was authorized by the AEC to begin design and construction of the proposed facility. By April 1952 the reactor was completed, and after a series of tests and safety measures were enacted, it produced small quantities of electricity in the spring of 1953. The Homogeneous Reactor Experiment at Oak Ridge thus became the world's second atomic reactor to produce electricity.[30] Briefly, these were some of the results of the AEC's first Reactor Development Program.

Additional Projects of the Reactor Development Program

The duration of the first Reactor Development Program saw three new developmental projects added between the years 1950-1952.[31] Two of these projects were for the military--one each for the Navy and the Air Force--with the remaining project being for civilian power purposes.

The civilian power project was contracted out to the North American Aviation Company in the spring of 1949. North American thereby joined General Electric and Westinghouse as the United States' third major industrial firm to enter the nuclear power business. North American had been contracted to research and develop nuclear power plant hardware, materials, and reactor designs. The aim was to concentrate on nuclear components and designs that would be "suitable for the practical application of atomic power."[32] As the studies developed, North American's research centered around a third type of reactor, different from either the Westinghouse or General Electric designs, that would employ liquid-sodium for coolant, graphite for the moderator, and enriched uranium as fuel.[33]

Once again the AEC had demonstrated the strategy behind its Reactor Development Program: research not one or two, but a diversity of reactor designs.

The Navy project can be said to have been a direct outgrowth of Westinghouse's successful reactor work for the *Nautilus*.[34] In fact, the work had been so successful and progressed so rapidly that nuclear scientists felt a much larger pressurized-water reactor could be built to operate frigates, cruisers, and even aircraft carriers. Thus Chief of Naval Operations, Forrest P. Sherman, immediately requested Hyman Rickover, head of the Navy's nuclear propulsion program, to begin study of the matter in August 1950. The Rickover staff concluded the project was feasible, and with luck, could be completed by 1955. Westinghouse was approached to study the details of reactor design for an aircraft carrier and produced a 133-page report in January 1952. The study examined the strengths and weaknesses of six different reactor designs, concluding that five of the six were feasible for a carrier. Within a few days, the Rickover group submitted a recommendation for a reactor that used water as both moderator and coolant--that is, the so-called light-water technology. Both the Commission and the Navy endorsed the Rickover plan. The project would take an estimated four years to complete and cost the taxpayer nearly $150 million.[35]

The third project added to the development program was for the Air Force. After terminating its NEPA (Nuclear Energy for the Propulsion of Aircraft) contracts with Fairchild Engine and Airplane Corporation in 1951, the AEC decided to award contracts to General Electric for continued development of a nuclear reactor suitable for aircraft. Oak Ridge was to assume most of the technological and nuclear work, with General Electric completing the engineering work. With the addition of extensive test facilities at the Idaho test site in 1952, the AEC had spent $33 million, plus some $16 million per year for work on the project at the Oak Ridge facility alone.[36] While it is not possible to go into a complete history of this project here, let us simply remark that the aircraft propulsion program encountered a host of difficulties, technological and otherwise, from the outset. In 1953 the Department of Defense made the decision to cancel the project. Only with bitter outrage from the Joint Committee on Atomic Energy was the program reinstated, finally to be struck down for good by President Kennedy in 1962.[37]

Summary and Conclusions

From the above treatment of the nation's first Reactor Development Program, several conclusions stand out. First, in their attempt to develop atomic reactors suitable for various applications, the Commission opted for a strategy of concentrating on a number of diverse reactor types, to be used for several different purposes. In so doing, the program showed the essential practicality and use of nuclear power reactors at several levels of operation. In military applications (where the program was the most successful), for example, the Westinghouse enriched uranium, pressurized-water reactor that was installed in the *Nautilus* had literally revolutionized naval strategies. Likewise the record-breaking voyage of the *Seawolf*, utilizing a General Electric uranium enriched, sodium-cooled reactor, demonstrated to the world the new vistas opened up by nuclear power. As for possible civilian application, the production of electricity at the Idaho and Oak Ridge facilities showed that atomic plants could probably be adapted to produce electricity for large-scale industrial and commercial use in the near future. Moreover, the reactor program demonstrated that homogeneous and fast-breeder reactors could be used successfully on a small-scale for experimental and testing purposes, and that sodium-cooled reactors, while not suitable for submarine use, could most probably be modified to function smoothly on land.

However, the program had been very expensive and much more complex than at first believed. Indeed,

Lilienthal had been more than right to emphasize the incredible organizational and technological complexity of putting the atom to work. As a consequence tremendous amounts of resources, materials, and man-hours of work had been expended to accomplish the admittedly impressive results of the Commission's first development program. Yet this was only the beginning. As will be shown below, the United States' nuclear energy program was rapidly becoming one of the most expensive technological ventures in history. This, it can be argued, is a very significant fact, and one that influenced the course of subsequent AEC reactor development programs. Because investments had been so huge, the present pressure to make them pay-off by means of proliferating nuclear generating stations is literally awesome, yet completely understandable from the economic standpoint of industry and the government.

Third, while some research and development work had been contracted out, the AEC seemed to be following the general policy of conducting most of the basic research and development work at government-owned laboratories and test sites. The limited number of United States industrial firms involved in atomic energy were financed almost entirely by government funds as they worked on what might be termed "government directed projects"; there were few independent, private projects on the drawing boards at this time. The obvious outcome of this situation was a continuance of the federal government's participation and supremacy at the basic research and development levels of the nuclear energy programs, which at the same time, served essentially to maintain its monopoly of the fundamental scientific and technical information on nuclear energy.

Consequently, the early years of the Reactor Development Program indicated a general lack of industry participation. Due in part to military and defense requirements, this lack of participation was remedied only very slowly. In fact by the early 1950s there were relatively few United States industrial firms who knew anything at all about nuclear energy. General Electric, Westinghouse, Phillips Petroleum, North American Aviation, and Union Carbide were the only major United States firms involved in the actual design and construction of nuclear reactors and power plants at that time. Yet, as the years progressed, more and more companies became interested in the incredible possibilities of nuclear energy. As a full-scale effort from the world's greatest industrial machine seemed forthcoming, perhaps the atom could be put to work to serve mankind for peaceful purposes after all.

THE REACTOR DEVELOPMENT PROGRAM, PHASE TWO: THE FIVE-YEAR POWER PROGRAM

An Invitation for Greater Industry Participation

While AEC Chairman David Lilienthal had pointed out the need for greater industry participation as early as 1948, the initial years of the United States reactor program was suffering from an acute lack of it. Not only did the Commission realize the need for greater inputs from private industry, but industry itself began to consider the enormous potential of the nuclear energy business. In fact, by the spring of 1950 in an article published in Collier's,[38] Lilienthal called for a termination of government monopoly in the non-military and commercial uses of nuclear energy. Further recognizing this need, the Oak Ridge School for Reactor Technology was established by the AEC in the spring of 1950 to educate engineers and scientists in nuclear principles.[39] By July 1950 the Commission had established a bi-weekly publication, *Nuclear Science Abstracts*, for the dissemination of technical reports.[40] But perhaps most indicative of the tenor of these events was a proposal offered to the AEC on June 20, 1950 by Charles A. Thomas, President of Monsanto Chemical Company. Thomas had said:[41]

> It is proposed that American Industry design, construct and operate one or more atomic power plants with its own capital. Power and plutonium would under such a plan be produced in the same plant from government-owned uranium... It is believed that the combined cost of making plutonium and power by the suggested means can be significantly less than by making the same quantities separately. The opportunity to design, construct and operate such a plant should be offered by the government to all responsible industries needing power and willing to venture capital to obtain it.

The so-called "dual-purpose" reactor proposed by Thomas would produce both power and plutonium--

power that could be made into electricity and plutonium that could be utilized for government needs--and was highly attractive to both the Commission and the public utilities. The Commission therefore decided to let Monsanto study its existing reactor projects before proceeding with the actual development and construction of the dual-purpose reactor.[42] But the ice had been broken: industry was for the first time allowed access to Commission research materials and to documents which heretofore had been classified information. Several months later Dow Chemical Company and the Detroit Edison Company submitted a joint proposal to the Commission asking their cooperation in conducting a study leading to construction of a "'a type of reactor which will permit economical production of power, fissionable material and fresh fission radioactive products on a very large scale and with optimum raw-material utilization'."[43] These proposals, together with the general attitude that prevailed within the AEC regarding industrial participation, then, led the Commission to issue "a general invitation to industry to conduct studies of so-called 'dual-purpose' reactors (that is, reactors for the production of plutonium for weapons and power for civilian use)."[44]

The initial response to the invitations was encouraging. The Detroit Edison-Dow Chemical Group, in cooperation with the Commission, proposed construction of a fast-breeder reactor similar to the Idaho version. The proposal was accepted in the spring of 1952. The Monsanto Chemical-Union Electric Group offered a second proposal. In cooperation with the Commission they asked to design and build a large dual-purpose reactor that would be capable of producing 150,000 kilowatts of electricity for commercial use and plutonium for military use. A third proposal, offered by the Pacific Gas and Electric and Bechtel Corporation Group, asked to build a similar dual-purpose reactor if it could gain the Commission's assistance and support. Other companies expressing similar interest in the dual-purpose reactor included Northern Illinois Public Service Company and General Electric. Thus by 1952 the AEC was sufficiently convinced of industry's eagerness to participate in atomic power development and it issued a second invitation for industry participation in April of that year. Industry response was immediate and soon the number of United States firms involved in atomic energy swelled to twenty-five. With such a convincing show of interest from private industry, the Commission's next task was to establish a sound policy of atomic power development based on extensive industry participation. This they began in the fall of 1952.[45]

Toward a Policy for Civilian Nuclear Power

While the AEC was doubtless aware of the importance of formulating a sound policy for civilian power development, its importance was reemphasized in a letter to the AEC in August 1952 from Representative Carl T. Durham, Chairman of the Joint Committee on Atomic Energy. Durham indicated that the Joint Committee was planning a series of hearings in early-1953 in order to determine the nature and state of industry participation in the nation's atomic reactor program, and that the Commission should be prepared to state its policy regarding this matter.[46] In May of 1953, the Commission responded with a policy statement stressing that cost-competitive nuclear power could be realized as an important national objective in the near future. This could be attained, the Commission asserted, by encouraging and offering such incentives as private ownership and operation of facilities to "'qualified and interested groups outside the Commission'."[47] As retiring AEC Chairman Gordon Dean described it to the Joint Committee:[48]

> It is the judgment of the Commission that now is the time to announce a positive policy designed to recognize the development of economic nuclear power as a national objective. An important element of this policy is to *promote and encourage free competition and private investment in the developmental work, while at the same time accepting on the part of government certain responsibilities for such development*... It would be a major set-back to the position of this country in the world to allow its present leadership in nuclear power development to pass out of its hands.

By the time the hearings had ended several things seemed clear. First, greater industry participation was not only desirable, but necessary. But in order to insure such participation, incentives seemed imperative. This meant, among other things, that the 1946 Atomic Energy Act would have to be amended to permit ownership and operation of nuclear facilities by private industry and utility companies, for at that time ownership and control was entrusted to the Commission alone. Second, if Dean's policy statement was to be effected, the Commission had to establish a more well-organized *civilian* research and development *program*. Indeed, Representative W. Sterling Cole, the new Chairman of the Joint Committee, had specified such a program in 1953 in a letter to the incoming AEC Chairman, Lewis L. Strauss.[49] Cole suggested implementing a three to five-year research and development plan to concentrate on nuclear plant hardware, materials testing, pilot plants, and prototypes, and one that would insure participation of all interested companies and organizations.[50]

In response to Cole's request for establishing a more well-defined civilian power program, Chairman Strauss proceeded to cancel the dual-purpose reactor projects. He declared that the AEC was now more interested in developing full-scale nuclear reactors for power production on a civilian basis since the military and the government's plutonium needs were being adequately fulfilled by the AEC's already existing materials production reactors. Consequently, none of the dual-purpose reactor projects first suggested by Monsanto president Charles A. Thomas was accepted, and the AEC asked study groups to shift to the civilian power projects instead. And in February of 1954, the AEC announced the United States' second[51] full-scale nuclear power reactor program, the Five-Year Power Program.[52] With the dual-purpose reactor now disbanded in favor of the civilian power projects, Monsanto Chemical Company, the initial proponent of greater industry participation, withdrew from the project and subsequently dismantled its nuclear reactor department.[53]

The Five-Year Power Program: The Power Reactor Demonstration Program, First Round

As the AEC was busy formulating the details of its Five-Year Power Program, the 1946 Atomic Energy Act was rewritten in order to more effectively accommodate large-scale private business and industry participation in nuclear power development. Under the new Act, the Atomic Energy Act of 1954, the section dealing with commercial licensing had been almost totally revised to permit private ownership of nuclear reactors under AEC license, while the AEC retained ownership of nuclear fuels, which it would lease to private users.[54] The new Act also spelled out more clearly new methods and principles of contracting vital research and development that were designed to promote and encourage greater industry participation.[55] In addition, the Act called for a somewhat revised policy regarding information dissemination. As the Act put it: "The dissemination of scientific and technical information relating to atomic energy should be permitted and encouraged so as to provide that *free interchange of ideas and criticism which is essential to scientific and industrial progress* and public understanding and to enlarge the fund of technical information." (emphasis added)

Further impetus to revise the Act resulted from the general failure of United States international policies of atomic energy. By late-1953 it was clear that the policy of relying upon secrecy would not deter other nations in the world from developing their own weapons programs; in fact, the Soviet Union had detonated a nuclear device as early as 1949 and Britain was well on its way to testing its first nuclear weapons in 1953. Signifying a break-up in the United States monopoly over atomic energy information, President Dwight Eisenhower addressed the United Nations General Assembly on December 8, 1953 and declared in his famous "Atoms for Peace" speech that the peaceful development of atomic energy ought to proceed through an international agency which would supervise and stockpile fissionable material, to be used to "serve the peaceful pursuits of mankind... and to provide abundant electrical energy to the power-starved areas of the world." The idea was to strengthen peace and create an international framework for cooperation in which the "contributing powers would be dedicating some of their strength to serve the needs rather than the fears of mankind."[56] Besides serving domestic priorities, the revised Atomic Energy Act would thus help establish a more realistic United States international policy for atomic energy development and control.

As the AEC continued working out its own Five-Year Power Program, the nature and results of which are summarized in Table 3.1,* the way was now cleared for a new development program by non-government agents. In January 1955, the Power Reactor Demonstration Program (PRDP) was announced by the AEC as "designed 'to open the way for

*see page 68.

American industry to develop, fabricate, construct and operate experimental nuclear power reactors' and offered to consider on a competitive basis proposals for AEC cooperation in privately financed power reactor projects."[57] More specifically, the program "proposed to waive use charges for materials, to undertake certain mutually agreeable research and development in AEC laboratories, and to enter into fixed-sum research-and-development contracts for buying technical and economic data from the applicant."[58] With the reactor work in the AEC's own Five-Year Power Program as its technological basis, the PRDP provided Commission assistance to private industry, but the companies were assumed to be responsible for ownership, construction, and operation of nuclear power plants.[59] By April of 1955, three proposals were received by the AEC in response to the First Round PRDP invitations.[60]

The first proposal was received from the newly formed consortium of New England electric utilities, Yankee Atomic Electric Company. Yankee Atomic proposed construction of a pressurized-water reactor similar in design to the AEC's Shippingport, Pennsylvania reactor (see Table 3.1), with a capacity of 100,000 kilowatts. The reactor was to be designed and built by Westinghouse at a site located in northwestern Massachusetts.[61]

Consumers Public Power District of Columbus, Nebraska submitted a second proposal. The utility proposed construction of a 75,000 kilowatt sodium-graphite reactor near Hallam, Nebraska. North American Aviation, Inc., which had been working on the Sodium Reactor Experiment at Santa Sussana, California, was selected as the reactor designer.

The third proposal submitted came from the Detroit Edison Group. The utility requested to build a 100,000 kilowatt fast-breeder reactor at Monroe, Michigan. Similar to the AEC's experimental breeder reactor, the reactor would be designed by the newly created Power Development Company.

The AEC approved all three proposals and construction on the plants began. While the Yankee Atomic plant was scheduled for operation by 1957, it did not begin full-power operation until early-1961. The final cost was over $55 million, revised upward from an earlier $35 million estimate. The Consumers Public Power District's sodium reactor did not go into operation until 1963; and it, too, suffered a cost overrun, from an estimated $24 million to a final $40 million. Lastly, the

Detroit Edison project was scheduled for operation in late-1958, but was not completed until 1964. Unexpected technological difficulties and construction delays by AFL-CIO labor organizations claiming public health and safety hazards in 1958 were responsible for the delay, but no cost overrun was experienced, with the completion cost being around $43 million.

Non-Government Private Power Projects

Besides the three projects in the First Round of the PRDP that received substantial financial support from the AEC, several additional applications for construction permits were received from companies willing to foot the entire cost of construction themselves. The Commonwealth Edison Company of Chicago requested from the AEC in August 1955 a permit to build a 180,000 kilowatt boiling-water facility at Dresden, Illinois with General Electric as the intended contractor.[62] Similarly, Consolidated Edison Company of New York requested a permit to build a pressurized-water reactor in March 1955. Babcock and Wilcox Company, a fledgling in the nuclear power industry, was selected to construct the 163,000 kilowatt power plant at Indian Point, a site located on the Hudson River, for an estimated cost of about $70 million.[63] The third concern to request a construction permit without government assistance came from General Electric. General Electric wanted to build a 5,000 kilowatt prototype of the Dresden, Illinois plant at their newly opened laboratories in Vallecitos, California.[64] All three requests were approved by the AEC.

The Power Reactor Demonstration Program, Second Round

By October 1955 the AEC had issued a second invitation for industry participation in the reactor program. The second round invitations called for industry construction of several government-owned power reactors. The government would finance the projects and the electric companies were to build and operate the facilities, with the option of purchasing the steam produced from the reactors. The reactors were to be in the range of 5,000 to 40,000 kilowatts, significantly smaller than some of the earlier models and suitable in size for use by electric companies serving rural areas.[65]

Several proposals were initially received in the Second Round invitations of the PRDP, but only three of the proposed plants were constructed and put into operation: (1) a 22,000 kilowatt boiling-water plant at Elk River, Minnesota owned by the Rural Cooperative Power Association, and built by ACF Industries, Inc.; (2) a 12,5000 kilowatt organic-moderated reactor at Piqua, Ohio, and constructed by North American Aviation, Inc; and (3) a 16,300 kilowatt boiling-water plant constructed by the General Nuclear Engineering Corporation (a division of Combustion Engineering, Inc.) for the Puerto Rican Water Resources Authority. All three plants reached full power operation in 1964, some nine years after the original 1955 invitations had been issued.[66]

The Power Reactor Demonstration Program, Third Round

While the reactor program seemed to be moving ahead smoothly in early-1956, the democratic members of the Joint Committee were of a different opinion. In view of the advances in nuclear technology made by the United Kingdom, France, and the Soviet Union, as well as the recommendations made by the McKinney Panel on the Impact of the Peaceful Uses of Atomic Energy, the Joint Committee felt a sizable new effort was needed to bring civilian nuclear power to fruition. These concerns were reflected in the Joint Committee's 1956 Gore-Holifield Bill, which called for a $400 million government appropriation for a new reactor construction program.[67] There was a heated debate between the proponents of so-called government financed "public power" (similar to TVA) which Gore-Holifield proposed, and the supporters of development and commercialization by private enterprise and the utility companies. The basic exchange concerned these value and policy implications of the bill, as well as some questions regarding the amount and availability of trained personnel and manpower in the nuclear industry. However, the main thrust of Gore-Holifield pointed out that no United States nuclear facility was yet producing commercially usable power. The bill passed in the Senate but was defeated in the House despite substantial modification. Notwithstanding this defeat, the message of the Joint Committee was clear and in January 1957 the AEC issued a

Third Round invitation for industry to construct with government assistance two large, new power reactors.[68]

While the announcement of the Third Round PRDP continued to strengthen the fast-growing government-industry partnership in nuclear energy, the year 1957 was marked by other significant developments important in consolidating this partnership. The AEC's first large-scale safety study, *Theoretical Possibilities and Consequences of Major Accidents in Large Nuclear Power Plants*,[69] contracted to the Brookhaven National Laboratory by the AEC in 1956, was published in 1957. The study indicated that a major reactor accident might cause thousands of deaths and injuries at distances up to seventy-five miles from the point of origin, and that property damages could reach as high as $7 billion. To many, the report was seen as a major deterrent to full-scale industry involvement in nuclear power, since the financial liabilities of a catastrophic accident would obviously bankrupt any equipment vendor or utility company. Furthermore, what insurance company would be willing to insure an enterprise whose liabilities were of this magnitude? Unless some drastic new policies were undertaken, clearly there would be little or no large-scale capital investment in nuclear power by non-government agents.

Thus in 1957, Congress reponded by enacting an amendment to the Atomic Energy Act of 1954, the Price-Anderson Act.[70] In addition to requiring any licensee of a nuclear facility to carry the maximum liability coverage available from the insurance industry, the Act provided up to $560 million in government indemnity to any person or party held liable for a nuclear accident causing substantial injury and property damage. Damages beyond the $560 million ceiling automatically would be cut off. The result, of course, was neither utility companies nor vendors of nuclear plant hardware and equipment could be held responsible for financial liabilities in the event of a serious accident; the federal government had almost totally underwritten their financial responsibility. This was a great boon to increased industry investment in nuclear power, for, as Harold Green has remarked:[71] "It is clear that in 1957, when Price-Anderson was enacted, there would have been no investment in nuclear power so long as the threat--even the remote possibility--of such astronomical liability remained." The

Price-Anderson Act, then, was a major legislative step in bringing increased industry involvement to nuclear power development.

In addition to the financial "umbrella" now provided by Price-Anderson, the Third Round invitations proposed that the AEC finance all research and development costs, as well as waive entirely uranium lease charges for up to seven years.[72] Of the three proposals received from industry for the Third Round program, two were authorized by the AEC. The Northern States Power Company of Minneapolis, Minnesota proposed building a boiling-water reactor to be manufactured by Allis-Chalmers Manufacturing Corporation, a major subcontractor to the Argonne National Laboratory.[73] The plant would be a 62,000 kilowatt facility located at Sioux Falls, South Dakota. The second approved proposal had been received from the Carolinas-Virginia Nuclear Power Associates. The group proposed construction of a 17,000 kilowatt nuclear facility at Pan Shoals, South Carolina. The reactor was a heavy-water moderated type to be designed and constructed by Westinghouse. Both plants began operation in 1964.[74]

By June 1959 a third plant had been approved by the AEC under the Third Round invitations. The Consumers Power Company of Jackson, Michigan had chosen General Electric and Bechtel Corporation to design and construct a boiling-water reactor with a 50,000 kilowatt capacity at Big Rock, Michigan. All construction permits and licensing procedures were settled by June 1960 and construction was completed in mid-1962.[75]

Two additional plants were constructed under the Third Round invitations, bringing the total to five. The first of the additional plants was a graphite-moderated, gas-cooled reactor (similar to those developed in England) of 45,000 kilowatts proposed by the Philadelphia Electric Company. The proposal was accepted in 1959 and General Atomics (a division of General Dynamics Corporation) began construction at Peach Bottom, Pennsylvania in 1960. The plant was scheduled for full operation in 1965.[76] The second additional plant was a large 370,000 kilowatt pressurized-water reactor proposed by Southern California Edison Company of Los Angeles. Westinghouse had been chosen to design and construct the plant at Camp Pendleton, California for a total estimated cost of around $78 million. Construction began in 1964.[77]

Summary and Conclusions

In evaluating the results of the AEC's second full-scale nuclear power reactor program, several conclusions are worthy of mention. First, the AEC continued its policy of diverse reactor design. Not only were there many different types of nuclear reactors now in existence, but the sizes also ranged from General Electric's 5,000 kilowatt prototype reactor at Vallecitos to the 370,000 kilowatt pressurized-water facility proposed by Southern California Edison.

Second, the program continued to be expensive. Not only were the power plants expensive to begin with, but in nearly all cases cost overruns were experienced to the tune of almost twice the original estimates. This trend continued throughout the 1960s and 1970s, with inflation and construction delays forced by citizen protest further adding to the costs.

Third, while the first development program experienced a general lack of industry participation, the second program succeeded in gathering an impressive number of the country's leading industrial concerns to join the atomic energy effort. Not only did industry participation lead to what can only be termed spectacular technological achievements in the nuclear energy field, but also, such participation lead to a *redefinition* of the approaches and general policies of the atomic energy programs, represented most conspicuously by the rewriting of the Atomic Energy Act of 1946. Thus the Atomic Energy Act of 1954 called for a significantly revised approach to atomic power development in the United States. Ownership and control of nuclear facilities no longer remained the sole responsibility of the Commission. The AEC did, however, retain title and rights to the control of nuclear fuels, but ownership, construction of facilities, and power plant operation was now left to private industry and the utility companies. One might also add, however, that while a number of additional industrial firms had become involved in nuclear energy, General Electric and Westinghouse continued to design and construct most of the new power plants.[78]

Fourth, the second reactor program continued the policy of conducting basic scientific and technological work at the nation's government laboratories, but now allowing private industry greater access to research results. Clearly, the government had decided to remain at the center of nuclear energy research by engaging in this strategy. Besides, research conducted through the federally funded national laboratory was an effective method of insuring that the government's military research needs would be adequately met, and presumably would also fulfill the section of the 1946 Act which specified a "program of federally conducted research to assure the Government of adequate scientific and technical accomplishment."

Fifth, as the second development program took shape, it appeared that the Joint Committee on Atomic Energy would assume a more central policy role in nuclear power development. It not only monitored more closely the activities of the AEC, but it also began demanding more accountability and planning of the nation's atomic energy programs. In addition, the Joint Committee began to more forcibly demonstrate its policy wishes, as evidenced, for example, by the Gore-Holifield Bill. But more than anything else, the Joint Committee seemed committed to developing civilian nuclear power as fast as practicable and thus provided a favorable political climate that insured adequate funds, conducive legislation, and other forms of vital encouragement for the fledgling nuclear power industry. The Price-Anderson Act is a case in point.

In sum, the Power Reactor Demonstration Programs marked the consolidation of the government-industry partnership in nuclear energy development. In fulfilling the requirements of the Atomic Energy Acts, and as civilian nuclear power became envisioned as a major energy alternative and national objective of the future, the AEC established by 1959 a solid research and financial base on which to build industry participation in the nation's nuclear energy effort. With the newly revised Atomic Energy Act of 1954 providing industry with greater incentives and opportunities than had existed previously, and with the relief of financial responsibility provided by the Price-Anderson Act in 1957, it seemed an era of full-scale industry participation in nuclear energy had finally arrived.

THE TEN-YEAR CIVILIAN POWER REACTOR PROGRAM

Overview

At the so-called "202" hearings in 1959,[79] the newly appointed AEC Chairman John McCone announced plans for a new atomic energy program. The new plan would continue the policy of inviting industry participation, as well as continue the vigorous experimental design and construction of reactor prototypes at all AEC-operated sites. In addition, McCone stressed the desire to make nuclear power cost-competitive with other energy sources by 1968, meaning continued emphasis would be placed on large reactor types such as the 370,000 kilowatt facility proposed by Southern California Edison for the Camp Pendleton, California site. And finally, asserted McCone, the new program would aim at maintaining United States leadership in the nuclear technology field.[80]

With respect to the reactor development program, it would follow a "three-phase sequence." As Nehrt summarizes:[81]

> This program was to follow a three-phase sequence for the development of individual reactor types: an experimental reactor would be constructed and operated bv the USAEC; prototypes would then be built and operated by electrical utilities, either independently or in cooperation with the USAEC, (Although prototypes could in some cases be built by the USAEC); the utility industry would then be expected to assume primary responsibility for the large, commercial-size plants, although the USAEC would consider giving various types of assistance where the plant was useful for demonstration purposes.

In accordance with the Ten-Year Program, in December 1959 the AEC issued invitations to utilities for construction of two 50,000 kilowatt prototype nuclear power plants: a boiling-water reactor with an improved cycle and an organic-moderated reactor.[82] While the organic-moderated reactor was never constructed and the project subsequently dropped, a 50,000 kilowatt boiling-water reactor was designed and constructed with considerable AEC assistance by Allis-Chalmers Manufacturing Company, to be operated by Dairyland Power Corporation of La Crosse, Wisconsin when start-up was reached in 1966.[83]

Two additional plants, independent of governmental programs and financial assistance, also began construction during this period. Both had been proposed by Pacific Gas and Electric of California. The first plant was a 50,000 kilowatt facility to be designed and constructed by General Electric and Bechtel Corporation at Humbolt Bay, near Eureka, California. The construction permit was issued by the AEC in 1960, with start-up scheduled for 1966.[84] The second Pacific Gas and Electric plant was a 325,000 kilowatt boiling-water facility to be designed and constructed by General Electric just outside San Francisco, at Bodega Bay, California. Citizen opposition, however, delayed construction of the proposed $62 million facility for over three years, and the project was eventually cancelled.[85]

But the most salient characteristic to be noted about the Ten-Year Program was it seemed to indicate a nearly institutionalized pattern of relationships between government and industry in nuclear power development. The kernel of this pattern is easily gleaned from McCone's statement at the 202 hearings: the government would continue to invite industry participation in nuclear energy development; it would offer industry continued scientific and financial support; and it remained convinced that full civilian application of nuclear energy would be shortly forthcoming. Further, the "three-stage sequence" of implementation of power reactors--construction and operation of experimental reactors by the AEC, construction and operation of prototypes (with AEC assistance) by utility companies, and construction and operation of the large commercial plants by the utilities--seemed to firmly knot the essential pattern of the government industry partnership by the early 1960s.

SUMMARY AND CONCLUSIONS

While the above is not, of course, a wholly exhaustive overview of the complex nature of nuclear power programs, it is nonetheless clear how the government-industry partnership was consolidated and how the commercial application of nuclear energy was initially achieved. At this point a summary and the main conclusions of the chapter are presented.

Perhaps the most salient characteristic of the civilian power programs promulgated by the Atomic

Energy Commission was what might be termed "multiple development." From the earliest days of the Manhattan Project, the AEC inherited the practice of embarking upon multiple reactor designs and approaches to technology development. Clearly, the strategy was successful for it prevented the program from being stalled when certain designs proved unworkable. This strategy also had the decided advantage of testing several different designs for different applications, thereby providing the Commission with the widest possible variety of information on which deployment decisions could be based. There is little question that the policy of multiple development must be seen as one of the major elements in the Commission's success in bringing commercial reactors on-line in such a short period of time.

Second, it was plain that the development strategy tended to rely on rigorous, small-scale testing by the AEC and the vendors of nuclear plant hardware, as well as on the construction of reactor prototypes by firms such as General Electric and Westinghouse. This allowed comprehensive testing of all major hardware and plant components, and provided experimental data that could help predict the outcome of actual, full-scale operation when the plants finally went on-line. Coupled with the AEC's practice of sequential development and the gradual scaling-up in size of new plants, as discussed above, the AEC could be reasonably certain that the new plants would perform adequately.

A third characteristic of the reactor programs concerned the influence exercised by the military, and especially the Navy's drive to build a nuclear submarine fleet. Not only did the military's needs for procurring plutonium result in certain developmental efforts--such as in the case of the proposed dual-purpose reactors--but Admiral Rickover's zeal to build a reactor suitable for submarine use resulted in a viable, dependable design that could be scaled-up for civilian purposes. Indeed, both the boiling-water reactors and the pressurized-water reactors designed by General Electric and Westinghouse, and which remain the predominant types of commercial reactors now in service in the United States, owed much of their design impetus to the Navy's submarine program. The influence of military objectives cannot be underestimated in their influence on the civilian power reactor effort.

Fourth, as the reactor programs got under way,

it became clear that major United States industrial firms were unlikely to make large capital expenditures in uncertain technical areas without more adequate technical demonstration and financial help from the government. As a result, the AEC was forced to declassify major technical information and provide substantial incentives to private industry--such as independent, private ownership of reactors and fuels, and government research and development and financial assistance. This became the guiding philosophy of the AEC's three rounds of the Power Reactor Demonstration Programs, where industry was approached by the AEC with direct invitations and offers of considerable assistance.

Fifth, as time went on the Joint Committee on Atomic Energy began to assume a more formidable role in the civilian power programs. On the one hand, the Joint Committee became more involved in basic policy-making and in determining the objectives of the reactor programs. Of this they made no secret, and was made clear, for example, in the numerous letters by Joint Committee Chairmen to the AEC and the annual "202" hearings cited in several places above. On the other hand, the Joint Committee also provided favorable legislative concessions to the nuclear industry, including the rewriting of the Atomic Energy Act in 1954 which allowed industry easy access to the programs already being conducted by the Commission; and the Price-Anderson Act in 1957, which provided government funds to cover all accident liabilities of the nuclear industry. These are only two of the more important examples of how the Committee devised legislation that would encourage industry involvement in nuclear energy development.

Finally, some mention must be made on the negative side, and which perhaps helps explain some of the controversy which envelops civilian nuclear power today. That is, although the civilian power programs had been spectacularly successful in their own terms, the AEC and the nuclear industry for the most part failed in nearly every case in terms of cost-estimation and predicting time schedules for construction of new facilities. Moreover, there seemed to be a clear lack of comparison of nuclear technology with other ways of generating electricity; different reactor designs were certainly vigorously compared with each other, but not with other technologies such as solar energy, coal gasification, or other methods. Together with the failure to estimate costs and construction times, the lack of comparison with alternative energy-generating technologies left the wisdom of the enthusiastic promotion of nuclear power open to serious question. While one cannot deny the apparent technical success of the civilian power programs in the United States, the question of whether the nuclear option should have been pursued to the extent it was is another matter. And when one adds to this unexpected problems such as those regarding basic safety questions and the unresolved difficulties posed by the disposal of radioactive wastes, the point is underscored.

Be this as it may, in the early 1950s it was believed that the key to making nuclear energy practical for civilian use lay in coordinating a massive effort by United States Government agencies and private industry. Certainly, the Power Reactor Demonstration Programs can be said to have made impressive strides in this direction. By the early 1960s and the initiation of the Ten-Year Program, it seemed the peaceful uses of the atom were at last within the grasp of humanity. Yet the nuclear programs began raising an entirely different set of questions for which there seemed no clear-cut answers. Already the cries were echoing throughout the nation: at Monroe, Michigan AFL-CIO construction workers had walked off the job, claiming the new plant posed serious health and safety hazards to themselves, the surrounding community, and the environment. Similarly, citizen groups had organized at Shippingport, Pennsylvania and at Bodega Bay, California to protest the nuclear plants being built there. And the AEC's own radiation standards were being assailed from many camps within the scientific and academic communities.[86] To those who had worked so tirelessly on nuclear energy since the days of the first programs, civilian nuclear power seemed a tremendous technological achievement that promised a great bounty for mankind. But suddenly, nuclear energy had begun raising some perplexing new concerns which scientific and technological sophistication seemed, so far, unable to answer.

Thus atomic energy--what many observers considered after the frightful nightmares of Hiroshima and Nagasaki the scourge of mankind--was still faced with the familiar old question in 1960: Could the atom serve mankind for peaceful purposes after all? The events which began with the first Congressional debates in late-1945 and early-1946, and which set into motion the wheels of civilian nuclear power development rooted in a broad based government-industry partnership, did not yet offer a satisfactory answer. By 1960, the first rumblings of the nuclear power controversy were already being felt.

TABLE 3.1:* FIVE-YEAR POWER PROGRAM

Reactor* Name	Location*	Reactor Designer* and Manufacturer	Completion+ Date	Cost	Electrical* Output
Pressurized-Water Reactor (PWR)	Shippingport, Pennsylvania	Westinghouse	December, 1957	$55 million $5 million by Duquesne Light Company	60,000 kw
Experimental Boiling-Water Reactor (EBWR)	Argonne National Laboratory (near Chicago)	Argonne National Laboratory	December, 1956	$6.1 million	5,000 kw
Sodium Reactor Experiment (SRE)	Santa Susanna, California	North American Aviation	April, 1957	$15.6 million of which $2.9 million by North American Aviation	6,500 kw
Homogeneous Reactor Experiment No. 2 (HRE No. 2)	Oak Ridge, Tennessee	Oak Ridge National Laboratory	Abandoned in 1957 after many technical difficulties		designed for 5,000 kw
Experimental Breeder Reactor No. 2 (EBR No. 2)	Argonne National Laboratory	Argonne National Laboratory	November, 1957	$29.1 million	20,000 kw

*U.S. Atomic Energy Commission, *Nineteenth Semi-Annual Report, 1956*, pp. 40-45.

+Ibid., *Major Activities in the Atomic Energy Programs, January-June, 1957*, pp. 49-53.

NOTES

1. Harold P. Green and Alan Rosenthal, *Government of the Atom: The Integration of Powers* (New York: Atherton Press, 1963), p. 76.

2. Lee C. Nehrt, *International Marketing of Nuclear Power Plants* (Bloomington: Indiana University Press, 1966), pp. 27-28.

3. David Lilienthal, "Private Industry and the Public Atom," reprinted in the *Bulletin of the Atomic Scientists* 5 (Janaury 1949): 6-8.

4. Nehrt, *International Marketing of Nuclear Power Plants*, p. 29; and "Report of the AEC Industrial Advisory Group," *Bulletin of the Atomic Scientists* 5 (February 1949): 51-55.

5. "Report of the AEC Industrial Advisory Group," pp. 51-55; and Lawrence R. Hafstad, "Reactor Program of the AEC," *Bulletin of the Atomic Scientists* 7 (April 1951): 109-14. For additional materials see United States Atomic Energy Commission, *Semi-Annual Report to Congress, July-December 1948* (Washington, D.C.: U.S. Government Printing Office, 1949).

6. Cited in Oliver Townsend, "The Atomic Power Program in the United States," in American Assembly, *Atoms for Power: United States Policy in Atomic Energy Development* (New York: American Assembly, 1957), p. 51.

7. United States Congress, Hearings before the Special Committee on Atomic Energy, *A Bill for the Development and Control of Atomic Energy*, 79th Congress, 2nd Session, 1946 (Washington, D.C.: U.S. Government Printing Office, 1947), p. 31.

8. Nehrt, *International Marketing of Nuclear Power Plants*, p. 29. See also Frank G. Dawson, *Nuclear Power: Development and Management of a Technology* (Seattle: University of Washington Press, 1976), pp. 36-40 for a relevant discussion.

9. Richard G. Hewlett and Oscar E. Anderson, Jr., *The New World, 1939/1946: Volume One of the History of the United States Atomic Energy Commission* (University Park: Pennsylvania State University Press, 1962), see especially chapters 3-9.

10. Nehrt, *International Marketing of Nuclear Power Plants*, pp. 55-56.

11. Hewlett and Anderson, The New World, p. 112. See also Gordon Dean, *Report on the Atom* (New York: Knopf, 1953), p. 149.

12. Nehrt, *International Marketing of Nuclear Power Plants*, p. 55.

13. Ibid. For the complete story of Oak Ridge and its atomic energy facilities, see Hewlett and Anderson, *The New World*, pp. 76-173.

14. Nehrt, *International Marketing of Nuclear Power Plants*, p. 56. For a good discussion of the Hanford installation see Hewlett and Anderson, *The New World*, pp. 188-226.

15. Nehrt, *International Marketing of Nuclear Power Plants*, p. 56.

16. Hewlett and Anderson, *The New World*, p. 252 and Ibid.

17. Hewlett and Anderson, *The New World*, pp. 627, 631 and Nehrt, *International Marketing of Nuclear Power Plants*, p. 56. Additional information on these materials may be found in Walter H. Zinn, Frank K. Pittman, and John F. Hogerton, *Nuclear Power, U.S.A.* (New York: McGraw-Hill, 1964).

18. Townsend, "The Atomic Power Program in the U.S.," pp. 52-53.

19. For a full account of these and other details involved with the Navy's atomic submarine project see Richard G. Hewlett and Francis Duncan, *Nuclear Navy 1946-1962*, (Chicago: University of Chicago Press, 1974).

20. Ibid, pp. 216-220.

21. United States Atomic Energy Commission, *Major Activities in the Atomic Energy Programs, January-June 1953* (Washington, D.C.: U.S. Government Printing Office, 1953), p. 21. See also Nehrt, *International Marketing of Nuclear Power Plants*, pp. 57-58.

22. Townsend, "The Atomic Power Program in the U.S.," p. 53. See also United States Congress, Hearings before the Joint Committee on Atomic Energy, *Atomic Power and Private Enterprise*, 82nd Congress, 2nd Session, 1952 (Washington, D. C.: U.S. Government Printing Office, 1952). On the selection of the Idaho test site see Richard G. Hewlett and Francis Duncan, *Atomic Shield, 1947/1952: Volume Two of the History of the United States Atomic Energy Commission* (University Park: Pennsylvania State University Press, 1969), pp. 210-219. On Hafstad's appointment see *Atomic Shield*, pp. 209-210. Note also that the Idaho test site was operated for the AEC by the Phillips Petroleum Company. See Dawson, *Nuclear Power*, p. 49.

23. Townsend, "The Atomic Power Program in the U.S.," p. 54.

24. The materials in this section are drawn largely from Ibid., pp. 54-56 unless specified otherwise.

25. Hewlett and Duncan, *Nuclear Navy*, especially chapters 7-10. It might also be mentioned that the addition of missile-firing capabilities to the submarines in the late 1950s revolutionized not simply naval warfare but warfare in all respects.

26. Professor A. Hunter Dupree has pointed out that a "simulated accident" may be irrelevant in the case of nuclear plants, for if an accident can be simulated, then it can also be protected against. The most serious accidents are those which are totally unforeseen, and therefore *not* protected against.

27. For a good account of the start-up of the experimental breeder see Hewlett and Duncan, *Atomic Shield*, pp. 497-498.

28. Ibid., p. 423.

29. Hewlett and Duncan, *Nuclear Navy*, p. 370.

30. Nehrt, *International Marketing of Nuclear Power Plants*, p. 58. See also United States Atomic Energy Commission, *Major Activities in the Atomic Energy Programs, January-June 1953*, p. 21. And for related discussions of interest see Zinn, *et. al.*, *Nuclear Power, U.S.A.* and Dawson, *Nuclear Power*, pp. 36 ff.

31. Townsend, "The Atomic Power Program in the U.S.," pp. 57-58.

32. Ibid., p. 57.

33. Hewlett and Duncan, *Atomic Shield*, pp. 424-425, 429-430.

34. Townsend, "The Atomic Power Program in the U.S.," pp. 57-58.

35. Hewlett and Duncan, *Nuclear Navy*, pp. 196-198.

36. Hewlett and Duncan, *Atomic Shield*, pp. 516-517.

37. For a complete account of the nuclear aircraft program see W. Henry Lambright, *Shooting Down the Nuclear Plane* (Indianapolis: Bobbs-Merrill, 1967). A good summary discussion also is found in Green and Rosenthal, *Government of the Atom*, pp. 242-247.

38. David Lilienthal, "Free the Atom," *Collier's* 125 (June 1950): 13-15, 54-58.

39. Hewlett and Duncan, *Atomic Shield*, p. 436.

40. Ibid.

41. Cited in Townsend, "The Atomic Power Program in the U.S.," p. 59.

42. Hewlett and Duncan, *Atomic Shield*, p. 438.

43. Cited in Townsend, "The Atomic Power Program in the U.S.," p. 59.

44. Ibid. For additional materials on the dual-purpose projects see Dawson, *Nuclear Power*, pp. 49-50 and United States Atomic Energy Commission, *Semi-Annual Report to Congress, July-December 1952*, (Washington, D.C.: U.S. Government Printing Office, 1953), pp. 23 ff.

45. Townsend, "The Atomic Power Program in the U.S.," p. 60.

46. Green and Rosenthal, *Government of the Atom*, p. 252 and Dawson, *Nuclear Power*, pp. 53 ff.

47. Green and Rosenthal, *Government of the Atom*, p. 252.

48. Cited in Townsend, "The Atomic Power Program in the U.S.," p. 51; emphasis added.

49. Green and Rosenthal, *Government of the Atom*, p. 253.

50. Ibid. See also Townsend, "The Atomic Power Program in the U.S.," pp. 62-63, and Fritz F. Heimann, "How Can We Get the Nuclear Job Done?" in Arthur W. Murphy (ed.), *The Nuclear Power Controversy* (Englewood Cliffs: Prentice-Hall, 1976), pp. 89-92.

51. If one counts the Manhattan Project, this was actually the third formalized U.S. atomic energy program.

52. Green and Rosenthal, *Government of the Atom*, p. 253; Nehrt, *International Marketing of Nuclear Power Plants*, p. 58; and Townsend, "The Atomic Power Program in the U.S.," pp. 61-63.

53. Townsend, "The Atomic Power Program in the U.S.," p. 61.

54. See Public Law 703, "The Atomic Energy Act of 1954," in *United States Statutes at Large 1954*, V. 68, Part 1 (Washington, D.C.: U.S. Government Printing Office, 1955), pp. 936-939. See also Green and Rosenthal, *Government of the Atom*, p. 254.

55. Public Law 703, "The Atomic Energy Act of 1954," pp. 927-928.

56. A good account of the Atoms for Peace speech, as well as an extended discussion of the legislative history of the 1954 Act, is found in Dawson, *Nuclear Power*, pp. 58-75. Quotes are taken from United States Congress, House of Representatives, *Legislative History of the Atomic Energy Act of 1954*, 83rd Congress, 2nd Session,

1954, House Document No. 328 (Washington, D.C.: U.S. Government Printing Office, 1954), p. 1641.

57. Green and Rosenthal, *Government of the Atom*, pp. 254-55.

58. Ibid., p. 255. See also United States Congress, Joint Committee on Atomic Energy, *Five-Year Power Reactor Development Program Proposed by the Atomic Energy Commission* (Joint Committee Print, March 1954) for additional materials.

59. Nehrt, *International Marketing of Nuclear Power Plants*, p. 58. Note also that all experimental and technological work conducted at the government laboratories--i.e., Oak Ridge, Los Alamos, Hanford, Argonne, and Brookhaven--could be made available through the AEC to the power companies. See Townsend, "The Atomic Power Program in the U.S.," pp. 65-66.

60. United States Atomic Energy Commission, *Eighteenth Semi-Annual Report 1954* (Washington, D.C.: U.S. Government Printing Office, 1954), p. 42. For more on the effects of the Atomic Energy Act of 1954 for atomic power development, see a comprehensive article by Clinton P. Anderson, "The Atom--Everybody's Business or Nobody's Business?" *State Government* 29 (December 1956): 243-47.

61. Unless noted otherwise the materials on which the following pages are based are drawn from Nehrt, *International Marketing of Nuclear Power Plants*, pp. 61 ff. and Townsend, "The Atomic Power Program in the U.S.," pp. 71 ff. A related discussion can be found in Dawson, *Nuclear Power*, pp. 84-89.

62. Note that Commonwealth Edison of Chicago was affiliated with four other companies: Union Electric Company, Pacific Gas and Electric Company, American Gas and Electric Company, and the Bechtel Corporation. And the cost of the plant was estimated to be about $45 million. See Townsend, "The Atomic Power Program in the U.S.," p. 70.

63. Nehrt, *International Marketing of Nuclear Power Plants*, pp. 61-62. The cost of the Indian Point Plant was estimated at about $70 million. See Ibid., p. 70.

64. Nehrt, *International Marketing of Nuclear Power Plants*, pp. 61-62.

65. United States Atomic Energy Commission, *Twentieth Semi-Annual Report 1956* (Washington, D.C.: U.S. Government Printing Office, 1956), pp. 35-37. See also John F. Hogerton, "The

Arrival of Nuclear Power," *Scientific American* 218 (February 1968): 23-24 and Dawson, *Nuclear Power*, pp. 98-100.

66. Nehrt, *International Marketing of Nuclear Power Plants*, pp. 62-63.

67. Green and Rosenthal, *Government of the Atom*, p. 256. See also United States Congress, Hearings before the Joint Committee on Atomic Energy, *Report of the Panel on the Impact of the Peaceful Uses of Atomic Energy*, 84th Congress, 2nd Session, 1956, V. 1 (Washington, D.C.: U.S. Government Printing Office, 1956). Also related is Robert McKinney, "Impact of the Peaceful Uses of Atomic Energy," *State Government* 29 (December 1956): 248-52. For additional material on the Gore-Holifield Bill see United States Congress, Hearings before the Joint Committee on Atomic Energy, *Civilian Atomic Power Acceleration Program*, 84th Congress, 2nd Session, 1956, Parts 1 and 2 (Washington, D.C.: U.S. Government Printing Office, 1956).

68. Green and Rosenthal, *Government of the Atom*, pp. 257-258, and Dawson, *Nuclear Power*, pp. 102-107, whose excellent discussion is especially valuable. Most of Dawson's material is drawn from Joint Committee on Atomic Energy, *Civilian Atomic Power Acceleration Program*.

69. United States Atomic Energy Commission, *Theoretical Possibilities and Consequences of Major Accidents in Large Nuclear Power Plants*, WASH-740 (Washington, D.C.: U.S. Government Printing Office, 1958), pp. 576-79.

70. Public Law 85-256, "An Amendment to the Atomic Energy Act of 1954," in *United States Statutes at Large 1957*, V. 77 (Washington, D.C.: U.S. Government Printing Office, 1958), pp. 576-79.

71. Harold P. Green, "Nuclear Power Licensing and Regulation," *The Annals* 400 (March 1972): 119. See also Dawson, *Nuclear Power*, for additional materials on Price-Anderson.

72. Nehrt, *International Marketing of Nuclear Power Plants*, p. 63.

73. Townsend, "The Atomic Power Program in the U.S.," pp. 69-70.

74. United States Atomic Energy Commission, *Research on Power from Fusion and Other Major Activities in the Atomic Energy Programs, January-June 1958* (Washington, D.C.: U.S. Government Printing Office, 1958), p. 96. See also Nehrt, *International Marketing of Nuclear Power Plants*,

p. 63.

75. Nehrt, *International Marketing of Nuclear Power Plants*, p. 64.

76. Ibid.

77. Ibid.

78. General Electric and Westinghouse have been so dominant in the nuclear power plant business that some have called them a "Duopoly." See Richard S. Lewis, *The Nuclear Power Rebellion: Citizens vs. the Atomic Industrial Establishment* (New York: Viking Press, 1972), p. 40. As Lewis points out, of the 106 reactors that produced more than 100,000 kilowatts in 1970, General Electric built 42; Westinghouse 34, Babcock and Wilcox, 14; Combustion Engineering, 11; and Gulf General Atomics, 1.

79. United States Congress, Hearings before the Joint Committee on Atomic Energy, *Development, Growth, and State of the Atomic Energy Industry*, 86th Congress, 1st Session, 1959 (Washington, D.C.: U.S. Government Printing Office, 1959).

80. Nehrt, *International Marketing of Nuclear Power Plants*, p. 65, and Green and Rosenthal, *Government of the Atom*, p. 261.

81. Nehrt, *International Marketing of Nuclear Power Plants*, p. 65. Nehrt draws this material from United States Atomic Energy Commission, *Civilian Power Reactor Program, Part IV, 1959* (Washington, D.C.: U.S. Government Printing Office, 1959), p. 1.

82. Nehrt, *International Marketing of Nuclear Power Plants*, p. 66. See also Hogerton, "The Arrival of Nuclear Power."

83. Nehrt, *International Marketing of Nuclear Power Plants*, p. 66.

84. Ibid.

85. Ibid. It might be pointed out that the Bodega Plant was never built and plans for the construction of the facility, which was located too near a major earthquake fault, were cancelled in 1964. For one account of the Bodega controversy, see Joel W. Hedgepath, "Bodega Head--A Partisan View," *Bulletin of the Atomic Scientists* 21 (March 1965): 2-7.

86. Lewis, *The Nuclear Power Rebellion*, pp. 26-27.

4
The Development and Commercialization of Civilian Nuclear Power in the United States, 1960-1974

> Excitement and preoccupation with nuclear fission as a new energy source obscured the economics of nuclear power--both the economics first of releasing nuclear energy in atomic reactors and then of converting that energy to its electrical form. There has been the disposition to sweep certain difficult or unpleasant facts connected with nuclear technology under the rug, so to speak. Among these can be mentioned the cost of the fuel itself, the cost of insurance, the higher cost of operation and maintenance, and the higher cost of nuclear energy inventory tied up not only in the reactor itself but in the whole fuel cycle. Similarly, important economic factors relating to the conversion of nuclear to electrical energy, such as the effect on cost of size of units, temperature of heat cycle, pressure, superheat and/or reheat in the heat cycle and load factor, were given too little consideration in the early work on nuclear energy development.
>
> -Philip Sporn

INTRODUCTION

When the Ten-Year Power Reactor Program was announced by the Atomic Energy Commission in December of 1959, the government-industry partnership in nuclear energy development seemed firmly established. Indeed, since 1946 the AEC had invested nearly $2.5 billion for reactor research and development, including an additional $0.8 billion for construction of facilities, while industry had contributed monies on the order of $650 million.[1] By 1963, these investments in reactor technology would pour some one million additional kilowatts into the nation's electrical grid system.[2]

Yet the actual prospects for full commercial acceptability of nuclear power were not quite as bright as the impressive number of kilowatts seemed to imply. For one thing, as of June 1961 fully two-thirds of all research and development and construction activities of the AEC's total $3.25 billion reactor program continued to serve weapons and military applications, including naval reactors, army reactors, air force reactors, weapons technology and hardware, and other military research and development programs.[3] This apparent neglect of civilian nuclear power not only had reactor manufacturers grumbling over the lack of new business, but it didn't help in convincing them to make additional capital investments in nuclear energy research and development, since it still appeared that the government was more interested in the navy and missile programs.[4] Notwithstanding the engineering and technical feasibility demonstrated by the AEC's Power Reactor Demonstration Programs (PRDP) by the early 1960s, the AEC was still faced with the problem of making nuclear power economically attractive to the nation's utilities, who continued to harbor considerable uncertainty about the commercial viability of nuclear reactors.

In view of these facts, the goal of the present chapter is to trace the events which turned this situation around and which led to the commercial acceptability of nuclear power by 1974. Its primary purpose, therefore, is to follow the efforts of government and industry which brought civilian nuclear power to full commercial acceptability--that point where utilities would be inclined to consider nuclear power plants competitive with fossil fuel installations.

THE STALEMATE OF 1960-1963: THE QUEST FOR MARKET ACCEPTABILITY OF NUCLEAR POWER

In its *Annual Report to Congress in 1961*, the Commission began the section on civilian nuclear power with the following remarks:[5] "In summarizing reactor construction and operating activities during 1961, it can be stated in general terms that operating activities were encouraging while construction activities were discouraging." The

Report went on to say that several reactors scheduled to achieve criticality by 1961 had failed to do so because of delays in construction or technical difficulties.[6] Nevertheless, the Commission believed that such delays need not alter the basic short and long-term objectives of the civilian power program which were:[7] (1) "to make it possible by 1968 for utility owners in high energy cost areas to elect, on the basis of economic considerations, to build large nuclear plants rather than conventional plants"; and (2) "to achieve such technological advances as to enable ever-increasing numbers of United States utility owners in the 1970s to make such choices in widening ranges of locations using various reactor types and sizes." To carry out these objectives, the Commission continued the fundamental PRDP strategy of broad-based reactor development work embodying research and development on several different reactor concepts that showed both short and long-term promise.

On the basis of the PRDPs, it was already shown that nuclear power was technically feasible, and there was fairly good consensus among the AEC, the nuclear industry, and the utilities that nuclear reactors were a viable method of producing electricity. In fact, most of the early technical difficulties stemmed in large part from auxiliary equipment. The reactors themselves proved surprisingly trouble-free and achieved a high degree of dependability. Not only were the plants amenable to steady-state and fluctuating-load conditions, but their essentially conservative designs allowed increased power outputs, substantially higher than their nominal ratings.[8]

Despite these encouraging facts, the same could not be said for economic considerations. As shown in the previous chapter, nearly every plant had cost more than originally intended, with many nearly doubling in price by the time they went on-line. Even the lowest generating costs achieved were reported to be some fifty-percent higher than seven mills per kilowatt hour, the point at which nuclear facilities were seen to be competitive with conventional plants. Moreover, the steadily increasing flow of cheap, low sulfur Middle Eastern oil, the declining price of coal, and the improved efficiency of conventional plants, which offset rising labor and materials costs, all resulted in further economic setbacks for nuclear power in the early 1960s.[9]

Further complicating market acceptability of nuclear power was another often overlooked fact; namely, the decision process by which utilities arrive at a choice of power plant supplier. The extensive intermediate step of analyzing and comparing differences between alternative energy sources is time-consuming an expensive and is not usually included in the decision process. The need for extensive pre-selection analyses of different energy types is often precluded by utilities' geographic locations and previous operating experiences with various energy supplies. Therefore the utilities' selection processes are typically more interested in making fine distinctions among suppliers of a single type of energy--which will result in firm bids--than in making generalized comparisons of competing energy sources, which complicate the decision process considerably.[10]

Therefore, the commercialization of nuclear energy faced the formidable problem of competing with mature technologies that had been tried and tested by utilities, a problem of course worsened by the fact that performance, particularly economic performance, had to rely primarily on predictions and extrapolations rather than on firm operating experience.[11] But more significant, the utilities appeared to favor building generating plants that offered higher power outputs than the experimental plants developed under the AEC's PRDPs in the 1950s. This suggested that nuclear energy would be further disadvantaged.

These and other early difficulties posed by competition from large fossil plants of demonstrated technical and economic competence that affected a utility's committment to nuclear energy were well summarized by Arthur D. Little, Inc. in their report to the AEC and the Department of Justice in 1968:[12]

> Utilities had to be convinced in rough, aggregate fashion that the fossil/nuclear alternatives were within the same broad cost range, before they would undertake the expensive, refined analysis necessary to evaluate bids ... the evaluation of commercial bids would have to generate findings that demonstrated nuclear energy's competitiveness, and were sufficiently credible to justify a multimillion dollar committment to a nuclear option that might--at best--be only marginally preferable to fossil alternatives.

Thus by 1962 it appeared that substantial difficulties still stood in the way of competitive nuclear energy. While there was little question that its technical feasibility had arrived, serious economic questions remained, and it was not clear that utilities easily could be presuaded to give up their long and favorable relationship with fossil units. In view of this situation, the AEC concluded that the developmental efforts should continue to push forward with new incentives by inviting industry to begin work on commercial-size plants of proven technology, which, of course, meant scaling-up boiling-water and pressurized-water reactors manufactured principally by General Electric and Westinghouse. The outcome was the AEC's announcement in August 1962 of a Modified Third Round of the PRDP, which actually had begun in 1957.

Modified Third Round Power Reactor Demonstration Program

Doubtless the AEC's announcement of the Modified Third Round Program was prompted in part by President Kennedy's request some months earlier that the Commission prepare a comprehensive report on the status of civilian nuclear power in the United States. Chairman of the AEC, Glenn Seaborg, submitted the report on November 20, 1962, less than three months after the Modified Third Round invitations.[13] These two actions provided a perfect opportunity to reassess the status of nuclear energy development and its role in the United States economy, as well as to determine the nature and direction of future programs. Since the report was being written while the Third Round was getting under way, it provides a good framework in which to view the rationale and content of the Third Round invitations.

Almost emphatically, the 1962 report concluded that nuclear power "is on the threshold of economic competitiveness and can soon be made competitive in areas consuming a significant fraction of the nation's electrical energy; relatively modest assistance by the AEC will assure the crossing of that threshold and bring about widespread acceptance by the utility industry."[14] The report went on to forecast that some forty million kilowatts of nuclear generating capacity would be on-line by 1980, and that by the year 2000 nuclear energy would account for roughly half of the nation's electical output and largely all subsequent power plant construction.[15] Finally, the report summarized three goals for the nation's future nuclear power development efforts:[16] (1) The immediate construction of power plants based on proven technology and of commercial size; (2) the continued development of so-called "advanced converter" reactors with improved fuel utilization characteristics; and (3) a longer range objective of developing breeder reactors which would produce more fuel than they consume.

Guided by these goals, the AEC offered the Modified Third Round invitations. Proposals from industry and the utilities were solicited, and the AEC agreed to provide funds for research and development related to nuclear steam supply systems and plant design. As for pre-construction research and development, the AEC offered to pay only about ten percent of the total projected cost. The utilities were responsible for the remaining ninety percent and to provide the sites on which plants would be built, cover all major construction costs, and be prepared to operate the facilities for at least five years after initial start-up.[17] In attempting to avoid some of the complications and negative experience of the previous rounds of the PRDPs, the AEC also explicitly stated the kinds of supporting material required in the proposals, including organizational information, personnel involved in the project, construction schedules and cost figures, systems for reporting construction progress and deadlines, fundamental technical information regarding the proposed plant, and anticipated research and development programs related to construction plans.[18]

Three proposals were received pursuant to the Modified Third Round invitations. Connecticut Yankee proposed building a 490,000 kilowatt plant, to be completed by 1967, at Haddam Neck, just outside Hartford, Connecticut. The Los Angeles Department of Water and Power proposed two additional plants to be built in southern California, one at San Onofre (a 395,000 kilowatt facility) and the other at Corral Canyon, near Malibu Beach, California.[19] All three plants would be outfitted with Westinghouse pressurized-water reactors. The proposed AEC assistance was fixed at amounts of $13.2 million, $13 million, and $16.2 million, respectively,[20] although actual expenditures were $13.1 million, $12.6 million and $2.1

million.[21] Because of technical problems with the fuel assembly and strong public opposition to the proposed site of the Malibu plant, which was close to an active earthquake fault, it was terminated in 1970. The Connecticut Yankee and San Onofre plants, however, performed beautifully after a number of routine start-up problems (leaky valves, faulty pump seals, etc.) and continue to operate today, holding positions as numbers one and three in the world for total kilowatt hours generated by nuclear power reactors.[22] Thus, after the three Modified Third Round proposals had been accepted, with prospects for several additional large-scale projects on the immediate horizon, Congressman and member of the Joint Committee on Atomic Energy, Chet Holifield, declared: "I believe it can be said that nuclear power is on the move."[23]

New Incentives for Industry: The Private Ownership of Special Nuclear Fuels Act of 1963

By the spring of 1963 the government was again considering legislative strategies for removing commercial barriers to nuclear power. This time, the Congress was concerned about government ownership of fissionable materials. When the Atomic Energy Act was signed into law in 1946, it was stipulated that all fissionable material was to be controlled by the United States Atomic Energy Commission.[24] Such control seemed imperative at the time, for clandestine diversion of uranium or plutonium could result in the nightmarish consequences of nuclear blackmail and possibly great tragedy. Furthermore, and perhaps more important, strict control of fissionable material by government agents was likely to strengthen the United States bargaining position in the quest for international control, as well as later contribute to a more clearly defined "Atoms for Peace" program which was promulgated in 1954. On both domestic and international fronts, a government monopoly of fissionable material seemed to contain a number of advantages in the early days of the nuclear age.

Yet even after 1954 and the revision of the Atomic Energy Act, which considerably loosened the government's stranglehold on nuclear energy development, it was clear that further action was needed to alter the government's continued monopoly in the area of ownership of nuclear fuels. The situation was such that by 1963 many industry and utility representatives urged the government to change this discouraging arrangement. Commercialization could be greatly accelerated, they argued, by allowing private business and industry to own special nuclear fuels. Not only did the AEC share this position in its entirety, but by March 15, 1963 they were already submitting to Congress an amendment to the Atomic Energy Act that would permit the private ownership rights industry sought.[25]

According to the Commission, the proposed legislation would have several major effects on the future development and commercialization of nuclear power in the United States. Most important was that private ownership would end "the continued distortion of technology" that resulted from existing leasing arrangements between the AEC and industry. Private ownership, asserted the AEC, ostensibly would put "the design of power reactors on a sounder long-term basis" because it would allow utilities to achieve more realistic cost comparisons between nuclear and conventional generating technologies. According to the AEC's *Annual Report to Congress in 1963*, private ownership would:[26]

> Allow and eventually require electric utilities to obtain nuclear fuel under more nearly the same economic conditions that apply to coal, oil, and natural gas and thus permit a more realistic comparison of nuclear and conventional power. Competitive nuclear power cannot really be demonstrated until normal economic factors relating to ownership and uses of nuclear fuels exists.

Other important effects of the new legislation would be to reduce substantially, and eventually eliminate, the AEC's growing investment in nuclear fuels used by utilities for the commercial production of electricity. The AEC was concerned that "if the present policy of mandatory Government ownership were continued, the estimated AEC investment in fuel inventories for commercial power reactors would exceed one billion dollars by 1975 and would increase rapidly thereafter."[27] In this way, the new legislation would shift more of the costs upon the utilities, thereby requiring nuclear power to be more responsive to normal market conditions affecting the production of electricity. Thus, not only was private ownership of nuclear fuels a way of reducing the dependence of utility companies upon government agents, but it was also a step toward achieving greater normalization of the nuclear industry by allowing increased competition among private enterprises and businesses involved in supplying alternative energy fuels, technologies, and equipment.

It came as no surprise that most of the parties spoke in favor of the proposed legislation at the Joint Committee's hearings in the summer of 1963. The only disagreement concerned minor details and not the underlying philosophy of the bill. Representatives of the coal interests were especially receptive of the bill, and most agreed with the position advocated by Thurston Morton, the Senator from coal-rich Kentucky. Senator Morton argued that the average price of coal throughout the country did not offer any significant cost advantages over nuclear fuel, and therefore "there is no valid reason that henceforth the civilian nuclear power industry should be further coddled and nourished by the taxpayers of the Nation."[28] Similarly, the utilities largely supported the bill despite the fact it would mean potentially higher costs. Such disadvantages probably would be offset, they believed, by the fact that private ownership would permit more realistic and stable assessment of future power costs and price projections, still a major area of uncertainty regarding nuclear power economics.[29]

The only unfavorable response came from Andrew J. Biemiller, Director of Legislation for the AFL-CIO. Rapid development of nuclear power was not the issue, said Biemiller; in fact the AFL-CIO actually supported the expansion of nuclear power for it ultimately would mean more jobs for its members. The union opposed the measure on altogether different grounds that were basically ideological in principle; that is, they argued that the bill would "endanger public ownership and public control and will assist and encourage a big business monopoly."[30]

In order to satisfy the utilities, the coal and uranium interests, and, to some extent, the unions, the Joint Committee slightly revised the original bill. The Committee did not change the essential spirit of the proposal, although it did revise some of its specifics. We need not go into detail about the differences between the AEC and Joint Committee versions of the bill, but it is worth mentioning that the eventual bill--The Private Ownership of Special Nuclear Fuels Act--passed speedily through Congress and received high praise both for reducing government involvement in nuclear power development and for encouraging increased competition between private enterprise and business. As far as most observers were concerned, the new Act was a tremendous boon for all: taxpayers would be relieved of the burden of financing nuclear power's multibillion dollar fuel bills; the utilities would be able to achieve more accurate prediction of fuel prices, allowing ease of comparison between energy sources; and the uranium industry would be freed of their existing dependence on the United States government, enabling them to negotiate contracts in a more normalized fashion.[32] Perhaps Representative John Anderson of Illinois expressed the prevailing sentiment most succinctly: The act "is a rare bill in this day and age of expanding Federal power and authority... it sets an example which could well be followed in other fields."[33] Thus, when President Lyndon B. Johnson signed the Private Ownership of Special Nuclear Fuels Act into law on August 26, 1964, nuclear power appeared to have moved a step closer to economic acceptability in the United States.

NUCLEAR POWER ON THE MOVE, 1963-1967: THE TURNKEY PLANTS AND THE GREAT ORDER SURGE

While the Commission and the Joint Committee were busy with the Private Ownership Act in the spring and summer of 1963, events continued to move swiftly. In December 1963, the Jersey Central Power and Light Company announced an historic event for the commercialization of civilian nuclear power in the United States: it planned to purchase a 515,000 kilowatt nuclear plant from General Electric at the fixed price of $66 million. The event was historic for several reasons. To begin with, Jersey Central's decision was based on its determination that the Oyster Creek generating plant would produce electricity cheaper than a comparable fossil unit. This was the case because General Electric offered to build the complete generating facility, including obtaining construction permits and operating licenses for a fixed price, adjusted only to correct for monetary inflation. Once the plant was completed, all Jersey Central had to do was put the key in the door and crank up the generating equipment. Oyster Creek, therefore, was the first of many "turnkey" plants subsequently offered to the utilities by General Electric and later Westinghouse.[34]

Several underlying assumptions made this remarkable committment by vendors possible. First, vendors assumed that close cooperation with utility companies and careful attention to experience accumulated in the experimental PRDPs concerning the costs of design, building, and operating reactor plants could be effectively utilized to manufacture competitive plants of over 400,000 kilowatts. It was believed that economies of scale of the larger units would substantially reduce costs of building and operating the smaller plants which vendors had been building heretofore. Finally, vendors remained fairly confident of cost predictions since the costs of plant equipment independent of nuclear steam supply systems substantially resembled the turbo-generator systems which vendors had been building for years as part of conventional fossil plants. Taken together, such facts weighed on the side of optimistic and reliable cost estimates for the larger nuclear units--or so the vendors thought in 1963.[35]

As for the Jersey Central's decision to go nuclear, their reasons were actually quite simple. The utility declared that nuclear power, as per the General Electric turnkey offer, was far and away the most economical generating system and would considerably outstrip conventional power sources within five years of start-up. It was later reported that Jersey Central's decision was based on the fact that Oyster Creek eventually would operate at 640,000 kilowatts, more than twenty-five percent higher output than the plant's nominal rating of 515,000 kilowatts. This meant that coal prices to Jersey Central would have to have been less than 20¢ per million B.T.U.s, or approximately four to five mills per kilowatt hour, to have been competitive with General Electric's turnkey plant.[36] Furthermore, Jersey Central argued that since the nuclear plant could be operated at about an eighty-eight percent capacity factor (that is, the ratio of the amount of electricity produced per year by the plant to the amount it could produce if it operated non-stop at full capacity), it would offer additional cost savings over fossil units of similar size.[37] Meanwhile, celebrating the Jersey Central announcement, the major trade journal of the American nuclear industry, the *Atomic Industrial Forum Memo*, declared that Oyster Creek "confirmed in the strongest possible way" that economical nuclear power had arrived and that previous economic analyses of nuclear power were obviously "obsolete."[38]

By February 1964, General Electric began laying plans for more turnkey offers when Westinghouse joined the race by announcing its own turnkey proposals for their pressurized-water systems. In the end General Electric built some seven turnkey plants, while Westinghouse was awarded contracts for six more by the time the turnkey era ended in 1967.[39] If the Oyster Creek and turnkey optimism was justified, there seemed little question that economically competitive nuclear power had arrived. The question was, however, were the cost projections justified?

The Questionable Economics of Oyster Creek and the Turnkey Orders

Whether the Jersey Central's cost estimates were correct rapidly became the focus of debate and discussion. On one side stood the government and the utility companies who asserted that Oyster Creek confirmed the optimistic forecasts of the 1962 *Report to the President.* In the report it was explained that in 1962, power from large nuclear plants, such as the one proposed by Pacific Gas and Electric for Bodega Bay, California, would produce electricity for approximately 5.6 mills per kilowatt hour. The report also predicted that this figure could be reduced to 3.8 mills per kilowatt hour by 1980. Thus, it came as a welcome surprise that Oyster Creek evidently would achieve this goal in 1968, which was the plant's scheduled start-up time.[40]

Criticism of these remarkable estimates was at first surprisingly limited. Only Philip Sporn, President of the nation's largest coal burning utility, American Electric Power Company, seriously questioned these figures. Reviewing the 1962 report at the request of the Joint Committee, Sporn concluded that the comparative economics of nuclear and fossil generating plants had not received enough attention *vis-a-vis* the solid rate of progress achieved with conventional generating technologies in recent years. Because of this great progress, Sporn said the AEC had improperly estimated fossil fuel costs and the probable effect of ever-increasing amounts of fossil fuels--particularly oil, natural gas, and coal--on the nation's energy situation.[41] Clearly, such factors would affect nuclear power's competitive position considerably.

As expected, both the AEC and the nuclear power industry disagreed with Sporn's assessment. The

AEC criticized Sporn for his "pessimism," while General Electric charged that his choice of reactor systems was "unduly conservative" and overestimated the capital costs of nuclear power plants by some fifteen percent.[42] Yet the heart of the disagreement between Sporn and government-industry spokesmen actually indicated a more serious problem with estimating nuclear costs; that is, most of the costs cited by the adversaries were *estimates* or *extrapolations* and *not* costs gained through actual operating experience, and, therefore, it was relatively easy to make certain claims one way or the other in the absence of firm data. Consequently, neither side could prove or disprove their own or each other's contentions, for the data simply didn't exist.[43]

Sporn's assessment of the economics of Oyster Creek was much the same in general substance and tone as his earlier critique of the 1962 report. His analysis again stressed the great leaps made by conventional generating technologies, as well as pointed to the reduction in the delivered price of coal "in those areas of the United States where transportation accounts for a large portion of the total cost"[44]--precisely those areas likely to be most interested in the use of nuclear power. In short, it wasn't yet clear to him that nuclear power could compete with coal fired plants, except perhaps in those areas experiencing the highest fuel costs.

However, Sporn expressed a more serious reservation about economic rationale of the turnkey strategy itself. It was his judgment that the turnkey contracts allowed insignificant margins of profit, and therefore estimates of power costs were probably considerably overstated. Sporn admitted that the economic justification probably stemmed from the fact that the manufacturers expected to sell additional turnkey plants, thereby minimizing the risks incurred by the favorable pricing formula used in the Oyster Creek bid. Nevertheless, Sporn went on to say that a number of elements of the Oyster Creek arrangement "are not so clear":[45]

> With all the good will toward all the organizations involved in the Oyster Creek project, it is still my personal judgment that one of the effects of the competitive pressures of the marketplace was to induce the manufacturer to risk somewhat greater uncertainty in the costs behind the turnkey price than might be tolerable repeatedly, when he decided to combine the effects of these innovations

> together with the effect of a substantial size extrapolation. In addition, I am extremely doubtful, even in the case of the most fortuitous minimization of the effects of the manufacturer's financial risk, whether the Oyster Creek sale will yield the same financial return as the manufacturer would normally require as a matter of sound business; the kind of return he requires of his conventional turbine business, for example.

The upshot of this remark, of course, was that while nuclear plants constructed under the turnkey contracts *appeared* cost competitive, their competitive level might not be as high as the initial announcements seemed to indicate.

Yet apart from the apparently misleading economics which turnkey plants suggested, Sporn went even further by questioning the underlying philosophy of the turnkey arrangements. As far as he was concerned, the turnkey strategy did more than merely jostle economics and cost estimates in favor of nuclear energy; in fact, Sporn asserted that such contracts could jeopardize the long-term economic and technological well-being of the electric power industry itself, including both utility and manufacturing segments. It is worth quoting him at length on this point:[45]

> The concept of a turnkey electric generating plant deserves more comment. It is in my judgment a concept which, if generally adopted, can lead only to an eventual decline in the technological and economic well-being of the electric power industry in both the utility and manufacturing segments. For the utilities, it will lead to a decline in the quality of what has been a most dynamic segment of its manpower, that is, it will discourage people of quality and imagination from joining its ranks. Furthermore it will eliminate the invaluable contribution of utility operating experience as an indispensible element in providing the direct feedback to plant design and to manufacturing organizations that for a half-century and more has stimulated so much progress in electric power technology. The manufacturing segment of the industry, deprived of the technical contributions of knowledgeable and expert user organizations, will gradually lose its vitality which has been kept alive to a

significant degree by the challenges and ideas presented by user technologists. I fear the net result would be the decline of U.S. electric power technology from its present position of world leadership and, eventually, higher cost power to the consumer.

I mention all this because a superficial look at the recently announced nuclear plant costs might leave the erroneous impression that the turnkey job offers a means of reducing nuclear costs. Not only is this untrue, but the turnkey plant shortcircuits the development of badly needed utility technological organizations and this in the long run can only be detrimental to the development of nuclear technology.

If there was ever any doubt about Sporn's earlier position on the 1962 report, these remarks seemed to firmly establish his skepticism concerning the purported economic advances made by nuclear technology in general, as well as the veracity of the turnkey strategy's rosy economic forecasts. As it turned out, however, only a disappointingly small number of experts shared this view--a view which later could not be dismissed simply because it had been a minority position in the early 1960s.

By now it is of course possible to determine whether the cost optimism of the turnkey era was warranted. Some of the figures remain speculative, but they appear to support Sporn's initial assessment. Rand Corporation, for example, reports that General Electric and Westinghouse lost on the order of $875 million to $1 billion on the thirteen turnkey plants constructed between 1963 and 1967. Excluding the San Onofre plant, this averages out to losses of about $73 to $78 million per plant.[46] In retrospect, the turnkey plants appeared to have cost about the same as their non-turnkey equivalents.[47] Yet at the same time, they served their purpose by announcing, however prematurely, that nuclear power was competitive with conventional power generating technologies. The turnkey orders piqued the utilities interest and doubtless played a significant role in the great order surge for nuclear power that would occur in 1966-1967, less than three years after Jersey Central's historical Oyster Creek contract with General Electric.

Aftermath of Oyster Creek: The Great Order Surge of 1966-1967

General Electric and Westinghouse turnkey offers appeared certain to whet the utilities appetites for nuclear power, but it is interesting to note that during the years of the turnkey era (1963-1967) General Electric and Westinghouse sold twenty-seven non-turnkey plants, more than double the number of fixed price offers.[48] While a number of questions were raised concerning why the utilities preferred non-turnkey plants,[49] which presumably would be more expensive, one fact seemed absolutely clear: the commercialization of nuclear energy in the United States had reached a watershed; altogether, the utilities had ordered some fifty nuclear power plants in 1966 and 1967 alone, accounting for nearly half of all the new power generating capacity ordered by United States utilities during that time.[50]

Several factors explained this great order surge. To begin with, there is considerable evidence that coal prices began to stiffen around 1965. Coal was then enjoying a rapidly expanding volume of business and was preparing to meet the demands of record numbers of coal-fired power plants under construction. In addition, the average price of nuclear plants had nearly doubled since the first orders, thus coal interests could be threatened only in areas of high cost coal, areas they could easily afford to write off in the face of a coal market that was doubling every ten years. Coal producers simply had little incentive to continue offering favorable prices to utilities contemplating nuclear plants. Unable to count on declining coal prices, and perhaps for use as a bargaining clip in future negotiations, utilities began to look toward nuclear energy in late-1965.[51]

A second factor responsible for the great order surge, ironically, was the growing awareness of environmental pollution. This was particularly true for utilities serving highly congested urban-industrial areas, where local ordinances began requiring stricter controls on sulfur-dioxide and other stack gas emissions to help curb air pollution. Low sulfur oil and coal, harder to develop and in short supply in many areas of the United States, obviously aggravated the utilities' situation. The removal of sulfur by means of scrubbers and other methods was extremely expensive, as was the possibility of erecting long-distance transmission lines which were likely to encounter a host of difficulties in obtaining right-of-way permits and the like. Coal mining itself increasingly was looked down upon for stream and river pollution, strip mining, and other environmental considerations, hence the utilities were encouraged to turn toward nuclear power for large central station application.[52] All in all, utilities began to perceive in the mid-1960s a positive public attitude toward nuclear energy, an attitude that might be enough to tip the balance in favor of the new technology in the years to come.

A third factor important for the great order surge can be traced to the northeast blackout in 1965. The blackout prompted the Federal Power Commission to push for interconnection and pooling of regional utility companies. This move favored adoption of nuclear plants on two fronts: in the event of a sudden nuclear plant shutdown, regional poolers could easily call upon their neighbors for additional power; and, second, joint participation would minimize any single utility's investment risks of building large new plants--nuclear or otherwise.[53] A strong correlation existed between regional pooling, joint ventures, and the great drive toward nuclear power that occurred in 1966-1967.

Another factor believed important in the push toward nuclear power has been advanced by Bupp and Derian. They argue that the investor owned utilities were afraid that if they didn't make some sort of committment to nuclear power soon, the insistence of the Joint Committee and the AEC on advancing civilian nuclear power would eventually lead to what Bupp and Derian called "massive atomic TVAs." Just as the Tennessee Valley Authority had exploited cheap coal to become a regionally dominant electricity producer, the utilities feared that the same thing could happen with nuclear energy, whereby government programs would preempt the public utilities if they failed to invest in nuclear power. This would severely cripple the public utilities in the event that nuclear power became the dominant electricity generating technology of the future, as indeed it was beginning to look from the perspective of the middle 1960s.[54]

In any case, by the end of 1967 seventy-five nuclear plants had been ordered by United States utilities, totalling some forty-five million kilowatts of generating capacity. In the AEC's

Supplement to the 1962 *Report to the President*, forecasts for nuclear power were revised upward from the optimistic 1962 projections. It was predicted that nuclear energy would produce between sixty and ninety million kilowatts of electrical power by 1980.[55] Understandably, proponents of nuclear power were ecstatic and brightly enthusiastic of future prospects. Alvin Weinberg, Director of the Oak Ridge National Laboratory, told the National Academy of Sciences, that a "nuclear energy revolution" had arrived, and that cheap power would be guaranteed for generations to come.[56]

Meanwhile orders for nuclear plants continued to surge forward in 1968 with utilities signing contracts for fourteen more units with higher power ratings, scheduled to produce some 12.8 million additional kilowatts for the nation's grid. Although orders fell off somewhat in 1969, with vendors receiving only seven orders for 7.2 million kilowatts capacity, the reactor business again leaped forward in 1970-1971. Fourteen more plants were ordered in 1970, totalling 14.3 million kilowatts, compared to twenty plants with nearly 19.8 million kilowatts capacity ordered in 1971.[57]

Thus by 1971 the tide for nuclear power in America could not have been higher. Orders and power projections exceeded even the bullish estimates of the early 1960s as each new order came in. Some utility companies were placing orders two at a time, and nuclear energy appeared to be the way of the future. Indeed, while the age of nuclear power finally seemed to have arrived, and with the long-nurtured dreams of the government-industry partnership taking on a bright new reality, the 116 nuclear plants ordered between 1963 and 1971 promised some real licensing and regulation problems that the AEC was only beginning to realize. In the meantime, Philip Sporn and a few others remained skeptical amid all the fanfare over nuclear energy; they must have been watching on, wondering about this great surge toward nuclear power and what it might mean when the dust settled and the hoopla was over.

REACTOR LICENSING AND REGULATION IN THE AGE OF COMMERCIALIZATION

Siting

The rapid commercialization of nuclear power in the middle 1960s was cause for great jubilation within the nuclear establishment. At the same time, however, the great order surge had created a licensing and regulation log-jam within the AEC. The problem was aggravated by the fact that reactors were being constantly scaled-up and improved, from an average size of 550,000 kilowatts in 1963 to over 800,000 kilowatts in 1966. To use Harold Green's term, unit sizes "leapfrogged" to larger and larger reactors, and hence design changes were based mostly on theory rather than on firm operating experience. Together with the huge number of orders for more reactors, the new generation of larger plants promised significant licensing and regulation problems for the AEC in the age of commercial acceptability.[58]

From the industry's standpoint, several new regulatory policies could affect nuclear power's competitive position. One important consideration was to test the AEC's policy of reactor siting near metropolitan areas. Industry felt that if the AEC would relax its regulations in this regard, transmission costs could be reduced significantly and an improved competitive position for nuclear power could be achieved.[59]

By and large, the AEC seemed opposed to urban siting of nuclear power plants on the grounds that more operating experience, research data, and improved testing and inspection criteria were needed. Consequently, the AEC never issued construction permits to Consolidated Edison of New York for a proposed one million kilowatt reactor that would have been located in Queens, New York, in the heart of New York City, just opposite Manhattan at 72nd Street. Perhaps the ordinance barring reactors from the city introduced by the City Council, and former AEC Chairman, David Lilienthal's statement in the *New York Times*, which called Consolidated Edison's proposal "a very risky business," prompted the utility to withdraw its application for the Queen's plant in 1962.[60]

Similarly, on the grounds of urban proximity the AEC denied construction permits to the Los Angeles Department of Water and Power and to Public Service Electric and Gas Company, which wanted to build a plant near Burlington, New Jersey. The AEC's Advisory Committee on Reactor Safeguards (ACRS) had strong reservations about siting problems and the sites in both cases were subsequently shifted.[61] By 1967 the AEC still had not developed any standards to guide urban siting policies, and it looked as though they would not do so in the near future either.[62]

Special siting difficulties also were encountered in areas of seismic activity. Perhaps the most publicized case was Pacific Gas and Electric's (PG&E) 1962 proposal to construct a boiling-water reactor plant at Bodega Bay, California, a small fishing village just outside of San Francisco. The plant was to be built close by the San Andreas Fault, one of the world's most active earthquake faults. The AEC staff review doubted whether PG&E could build a plant that would withstand the shock of a major quake even though the utility assured them that special buildings and containment procedures could be used. The ACRS was inclined to agree with PG&E and advised the AEC to let the project proceed.

However, while the AEC and the ACRS were attempting to iron out their differences, stiff opposition from local citizen groups emerged. One organization, the Northern California Association to Preserve Bodega Head and Harbor, led by attorney David Pesonen, marshalled an impressive amount of testimony which contradicted PG&E's seismic analyses. Seismic experts from the Naval Ordinance Testing Station at China Lake, California, the United States Geological Survey, and other noted experts offered data which cast serious doubt on the plant's ability to withstand a big quake. After considerable debate and expense, PG&E finally abandoned its plans for the Bodega Bay plant in late-1964 and agreed to work jointly with the Sierra Club to find an alternative coastal site.[63]

The AEC and the utilities ran into other siting imbroglios on the Pacific Coast. Additional opposition over seismic problems was encountered by the Los Angeles Department of Water and Power at is proposed Malibu site. After heated debate over the proposal, the AEC ruled in favor of the opposition groups and the utility abandoned the project in 1967. Likewise, Southern California Edision and PG&E applied for and received construction permits for their San Onofre and Diablo Canyon plants, respectively, but the AEC nevertheless required additional seismic data before the plants could be built.[64]

The Licensing and Regulation Program

Siting criteria were a constant source of difficulty for the AEC. Yet by the middle 1960s, the inability of the AEC's licensing and regulation program to keep pace with new construction applications became a more significant problem which nearly crippled the commercialization of nuclear power. A slow moving licensing process would hurt both fossil and nuclear plants, but builders of nuclear plants would suffer relatively more since they had higher capital costs. Moreover, the competitive position of nuclear power was fairly narrow and extra costs caused by licensing delays promised to cut into its market position. Understandably, both vendors and utilities pushed hard to expedite the licensing process.

Up until about 1966, the AEC's licensing programs and staff reviews handled new applications satisfactorily. But as the volume of applications increased and plants were scaled-up in size, the work load burgeoned and the safety review process necessarily became more complex. The Commission increased its technical and licensing staff measurably, but little headway was made in significantly reducing the nine and one-half month review time; in fact, as orders swelled in 1966 and 1967, the review time was likely to increase rather than decrease.[65]

Anticipating this application glut, the AEC appointed William Mitchell to head a special seven member outside review panel to consider ways to expedite the licensing program. According to a recent Rand Corporation report, the Mitchell Panel identified four major problem areas and proposed remedies:[66]

> (1) the length of the review process; (2) an absence of well-defined safety criteria and requirements; (3) increasing regulatory manpower requirements; and (4) duplication of review and evaluations. As remedies, it proposed that the AEC (1) get on with the job of developing criteria and standards, but limit its specifications to genuine safety needs, not general design specifications; (2) coordinate its safety research program with regulatory requirements; (3) define more

precisely and realistically the information the applicant required in all license application; and (4) give the AEC staff primary safety review responsibility by limiting the Atomic Safety and Licensing Board's review to the *adequacy* of the Safety Evaluation Report (precluding *de novo* safety evaluations) and by eliminating the *mandatory* Advisory Committee on Reactor Safeguards review of each application.

The AEC tried hard to implement the Mitchell Panel's recommendations and had some initial success by increasing regulatory manpower and cutting down on duplication. However, the general design criteria adopted by the Commission were supposed to help applicants establish principle design criteria for nuclear plants but were too vague and ambiguous to have much impact, especially considering the rapidly changing design parameters involved in plant size scale-ups. In short, without operating experience with the larger plants for which design criteria were being devised, standards were necessarily vague and nondefinitive. The ambiguity of the standards, then, resulted in a case-by-case, somewhat *ad hoc*, evaluation of plant designs which did little to reduce delay time.[67]

Related to the standards problem were the AEC's policies on "backfitting" and "ratcheting." Backfitting refers to mandatory modification of operating facilities, often requiring addition of new components, safety systems, and other large modifications. Ratcheting usually does not call for any retrofitting, but refers to revision of applicable requirements and standards for plants still in design and construction phases. Oftentimes, racheting standards may lead to significant construction and engineering changes. Because of the leapfrog effect spoken of above, as well as the lack of operating experience, industry was worried that the AEC would employ racheting and backfitting as ways of meeting constantly evolving regulatory standards. Thus as far as industry and the utilities were concerned, ratcheting and backfitting would be expensive and lead to endless irritation in meeting new design and construction criteria over the life of a given plant.[68]

Fortunately for the nuclear industry, however, the AEC rarely ordered major backfits. Most retrofits were determined on a case-by-case basis rather than in generic fashion, and the AEC promised to examine feasible alternatives before asking for any retroactive action by industry and the utilities.[69] All of this, of course, added months of delay to the already overloaded regulation program, and stalled utilities' efforts to bring new plants into operation.

The AEC's Safety Research Program

A final area of reactor licensing and regulation affecting the commercialization of nuclear power was the AEC's safety research "program." Industry considered such a program an integral part of the overall drive to establish safety standards and design criteria on which licensing a nuclear power reactor would be based. To be sure, a well defined AEC-supported safety research program could contribute to improved component reliability and help solve various engineering problems faced by the nuclear industry. The AEC, on the other hand, seemed more interested in a loosely structured program focusing on the physical effects and consequences of serious accidents such as loss-of-coolant mishaps. In fact, the AEC had been engaged in just such a safety program with the loss-of-fluid tests at the National Reactor Testing Station in Idaho since at least 1963. Later, such experiments were to be the basis of testing emergency core-cooling systems, providing additional data for validating analytical models, assessing the performance of related safety systems, and for developing AEC standards used in design and construction of nuclear plants.[70] The AEC's program, by concentrating on the large accidents, was therefore considerably different than what the nuclear industry had in mind.

However, the AEC's loosely knit safety research program came to an abrupt end in 1965 when the Commission appointed Milton Shaw, a former aid to Admiral Hyman Rickover, to head the new Division of Reactor Development and Technology. While Shaw, in typical Rickover fashion, pursued a vigorous and demanding program, many criticized his apparent preoccupation with the rapid commercialization of the breeder reactor. Critics charged that Shaw's enthusiasm for the breeder, and the commercialization of civilian nuclear power in general, resulted in a reluctance to raise safety questions or engage in research that might retard reactor diffusion by hampering industry with additional requirements. Furthermore, under Shaw's direction, safety research largely concentrated on the reactor itself and slighted other difficulties related to the various stages of the nuclear fuel-cycle--from problems of mining and milling uranium ore to the difficulties presented by the disposal of radioactive wastes.[71]

This myopic safety program caused great concern. By 1966 it became evident that something had to be done since safety assessment of new plants was based on data and assumptions gained largely from the small-size experimental plants developed under the PRDPs. Clearly, the increased numbers and sizes of new reactors suggested that risk assessments were understated and required reformulation in view of the larger amounts of nuclear fuel and radioactive wastes produced, as well as the fact that the larger reactors burned hotter and required more cooling water in the event of a loss-of-coolant accident. Without new information and experimental data on which to base assessments, the AEC's regulatory staff was simply extrapolating on the basis of old data.

The adequacy of untried emergency core-cooling systems installed in the larger plants, therefore, quickly emerged as the central issue with Consolidated Edison's (Con Ed) application in 1965 to build a 873,000 kilowatt plant at Indian Point, New York.[72] No one knew whether the plant's untried emergency core-cooling system would work and construction permits were issued by the AEC with considerable reluctance.

The problems of insufficient experimental data on back-up containment procedures, such as with Con Ed's safety system, were further underscored by the Advisory Committee on Reactor Safeguards. In order to obviate the threat of a formal letter from the ACRS spelling out its reservations with AEC guidelines on containment procedures, the Commission appointed on outside task force to review loss-of-coolant accidents and assess whether emergency safety systems proposed for new plants were adequate. Headed by William Ergen from the Oak Ridge National Laboratory, the formation of the task force thus officially marked the AEC misgivings about the safety of light-water nuclear technology.[73]

The Ergen task force presented its report to the AEC in late-1967. Basically, the tone of the 221-page report was one of uncertainty regarding the adequacy of emergency core-cooling systems. The report indicated that a malfunctioning system probably would lead to a breach of containment, releasing large quantities of radioactive material into the environment. Improvements in existing emergency core-cooling systems and simulation models for estimating accident parameters would help, said the report, but it was urgent that the AEC get on with the job as soon as possible. In a letter to the AEC, the ACRS concurred with the Ergen Report and suggested additional measures for improving back-up containment systems.[74]

Thus by 1970 the AEC was faced with a remarkable paradox: on the one hand the age of commercial acceptability of nuclear power seemed to have arrived as orders for new plants poured in; yet on the other hand, the AEC had been forced to admit the basic incompetence of its safety review programs. The AEC's regulatory staff was swamped with reviews for new power plants, which in itself was enough to increase licensing and regulation delays. But exacerbating delays was the fact that the AEC had failed to develop a number of licensing, regulation, and siting criteria as each new generation of nuclear power plants evolved. Siting criteria for both metropolitan locations and areas of seismic activity were non-existent and the rapid pace of evolution of scaled-up plants precluded the smooth and rational development of generic licensing and regulation criteria, thereby forcing the AEC more or less to review each application on an individual basis. Consequently, the AEC's regulatory apparatus could be assailed easily, for it was clear that the jumble of constantly evolving regulatory procedures--coupled with a lack of operating experience with new generation plants--provided an easy target for critics of the Commission and its programs. This became a growing problem in the late 1960s.

Yet it was probably the 1967 Ergen Report that caused the greatest concern. By casting serious doubt on the adequacy of emergency core-cooling systems to function in the event of a serious accident, the report forced the AEC to admit to a total reassessment of the safety problem and to reconsider existing standards and criteria for plant design and construction. The AEC was therefore left in the impossible position of guaranteeing that accidents would not occur because they had considered every possible engineering safeguard. Obviously the Commission could never "prove" in a mathematical sense that they had addressed the infinite variety of accidents which might occur in a large nuclear plant. Working from such a regulatory position, it didn't take much for a shrewd critic to cast aspersions on the integrity of the AEC's regulatory strategy. Therefore rather than shortening delay times, the AEC was instead forced to extend the licensing and review time for new power plants which was, of course, to the detriment of rapid commercialization of nuclear energy. By 1970, it looked as if the AEC and the nuclear establishment had opened the door to public debate by their own hands and their failure to keep regulatory pace with a rapidly evolving technology. Indeed, the growing concern over safety indicated that perhaps nuclear technology was not yet in hand.

INFLATING FOSSIL FUEL PRICES: A BOOST FOR NUCLEAR POWER

In spite of the AEC's growing licensing and regulation woes, the move toward nuclear power did not abate in the early 1970s. In fact, the AEC's *Annual Report of Congress, 1972-1974* was very optimistic about the future prospects of nuclear power plants. During 1972 alone, the report indicated that thirty-five new plants had been ordered, with a total design capacity of about 37.9 million kilowatts. At the end of 1972, twenty-nine nuclear plants (14.6 million kilowatts) were in operation, fifty-five under construction (47.7 million kilowatts), and seventy-six contractually ordered (80 million kilowatts). The report estimated that their combined capacity of 142.4 million kilowatts was enough to serve about 70 million people.[75] This trend didn't slow down at all in 1973, as thirty-eight more orders were accepted adding some 43 million kilowatts to the projected nuclear generating capacity in the United States.[76]

What explained the utilities' continued acceptance of nuclear power in the face of questionable economics and growing safety and regulation difficulties? Bupp and Derian argue that the skyrocketing price of fossil fuels after 1972 was perhaps the principle reason.[77] Especially important were the huge price jumps for Middle Eastern crude oil that hit the industrial world in the form of the oil embargo of 1973-1974.

As early as 1970 the trend toward higher oil prices was apparent. Syria had blocked the trans-Arabian pipeline in an effort to obtain higher revenues for transit rights, while Libya began imposing significant production cut-backs to force increased taxes from foreign oil companies. The immediate effects of these actions were relatively small. However, it looked as though the long downward trend in crude oil prices experienced throughout the 1960s would be reversed in the years ahead.[78]

Eventually, the companies producing in Libya agreed to a tax increase, prompting other Persian Gulf countries to seek similar increases, which they received. Libya then demanded another round of price boosts and the Persian Gulf producers followed suit. Finally, compromises were reached in February 1971 with the signing of the Tehran Agreement which provided automatic tax increases for the next five years.[79] However, Libya was once again dissatisfied and negotiated a new tax deal in the Tripoli Agreement less than a month later on April 2, 1971.[80]

Throughout the early 1970s, one new agreement seemed to follow another as prices shot up dramatically. By 1973 the oil-producing countries negotiated the so-called "Participation Agreements," whereby producers acquired partial ownership of their concessionary companies. On October 6, 1973 Syria and Egypt invaded Isreal setting off the "Yom Kippur" war. Meanwhile, the oil-producing countries had convened a previously scheduled meeting in Vienna to discuss increasing oil prices once again. The oil industry was prepared to negotiate a price revision of somewhere between eight and fifteen percent, with authorization to bid as high as twenty-five percent. They were shocked when the Organization of Petroleum Exporting Countries (OPEC) asked for a one hundred percent price hike, which the industry immediately rejected out of hand. OPEC then flexed its muscles and unilaterally hiked the price about seventy percent--from $3.00 to $5.11 a barrel. At the same time OPEC cut production and imposed an embargo on the United States and the Netherlands in retaliation for their support of Isreal.[81]

The oil consumers had barely adjusted to the October price hikes when they were hit with a second, even greater increase. At an OPEC meeting in Tehran, the cartel announced a price of $11.65 a barrel, effective January 1, 1974. Thus in four years the price of OPEC oil had risen from $1.80 in late 1970 to $2.59 in early 1973, to $3.01 less than a year later, to $5.11 in October 1973, and finally to $11.65 in January 1974--a six hundred percent increase.[82]

The outlook for coal in the early 1970s wasn't much better. In 1969 the coal price began a slow upturn, and accelerated in 1973 with the OPEC embargo. Between 1973 and 1974 the price tripled to those utilities without long-term delivery contracts.[83]

This dramatic rise in fossil fuel prices particularly hurt the utility markets in the northeastern United States. Under heavy pressure from the Federal Clean Air Act of 1970 to reduce emissions, and the fact that coal from the Appalachian coal fields was more expensive to transport to the distant northeast, low sulfur Middle Eastern oil held particular attraction to the accessible northeastern ports. Thus when the OPEC embargo hit, the oil dependent northeast's energy situation was turned topsy-turvey. As Bupp and Derian explain:[84]

> Spot prices for residual fuel oil jumped almost 40 percent between October and November 1973. Coal prices soon followed. Spot coal prices rose about 10 percent in December 1973 and by an additional 30 percent in January. By March 1975, residual fuel oil had risen 282 percent above its price in June 1973. During the same month, the spot coal index rose about 216 percent above its June 1973 level.

The fossil fuel crunch in the early 1970s led many utilities to look upon nuclear energy as a viable alternative to tight markets and high prices. The simple fact of the matter was that few alternatives to oil, coal, and natural gas existed and drastic rationing and conservation programs were likely to meet with public outrage. Anticipated changes in life style brought on by severe curtailment of energy use would not be easy and promised a political backlash that few politicians were prepared to deal with. Together with the strong and optimistic forecasts made by the AEC and the nuclear industry, the "energy crisis" of the early 1970s vaulted nuclear power into a new economic position. And because economic forecasts for reactor generating costs were largely *expected* rather than actual, it was easy to see how proponents looked upon nuclear energy as the answer to OPEC. Once again it appeared that the atom's time had come, as the nuclear community's assurances looked evermore promising in the face of the new and powerful oil cartel.

IN SEARCH OF CREDIBILITY: REVISING THE REGULATORY PROGRAM FOR COMMERCIAL POWER REACTORS

By the early 1970s, several factors had strengthened nuclear power's commercial acceptability and buttressed its market position among electric generating technologies. The energy crisis seemed to have cemented nuclear power's position as the answer to OPEC, and proponents firmly believed that nuclear technology was the sign of things to come. Yet at the same time, the Commission's civilian power programs were subjected to increased public scrutiny as more and more reactors went on-line. Growing numbers of concerned citizens and environmentalists began to question the AEC's safety assurances, and it was nearly common knowledge that the Commission's regulatory process was in shambles. Thus, the most formidable barriers to commercial acceptability of nuclear power in the United States were no longer mainly technical and economic, but were questions concerning the AEC's credibility as a regulator and its growing lack of public support.

In an effort to rebuild the AEC's image as a defender and protector of the public interest, James R. Schlesinger was appointed Chairman of the AEC on July 21, 1971, replacing Glenn Seaborg. The economist Schlesinger had a reputation in the Bureau of the Budget as an adept administrator and organizer. Government officials believed he could restore public confidence in the AEC as well as overhaul the sputtering licensing and regulation program.

Schlesinger didn't waste any time in turning things around. He reversed earlier AEC policy and announced that the Commission would not appeal a court decision requiring it to implement all National Environmental Policy Act (NEPA) standards retroactively. In the months that followed, Schlesinger confirmed industry's worst fears. At a banquet of the Atomic Industrial Forum-American Nuclear Society meetings at Bal Harbor, Florida, on October 20, 1971, Schlesinger indicated that henceforth the AEC would act as the referee of nuclear power, not its promoter. It would not fight industry's battles in the courts or with the environmentalists, said Schlesinger, and the AEC was neither in the busines of supplying power nor selling power reactors. The AEC would be officially neutral, Schlesinger said.[85]

In defining the AEC's role as that of a referee serving the public interest, Schlesinger was attempting to improve the Commission's regulatory credibility by disassociating it from industry and a promotional image. Clearly, establishing the independence of the Commission was the first step for improving public confidence.

At the same time, Schlesinger recognized that the AEC also had a responsibility to the nuclear power industry and to further the commercialization of nuclear power, as per the mandate of the Atomic Energy Acts. He believed this responsibility was best met by assuring expeditious licensing and review of power plant applications and construction permit proceedings. With licensing all but completely stalled in 1972, Schlesinger and his staff undertook a complete overhaul of AEC licensing procedures, which they hoped to achieve by early-1973.[86]

One of the first things the AEC did was to standardize the application process by providing clear guidelines on the content and preparation of applications and preliminary safety analysis reports. The AEC believed this would help shorten long review times by clarifying review criteria such that smoother, more uniform reviews would become possible. The AEC also returned incomplete applications with no further reviews until an application was letter complete.[87]

By April of 1972, the AEC rationalized and streamlined the regulatory staff by reorganizing it into three directorates: (1) Directorate of Licensing, (2) Directorate of Regulatory Standards, and (3) Directorate of Operations (or Compliance). The regulatory staff was also strengthened in areas of environmental impact and reactor safety. Meanwhile, the Directorate of Licensing was attempting to standardize application reviews, reduce construction permit reviews to twelve months, and be in a position to issue operating licenses immediately after plants were completed and ready for operation.[88]

The AEC's attempt to upgrade and settle on a fixed set of licensing criteria--perhaps the key to an expeditious licensing process--however, was more problematic. Additional research and development support would be needed and the AEC would have to discard the traditional case-by-case approach to licensing. The Commission responded by expanding the Regulatory Standards staff and increasing available funds to contract outside technical expertise. Seismic standards, criteria for emergency core-cooling systems, radioactive emissions guides, and quality assurance standards were all promulgated by 1973 with help of the American Institute of Standards. Although the AEC moved swiftly to implement the new standards, which were sure to cause problems for the utilities and industry, it permitted appeal rights in contested cases.[89]

But perhaps the most important ingredient in establishing public confidence, concerned the matter of public hearings and intervention in the reactor licensing procedures. At first the agency attempted to reduce licensing times by restricting public participation at construction permit proceedings, but Schlesinger immediately overruled this move. Instead, he supported streamlining the hearing format by scheduling prehearing conferences to identify major issues to be resolved, imposing time limits on various phases of the hearing process, limiting the types of issues that could be raised, and by providing private citizens with increased access to relevant licensing documents. The Commission also established so-called public "rulemaking hearings" to isolate generic issues in order to avoid duplication of argumentation in individual hearing cases.[90]

There is little doubt that Schlesinger's program incited tremendous changes in the basic licensing and regulation posture of the AEC. Many believed that the changes would speed the commercialization of nuclear energy and release the nation from its dependence on high-priced OPEC oil. But the very fact that the licensing process needed such drastic overhaul prompted critics to take a closer look at the nuclear energy programs and their basic rationale. Old issues were rapidly joined by new ones, and critics pointed to innumerable minor safety problems which called into question the adequacy of engineering safeguards in general. Meanwhile, the Commission had supported NEPA entirely and had made tremendous strides to further open the licensing process to public groups. More documents were made available, witnesses were permitted to cross-examine AEC spokesmen, and the AEC encouraged participation, debate, and reasoned criticism.

However, try as they may to improve public credibility, the Commission continued to engender skepticism among critics. As the orders for new power plants streamed in, the AEC still appeared in a promoter role, deeply committed to the rapid proliferation of nuclear power. Regulatory considerations appeared subordinated to the AEC's promotional activities in case after case of construction permit proceedings. Moreover, the opportunities for interaction between the Commission and the public, primarily through the medium of the mandatory public hearing at the construction permit stage, had done little to improve public confidence. In fact, the AEC seemed so intent on promoting nuclear energy that public groups were largely ignored and slighted, even though the AEC claimed to take them seriously. In any case, the public participation clause of the Atomic Energy Act would continue to provide concerned citizens with ample opportunity to state their concerns and disagreements with the AEC and the utilities who wanted to build nuclear power plants. And state them they did, for by the early 1970s reactor construction permits were being routinely delayed by disgruntled citizens, intent on stalling the rapid commercialization of nuclear power in any way they could.

SUMMARY AND CONCLUSIONS

The decade of the 1960s saw the rapid commercialization of nuclear power in America. To many observers it looked as if nuclear power had finally become a reality as each new reactor achieved criticality. Yet the push for commercialization had not been easy. The AEC and the nuclear power industry had to overcome a host of problems and barriers in convincing the utilities to invest in nuclear units. The principal problems in the early 1960s were largely economic: was the electricity generated from expensive nuclear power plants cost-competitive with that generated by conventional fossil fuel plants, particularly those which used coal? As things stood in 1961, the answer seemed to be negative.

But the AEC did not despair easily; it continued to harbor marked optimism for the future of nuclear power in America. The AEC's report to the President--1962 reaffirmed the nuclear committment, as did the AEC's announcement of new invitations to industry via the Modified Third Round Power Reactor Demonstration Program. The Modified Third Round Program offered substantial AEC financial and research and development assistance to industries and utilities willing to construct power reactors in the commercial range of 300,000 kilowatts. In addition, as the Modified Third Round proposals were being received, the AEC and the Joint Committee on Atomic Energy moved to eliminate another obstacle in the path of commercialization: the government's monopoly over special nuclear fuels. Under the Private Ownership of Special Nuclear Fuels Act of 1963, private industry and business were allowed to own fissionable materials for the first time. This had several advantages for commercialization, the foremost of which was the utilities could make more accurate cost estimates and comparisons between nuclear and conventional generating technologies.

The major breakthrough for commercialization, however, was reached between 1963 and 1967. Initially, it was achieved by fixed price contracts, or the so-called "turnkey" plants, offered by General Electric and Westinghouse. The turnkey plants promised generating costs that would be competitive with fossil plants, or so the nuclear industry claimed. However, some observers, notably Philip Sporn, remained skeptical. Sporn argued that the economics for the turnkey plants were probably misleading because they failed to account for increased progress made with existing generating technologies. Sporn also questioned the basic rationale behind the turnkey strategy itself, asserting that it would eventually undermine the technological and economic well-being of the electric power business. Despite Sporn's prognosis, the utilities eventually ordered thirteen turnkey plants from General Electric and Westinghouse between 1963 and 1967.

Yet during the same time period utilities also ordered twenty-seven non-turnkey plants at substantially higher costs. This suggests the turnkey offers were only partially responsible for the great order surge. The materials reviewed here indicate at least three other reasons for the large increase in nuclear starts and the move toward commercialization. First, and most important, was by the middle 1960s the fossil fuel picture began to change dramatically. Favorable coal prices to utilities thinking about going nuclear became a thing of the past by 1965. Coal producers had all the business they could handle and saw no reason to cut prices in order to compete with nuclear energy. As for nuclear power's other economic rival in the electric power business, oil, there was increasing environmental pressure to burn expensive low sulfur oil, meaning nuclear power would gain further economic advantage. Thus if utilities were thinking about fuel diversification in the middle and late 1960s, the 1973-1974 OPEC oil embargo provided further impetus for them to invest in nuclear energy. Perhaps this is why utilities ordered 108 more nuclear units between 1970-1973--seemingly a direct response to spiraling oil and coal prices.

Second, utilities were able to spread out investment risks and the high capital costs of nuclear power by entering into joint ventures and consortia. Much of this was encouraged by regional pooling which joined utilities together in electrical grid systems to prevent blackouts from unexpected down times of the large peak load plants. Pooling and increased numbers of joint ventures also coincided with the large commercial surge of nuclear power after 1963.

The third major factor responsible for rapid commercialization was something that harked back to the days of the Gore-Holifield Bill in 1956; that is, the utilities had to be thinking about the old public versus private power debate. It seemed unlikely that the government would give up on the nuclear option; indeed, it was something of a national committment and whole careers had been built around its successful commercialization. Therefore the utilities probably felt the government would simply go on without them if they failed to invest in nuclear power in a large way. The result would be increasing numbers of public nuclear power programs similar to TVA, something the utilities didn't particularly relish. Furthermore, if nuclear energy really was the great power source of the future, as many had claimed it would be, the utilities might get caught on a limb if they failed to have nuclear plants operating fifteen or twenty years down the road when the fossil fuel situation became more critical. Thus together with changing fossil fuel costs and the move toward pooling and joint ventures, the possibility of government-owned utilities created a favorable environment for rapid commercialization in the middle 1960s.[91]

The apparently successful commercialization of nuclear power, however, was not without a price of another kind. That is, while the events accompanying the great order surge seemed to confirm nuclear power's economic competitiveness, the strain on the regulatory program thrust the entire civilian power effort into headlong confusion and controversy. The AEC began encountering problems with seismic and metropolitan siting, lack of clear-cut criteria and regulatory standards, and the absence of a well-defined safety research program, particularly in regard to large-scale calamities such as the loss-of-coolant accident. These problems exacerbated criticism of the AEC and its programs, and seemed to support environmentalists' growing concerns about the safety of nuclear reactors and the Commission's overly promotional bias toward nuclear power.

Significantly, these concerns were confirmed by citizens and public groups' experiences in the AEC's public hearings. It was here that public groups first realized the incredible strength of the nuclear power establishment and their own relative impotence. Their largely unfavorable experiences with the nuclear establishment, under the guise of "public participation," convinced them that the AEC and the nuclear industry had been overly hasty in their enthusiasm for nuclear power; many serious questions still appeared outstanding. But more than that, the incredibly ritualistic treatment of public groups via the public hearing seemed to alienate them from both government and big business interests involved with nuclear power development. The result was the AEC's own licensing and hearing procedures became the source of significant dispute and disagreement among anti-nuclear groups, whose only alternative was to extend their efforts into other political arenas as time went on. Commercialization had arrived, alright, but so had the nuclear power controversy.

NOTES

1. United States Atomic Energy Commission, *Major Activities in the Atomic Energy Programs, January-December 1961* (Washington, D.C.: U.S. Government Printing Office, 1962), p. 509. See also Philip Mullenbach, *Civilian Nuclear Power* (New York: The Twentieth Century Fund, 1963), pp. 127-28.

2. United States Atomic Energy Commission, *Annual Report to Congress 1960* (Washington, D.C.: U.S. Government Printing Office, 1961), pp. 6-7.

3. Mullenbach, *Civilian Nuclear Power*, p. 129.

4. Ibid.

5. United States Atomic Energy Commission, *Annual Report to Congress 1961* (Washington, D.C.: U.S. Government Printing Office, 1962), p. 25.

6. Ibid.

7. Ibid.

8. John F. Hogerton, "The Arrival of Nuclear Power," *Scientific American* 218 (Feburary 1968): 24.

9. Ibid., p. 25.

10. This discussion draws on Arthur D. Little, Inc., *Competition in the Nuclear Power Supply Industry*, Report to the United States Atomic Energy Commission and the United States Department of Justice (Washington, D.C.: U.S. Government Printing Office, 1968), pp. 358 ff.

11. It is of course true that in the 1950s the PRDPs had accumulated a significant amount of operating experience, but it was largely with small-scale, experimental projects rather than with commercial applications, since commercial plants had been on-line only a few years.

12. Arthur D. Little, Inc., *Competition in the Nuclear Supply Industry*, p. 358.

13. United States Atomic Energy Commission, *Civilian Nuclear Power: A Report to the President--1962*, Washington, D.C.: United States Atomic Energy Commission, 1962).

14. Ibid., p. 13.

15. Ibid.

16. Ibid.

17. United States Atomic Energy Commission, *Major Activities in the Atomic Energy Programs, January-December 1962* (Washington, D.C.: U.S. Government Printing Office, 1963), p. 153. See also Wendy Allen, *Nuclear Reactors for Generating Electricity: U.S. Development from 1946 to 1963*, Rand Report R-2116-NSF (Santa Monica, Calif.: Rand

Corporation, 1977), pp. 73-74.

18. Allen, *Nuclear Reactors for Generating Electricity*, p. 74.

19. United States Congress, Hearings before the Joint Committee on Atomic Energy, *Cooperative Power Reactor Demonstration Program, 1963*, 88th Congress, 1st Section, 1963 (Washington, D.C.: U.S. Government Printing Office, 1963), p. 2.

20. Ibid.

21. Frank G. Dawson, *Nuclear Power: Development and Management of a Technology* (Seattle: University of Washington Press, 1976), p. 135.

22. Ibid.

23. Joint Committee on Atomic Energy, *Cooperative Power Reactor Demonstration Program, 1963*, p. 2.

24. See Chapter Two for a complete discussion of these points.

25. United States Atomic Energy Commission, *Annual Report to Congress 1963* (Washington, D.C.: U.S. Government Printing Office, 1964), pp. 17 ff.

26. Ibid., p. 18.

27. Ibid.

28. Cited in Dawson, *Nuclear Power*, p. 153. See also United States Congress, Hearings Before the Joint Committee on Atomic Energy, *Private Ownership of Special Nuclear Materials*, 88th Congress, 1st Session, 1963 (Washington, D.C.: U.S. Government Printing Office, 1964).

29. Joint Committee on Atomic Energy, *Private Ownership of Special Nuclear Materials*, pp. 46, 261, 294. See also the discussion in Dawson, *Nuclear Power*, pp. 154-55.

30. Dawson, *Nuclear Power*, p. 142.

31. Ibid., pp. 156-57.

32. See the comments of Representative John Anderson of Illinois in United States Congress, House, *The Congressional Record*, 88th Congress, 2nd Session, 1964 (Washington, D.C.: U.S. Government Printing Office, 1964), 110 part 15, pp. 20143. Cited in Dawson, *Nuclear Power*, pp. 157-58.

33. Ibid.

34. See the discussion in Robert Perry, *et. al.*, *Development and Commercialization of the Light Water Reactor, 1946-1976*, Rand Report R-2180-NSF (Santa Monica, Calif.: Rand Corporation, 1977), pp. 28 ff. See also Irvin C. Bupp and Jean-Claude Derian, *Light Water: How the Nuclear Dream Dissolved* (New York: Basic Books, 1978), pp. 42 ff.

35. The following discussion draws from Perry, *et. al.*, *Development and Commercialization*

of the Light Water Reactor, pp. 29 ff.

36. Hogerton, "The Arrival of Nuclear Power," pp. 26-27. It might be pointed out that some believed the Oyster Creek plant would generate electricity in the range of 3.42 to 3.97 mills per kilowatt hour. See "Report on the Economic Analysis for Oyster Creek Nuclear Electric Generating Station," Jersey Central Power and Light Company, February 17, 1964. Hogerton also reports that Jersey Central had been contracting coal for a delivered price of around 30 to 31 cents per million B.T.U.s, and could get a price no better than 26 cents offered for the Oyster Creek site. Therefore, nuclear appeared to be economically more competitive. See "The Arrival of Nuclear Power," p. 26.

37. Bupp and Derian, *Light Water*, pp. 42-44.

38. "The Jersey Central Report," *Atomic Industrial Forum Memo* 11 (March 1964): 3.

39. Perry, *et. al.*, *Development and Commercialization of the Light Water Reactor*, p. 31.

40. See United States Atomic Energy Commission, *Civilian Nuclear Power: A Report to the President--1962.*

41. United States Congress, Hearings before the Joint Committee on Atomic Energy, *Nuclear Power Economics 1962 Through 1967*, 90th Congress, 2nd Session, 1968 (Washington, D.C.: U.S. Government Printing Office, 1968), pp. 81-86.

42. Ibid., p. 90.

43. An excellent discussion of this point may be found in Bupp and Derian, *Light Water*, pp. 47 ff.

44. Joint Committee on Atomic Energy, *Nuclear Power Economics*, p. 41.

45. Ibid., pp. 45-46.

46. Ibid, pp. 50-51.

47. Perry, *et. al.*, *Development and Commercialization of the Light Water Reactor*, p. 35.

48. See General Electric Company, *1966 Annual Report* (New York: General Electric Company, 1967). See also Perry, *et. al.*, *Development and Commercialization of the Light Water Reactor*, pp. 37-38.

49. See Perry, *et. al.*, *Development and Commercialization of the Light Water Reactor*, p. 38.

50. United States Congress, Hearings Before the Joint Committee on Atomic Energy, *Nuclear Power Plant Siting and Licensing*, 93rd Congress, 2nd Session, 1974 (Washington, D.C.: U.S. Government Printing Office, 1974), p. 350 and Hogerton, "The Arrival of Nuclear Power," p. 28.

51. Hogerton, "The Arrival of Nuclear Power," p. 29.

52. Ibid.

53. Perry, et. al., *Development and Commercialization of the Light Water Reactor*, pp. 39-40.

54. Bupp and Derian, *Light Water*, pp. 74-75.

55. See United States Atomic Energy Commission, *Civilian Nuclear Power: The 1967 Supplement to the 1962 Report to the President* (Washington, D.C.: United States Atomic Energy Commission, 1967), p. 19.

56. Cited in Bupp and Derian, *Light Water*, p. 50.

57. Joint Committee on Atomic Energy, *Nuclear Power Plant Siting and Licensing*, p. 350.

58. See Elizabeth Rolph, *Regulation of Nuclear Power: The Case of the Light Water Reactor*, Rand Report R-2104-NSF (Santa Monica, Calif.: Rand Corporation, 1977), pp. 22-23.

59. United States Congress, Hearings before the Joint Committee on Atomic Energy, *Licensing and Regulation of Nuclear Reactors*, 90th Congress, 1st Session, 1967 (Washington, D.C.: U.S. Government Printing Office, 1967), pp. 659 ff.

60. Sheldon Novick, *The Careless Atom* (Boston: Houghton Mifflin Co., 1969), p. 53. *New York Times*, March 21, 1963.

61. Rolph, *Regulation of Nuclear Power*, p. 25.

62. Joint Committee on Atomic Energy, *Licensing and Regulation of Nuclear Reactors*, pp. 59 ff.

63. A good discussion of the Bodega Bay incident is found in Novick, *The Careless Atom*, pp. 38-45. See also Pierre Saint-Amand, "Geological and Seismic Study of Bodega Head," Northern California Association to Preserve Bodega Head and Harbor, 1963.

64. See Novick, pp. 45 ff.

65. Joint Committee on Atomic Energy, *Licensing and Regulation of Nuclear Reactors*, pp. 47 ff.

66. Rolph, *Regulation of Nuclear Power*, p. 29.

67. See the discussion in Ibid., pp. 28-32.

68. Ibid., pp. 33-34.

69. Joint Committee on Atomic Energy, *Licensing and Regulation of Nuclear Reactors*, p. 215.

70. United States Congress, Hearings before the Joint Committee on Atomic Energy, *The Status of Nuclear Reactor Safety*, 93rd Congress, 2nd Session, 1974, Part 2 (Washington, D.C.: U.S.

Government Printing Office, 1974), pp. 457-58.

71. See Robert Gillette, "Nuclear Safety (I): The Roots of Dissent," *Science* 177 (September 1, 1972): 771-76 and Gillette, "Nuclear Safety (II): The Years of Delay," *Science* 177 (September 8, 1972): 867-71.

72. United States Atomic Energy Commission, *Annual Report to Congress 1965* (Washington, D.C.: U.S. Government Printing Office, 1966), pp. 50-1.

73. Rolph, *Regulation of Nuclear Power,* p. 39.

74. Ibid.

75. United States Atomic Energy Commission, *Annual Report to Congress 1972-1974* (Washington, D.C.: U.S. Government Printing Office, 1975), p. 2.

76. Joint Committee on Atomic Energy, *Nuclear Power Plant Siting and Licensing,* p. 350.

77. Bupp and Derian, *Light Water,* p. 91.

78. See Morris A. Adelman, *The World Petroleum Market* (Baltimore: Johns Hopkins University Press, 1972), pp. 160 ff. and Morris A. Adelman, "Is the Oil Shortage Real?" *Foreign Policy* 9 (Winter 1972-1973): 77.

79. A good discussion of the events leading up to the Tehran Agreement is found in Ruth Sheldon Knowles, *America's Oil Famine* (New York: Coward, McCann and Geoghegan, 1975), pp. 77-96.

80. John M. Blair, *The Control of Oil* (New York: Pantheon, 1976), pp. 226-27.

81. Ibid., pp. 261-62.

82. Ibid., p. 262.

83. Bupp and Derian, *Light Water,* pp. 92-93.

84. Ibid., p. 93.

85. "AEC to Referee, Not Promote, Industry," *Science* 174 (October 29, 1971): 478.

86. See *Nucleonics Week,* October 18, 1971, p. 1.

87. Rolph, *Regulation of Nuclear Power,* p. 65.

88. Ibid.

89. Ibid., pp. 65-67. See also Joint Committee on Atomic Energy, *The Status of Nuclear Reactor Safety,* Parts 1 and 2 for more on the development of standards.

90. United States Atomic Energy Commission, *Annual Report to Congress 1972-1974,* pp. 29 ff. and Rolph, *Regulation of Nuclear Power,* pp. 67-68.

91. For related materials which bear on these points, see Arthur D. Little, Inc., *Competition in the Nuclear Power Supply Industry.*

5
The Evolution of Opposition to Nuclear Power in the United States (I): Reactor Licensing, Public Participation, and the Limits of Subsystem Procedures

> In practice, however, there has not been full, free, and frank discussion of the hazards (of nuclear power). The AEC has regarded public participation in the licensing process as a means of procuring public acceptance of its safety determinations. Risks of nuclear power plants are never discussed in explicit terms; to the extent that they surface at all, they are referred to only in passing as it is pointed out that there are numerous safety features which reduce risks, it is hinted, to virtually zero. There is no discussion as to the degree of certainty that the safety features have been subjected to actual testing or the degree to which, and the period of time in which, there has been actual operating experience with them. A calculated effort is made to invite the public to assume that the fact that the plant meets AEC standards means that there are no risks. Residual risks remaining after these standards are met are totally ignored.
>
> -Harold P. Green

INTRODUCTION

By the early 1970s the nuclear debate appeared to be gaining momentum. In this and the following two chapters, we probe the nature and meaning of this controversy, attempting to delineate the principal reasons for, and events involved in, the evolution of opposition to civilian nuclear power in America. In the previous chapter we suggested that the AEC's own reactor licensing and regulation procedures, particularly its procedures for public participation, seemed to do little more than create difficulty and increase distrust and suspicion of the government and the nuclear industry. Hence in this chapter we shall discuss the AEC's reactor licensing procedures more fully, in order to show how their promotional bias became the cause for public concern and cast a shadow of doubt on the integrity of the regulatory process itself. When it turned its face to the public, the AEC did not help its own cause but worsened it. Instead of assuaging conflict and debate, the very scope and breadth of reactor licensing and regulation worked to undermine public trust and political accountability--or so it must have seemed to interveners experiencing the limits of the regulatory subsystem's procedures of public participation.

NUCLEAR REACTOR LICENSING AND REGULATION: DEFINING THE ROLE OF PUBLIC PARTICIPATION

The Requirement of Public Participation in Reactor Licensing Procedures

With the massive revision of the Atomic Energy Act in 1954, it seemed that electricity produced by nuclear reactors would become a fact of modern industrial life in America.[1] At the same time, it was evident that a major push toward large-scale power production from nuclear reactors would require substantially new and increased efforts of regulation and control. While a nuclear power plant could not be detonated like a bomb, it was nevertheless possible for a large reactor accident to emit lethal doses of radioactivity into the environment. With safety considerations at the forefront, the 1954 Act widened the thrust of government control of atomic energy by requiring an "exceptionally stringent licensing and regulatory scheme"[2] for the construction and operation of nuclear power plants. Furthermore, the 1954 Act set provisions for outright public participation in the licensing and regulation proceedings, established by the phrase: "In any proceeding under this Act, for granting, suspending, revoking, or amending any license or construction permit ... the Commission *shall grant a hearing upon request of any person whose interest may be affected by the proceeding,* and shall admit any such persons as party to such proceeding."[3]

The decision to implement public participation seemed rooted in several considerations. To begin with, interlaced throughout the 1954 Act were variants of the phrase: "nuclear material must be regulated in the national interest and in order to provide for the common defense and security and *to protect the health and safety of the public*."[4] "To protect the health and safety of the public" could be enhanced, it was suggested, by permitting public access to the AEC's licensing proceedings, where the public could voice their concerns in cases that ostensibly affected their interests. Senator Clinton P. Anderson, speaking on the Senate floor on July 14, 1954 summed up the main thrust of this "open door policy:"[5]

> ... Because I feel so strongly that nuclear energy is possibly the most important thing we are dealing with in our industrial life today, I wish to be sure that the Commission has to do its business out of doors, so to speak, where everyone can see them.
>
> Although I have no doubt about the ability and integrity of the members of the Commission, I simply wish to be sure they have to move where everyone can see every step they take; and if they are to grant a license in this very important field, I think a hearing should be required and a formal record should be made regarding all aspects, including the public aspects.

In seeking to enforce the phrase "to protect the health and safety of the public," the hearing presumably would help insure that important AEC decisions regarding nuclear power plant licensing and operation would take place openly and with public knowledge.

Congress responded to the Joint Committee's requests for a public hearing in 1957 by enacting additional amendments to the 1954 Act which *required* a public hearing before a construction permit or operating license for a nuclear reactor was issued, *regardless* of whether any citizen or party requested one. As the amendment read:[6] "The Commission shall hold a hearing after thirty days notice and publication once in the Federal Register on each application ... for a license for a facility and on any application ... for a testing facility." Providing for the mandatory hearing seemed to coincide with the spirit expressed by the Joint Committee when drawing up the amendment in 1957:[7] "The

Joint Committee concluded that full, free, and frank discussion in public of the hazards involved with any particular reactor would seem to be the most certain way of assuring that the reactor will indeed be safe and that the public will be fully appraised of this fact."

The 1957 amendment required a mandatory hearing at both the construction permit and operating license stages, but the public hearing at the operating license stage was subsequently dropped in 1962 in order to expedite reactor licensing.[8] Nevertheless, a person whose interests might be affected by the issuance of an operating license retained the right to petition for a hearing at this stage of the proceedings. Further, the Commission reserved the option of ordering an operating license hearing in appropriate cases.[9] Although the operating license hearing had been dropped, the AEC believed that its procedures would still provide an "'...open forum in which matters of reactor safety...could be thoroughly aired and made known to the public, even in non-contested cases.'"[10]

From the above it seemed clear that the public hearing, by direct incorporation into the regulatory proceedings, would be an addition to the AEC's existing methods of assessing nuclear technology, as well as a way of informing the public of this assessment. By creating opportunities for public participation, it seemed the framers of the Atomic Energy Act of 1954 and its amendments had realized one crucial fact about nuclear energy: a technology with the potential to dramatically affect people's lives was too important to leave in the hands of any narrowly drawn body of elites, whether they were political decision-makers, scientists, technicians, lawyers, or otherwise. Important decisions involving tremendously powerful technologies such as nuclear power required a substantial measure of public participation and support, independent of whatever input might be realized through elected representatives. When the National Academy of Sciences stressed the importance and necessity of such participation in its seminal report on technology assessment in 1969,[11] it was simply underscoring a principle of participation that the Atomic Energy Act of 1954 had already applied to the application and deployment of nuclear power.

POWER PROJECTIONS, THE POLITICAL CLIMATE, AND CITIZEN OPPOSITION

The first few years after the enactment of the public participation clause saw a significant lack of organized citizen action. Apart from the more substantial opposition at Bodega Bay, Malibu, and Ravenswood facilities, most of the initial opposition via the public hearing was generally rather unorganized, and assumed the form of a town meeting where concerned citizens would simply meet with and question AEC and utility representatives.[12] However, several new developments were in the air during this time, and increased citizen involvement seemed eminent.

Perhaps most important in heightening citizen participation were the AEC's hefty power projections, particularly the anticipated role of nuclear power in the United States energy mix for the remainder of the century. As shown previously, the Commission was extremely optimistic about the future of nuclear energy. In the Commission's *Report to the President* in 1962, for example, the following statements were made:[13]

> Nuclear energy can and should make an important and, ultimately, a vital contribution toward meeting our long-term energy requirements, and, in particular, that: the development and exploitation of nuclear electric power is clearly in the near- and long-term national interest and should be vigorously pursued.

Furthermore, the Commission's 1967 *Supplement* to the 1962 report concluded that:[14]

> Total energy consumption is expected to increase by 50 percent between 1965 and 1980 and by 150 percent between 1965 and 2000... The proportion of energy consumed in the form of electricity is currently about 20 percent; it is expected to increase to 30 percent in 1980 and to over 50 percent by the year 2000... Whereas less than 1 percent of the electrical generating capacity in 1965 was nuclear, it is estimated that 23 to 30 percent will be nuclear in 1980 and about 50 percent in 2000.

Seemingly in concert with AEC's 1967 projections the President's Office of Science and Technology reported in 1968 that at existing rates of consumption, at least 492 new electrical generating stations would be required by 1990.[15] It was thus not entirely surprising to find nuclear power stations proliferating at an accelerated rate, as applications for construction of nuclear units reached an all-time high in 1967, when the AEC received twenty-nine new applications for construction permits, while at the same time, issuing twenty-three construction permits on pending applications.[16] With the AEC's goal for nuclear generating stations being to produce about fifty percent of the nation's electricity by the year 2000, it seemed likely that about 1,000 nation-wide nuclear stations would be required to generate this much power.[17]

The rather weak and unorganized anti-nuclear forces naturally found the above scenario rather shocking. On the one hand, the nation seemed on the verge of a crash nuclear development program--a thousand reactors by the year 2000--yet on the other hand, the safety of the reactors had not been convincingly proved. Indeed, the AEC's 1957 safety study, WASH-740 (*Theoretical Consequences of Major Accidents in Large Nuclear Power Plants*), had not yet received any substantial up-date. As WASH-740 indicated in 1957, a major reactor accident could kill thousands of people, injure tens of thousands more, and cause several billion dollars in property damages. So far as anyone knew, the figures were not just true for the 1957 period, but probably considerably *underestimated* the real danger since the utilities had brought larger reactors on-line. Moreover, the extension of the Price-Anderson indemnity legislation until August 1, 1977 by means of an amendment to the Atomic Energy Act in 1965,[18] meant, in effect, that atomic energy was still singled out from all other technologies and provided special government indemnity and limitations on liability.[19]

This combination of optimistic power projections and growing concerns over the safety of nuclear plants was exacerbated by the political "climate" which surrounded the civilian power programs: that is, neither the Atomic Energy Act of 1954 nor any other single piece of legislation *clearly* outlined the major goals and policies of this greatly expanded national commitment to civilian nuclear power. The policies and programs of atomic energy development, including the vigorous promotion of civilian nuclear power in the middle 1960s, occurred largely on the strength of the Joint Committee and the AEC's own discretion on how developmental efforts ought to proceed. One long-time observer of nuclear power, Harold P. Green, describes the situation this way:[20]

> The political structure of atomic energy is in reality a closed loop. Starting with the premise that atomic technology should be developed, introduced, and used, the JCAE and the AEC have usually cooperated symbiotically to resolve policy issues behind the scenes before legislative proposals can reach public view. By the time these proposals emerge, it can be said that they are "noncontroversial," and they usually breeze automatically through Congress. Benefits of nuclear technology have usually been presumed, while risks have been ignored or dismissed in boldly optimistic terms.

The result of this closed political structure was an extraordinary speed-up in the development of nuclear technology without the political debate that usually accompanies such policy decisions. With the government's financial subsidies eliminating many of the normal restraints imposed upon technological innovation, such as market pressures and legal and political obstacles, nuclear technology reached a state of development, which, under normal circumstances, would have required many more decades to achieve.[21] Accordingly, reactor licensing and regulation procedures by the early 1960s became, as will be shown below, predisposed to promoting the rapid spread of nuclear reactors and largely assumed *a priori* that the reactors were in fact safe.[22] This regulatory posture had some inevitable consequences for the nature and content of public participation, and it is not difficult to see how private citizens became angered over the fact that the public hearing was little more than a "showcase for unveiling and ratifying the results of prior, private negotiations"[23] that a nuclear plant should be built and operated in accordance with the wishes of the nuclear power establishment.

LICENSING A NUCLEAR POWER REACTOR: THE EXTENT OF PUBLIC PARTICIPATION AND THE PUBLIC HEARING

In this section, we attempt to demonstrate the perfunctory nature of public participation in the AEC's licensing and regulation process. In order to do this, it is necessary to describe in detail the general mechanics of the process to show that considerable momentum was already in favor of the utilities, and that public interveners tended to get "brushed aside." We begin by outlining the AEC's prehearing licensing requirements as they stood in 1974.[24]

In actuality the licensing process begins well in advance of the public hearing for a construction permit for a nuclear plant. Before a utility publicly announces its intention to construct a nuclear power facility it usually conducts several informal discussions with state regulatory agencies and with the AEC.[25] These discussions often span several months, sometimes years, of talks and negotiations.

Before any construction can begin, the applicant is required to file a formal application with the AEC for a construction permit. The application is generally accompanied by a Preliminary Safety Report (PSR) which must contain:[26]

> A description of the site and the proposed reactor with particular emphasis on the features of design which are pertinent to an appraisal of the safety of proposed operations; a discussion of the proposed operating limitations; a discussion of the proposed procedures in routine and other operations; a discussion of procedures and devices which are to come into play in the event of an accident or other unusual event; necessary meterological, hydrological, geological and seismological data; procedures for waste disposal and the sampling of wastes; and an evaluation of the measures designed to prevent radioactive hazards or to protect against the consequences of accidents.

Once received by the Commission, the applicant's PSR is then submitted for review to the AEC's Office of Regulatory Activities which attempts to evaluate and rule on the safety aspects contained in the report.[27] Often times other AEC staff personnel are called in for assistance, as are additional federal agencies as, for example, the Environmental Protection Agency or the Geological Survey. Individual consultants and outside experts also may be called in to assist with the PSR evaluation.[28]

As is generally the case, this evaluation turns up weaknesses, inadequacies of pertinent information and even serious substantive criticisms of the report. The applicant is then asked, either in a series of informal gatherings or by means of letters, to respond to the criticisms and to supply additional information as needed. After having supplied the necessary materials, the applicant and the staff again meet on an informal basis, at which time the remaining differences are addressed and ironed out as much as possible.[29]

When this process is completed, the AEC's staff then files for the public record what is known as a "Safety Evaluation Report". The report:[30]

> ... analyzes the site from the point of view of location and surrounding population, meteorology, geology, hydrology, and seismicity. It evaluates the adequacy of the containment and the design of the reactor plant, including reactor physics, the design of the core and fuel, the control rod drive system and reactor vessel, the coolant system, and the control and instrumentation. It also considers the adequacy of auxiliary plant systems, including power supply, fuel handling and storage, waste disposal and others. It analyzes the proposed research and development programs, and evaluates the technical qualifications of the applicant. It analyzes potential accidents in order to determine possible initiating mechanisms, the effectiveness of protective design features, and the consequences of possible dispersion of radioactive material into the environment. Attached to the safety evaluation are the reports of any other Government agencies and private consultants whose views have been invited, and one or more reports of the Advisory Committee on Reactor Safeguards.

Before the regulatory staff's study is completed however, the application is further reviewed by the Advisory Committee on Reactor Safeguards (ACRS), a body within the AEC first established by the Commission in 1953, and later made an independent statutory body by the 1957 amendment to the Atomic Energy Act.[31] The ACRS is a fifteen-member board appointed by the Commission on a part-time basis for terms of four years each. The members represent various scientific disciplines relevant to evaluating nuclear reactor safety and are responsible for advising the Commission in pending applications for construction permits.[32]

As is ordinarily the practice, the regulatory staff first submits a copy of the applicant's

Preliminary Safety Report to the ACRS for review by a subcommittee in order to determine whether sufficient information is available for full committee consideration, and whether novel aspects of the proposed facility deserve special attention.

After the ACRS subcommittee has had sufficient time to review the applicant's PSR, the regulatory staff provides the ACRS with its own preliminary evaluation of the project which underscores those areas likely to require special consideration. The regulatory staff's evaluation and the ACR's subcommittee report (neither of which are made public) are the essential elements involved in full committee consideration of the project.[33]

The next step, if relevant, is the ACRS subcommittee calls in the applicant for one or more informal discussion sessions in which various aspects of the project are discussed with both the applicant and the regulatory staff. The results of these discussions are reported back to the full ACRS committee which may opt for additional meetings with the staff and applicant, including some discussion with private consultants and experts. The proceedings of these sessions are not included in the public record.[34]

After these procedures have been completed, the ACRS makes a report to the AEC. The report is always in the form of a letter to the Chairman of the AEC and states the opinion of the ACRS regarding the construction of the reactor at the proposed site. Specifically, the letter states whether or not the proposed reactor can be operated without endangering the health and safety of the public, and which aspects it feels should be given further consideration by the Commission.[35] While the regulatory staff always takes the ACRS report into account, the staff may not necessarily reach the same conclusions in its own safety evaluation, and occasionally, therefore, the ACRS and the staff reports have disagreed.[36]

In addition to the above, before a construction permit or operating license can be issued, the applicant is required to submit 300 copies of an environmental report known as the "Applicant's Environmental Report--Construction Permit Stage." The report is required to contain the following: the impact of construction and operation of the proposed facility; adverse effects and irreversible depletion of resources relating to the proposed action; available alternatives; the balance between short-term use and long-term preservation of the environment; what will be the technical, economic, and environmental benefits of the proposed facility; how does the proposed facility comply with various governmental regulations and standards; and a detailed cost-benefit analysis which balances the facility's benefits together with the adverse environmental effects and the alternatives for reducing such effects.[37]

The regulatory staff then prepares its own environmental statement, known as a "Draft Detailed Statement of Environmental Considerations," and together with the applicant's Environmental Report, sends it to various federal agencies and the appropriate state and local officials of an affected area for their return comments.[38]

When all outside comments have been returned, the regulatory staff then compiles what is known as a "Final Detailed Statement of the Environmental Considerations," which is sent to the Council on Environmental Quality and becomes part of the public record. Since this statement presumably contains all the relevant information and comments of the interested parties, it is considered the final report on which all subsequent environmental action will be based.[39] Once the Final Detailed Statement is completed, the public hearing, which forms an integral part of the construction permit proceedings, is the next step in the licensing process.

As stated previously, the 1957 amendment to the Atomic Energy Act required a public hearing at both the construction permit and operating license stages. Thus when the construction permit stage is reached, the AEC must give notice to the public that a hearing will commence in thirty days. The notice sets the agenda, specifies time and place of the hearing, dates for filing petitions to intervene, and how interested parties may state their views on the proposed action without becoming a full intervener. In such instances, the Commission exercises some power in handling petitions such that "irrelevant, duplicative, or repetitive evidence and agreement" are barred from consideration, and such that "common interests (are) represented by a spokesman."[40]

Up until 1962, the hearing was a trial-type affair conducted before a single hearing examiner. The hearing examiner was ordinarily legally rather than scientifically or technically trained, meaning he was often criticized as incompetent to review relevant technical factors involved with nuclear plant operation. As a result, the Joint Committee's staff undertook a complete review of the licensing process in 1961.[41] The review ended in an amendment to the Atomic Energy Act in 1962 which created the Atomic Safety and Licensing Boards (ASLB).[42] The ASLBs are comprised of three members, "one of whom shall be qualified in the conduct of administrative proceedings and two of whom shall have such technical or other qualifications as the Commission deems appropriate to the issues to be decided."[43] The board members were to be selected from both within the AEC and from the private sector, and included biologists, lawyers, nuclear physicists, and health officials.

As for the function of the boards, it is largely one of technical review of the safety considerations and documents already compiled--the regulatory staff's safety evaluation, the ACRS report, the applicant's Preliminary Safety Report, and the Commission's Final Environmental Statement. The purpose of the boards, then, is to check whether the review process up to that point satisfies the necessary safety considerations stipulated for granting a construction permit.[44] This includes:[45]

> Determining whether the applicant has described the proposed design of the facility and identified major safety and health features; whether further technical information which can reasonably be left for later consideration will be supplied in the final safety analysis report; whether safety features and safety research and development programs are incorporated; and whether the proposed facility can be constructed and operated at the selected location without undue risk to the health and safety of the public.

Yet despite what seemed like a clear delineation of the boards' responsibilities, there has been much discussion of whether or not the ASLBs, in practice, should attempt to resolve disputes over the above issues, and whether or not they should re-do the work of the regulatory staff and the ACRS. It seems evident from a reading of the 1962 amendment however, that the boards' major overriding function is to clarify and promote safety issues.[46]

In any case, before a hearing can proceed, an initial prehearing conference is scheduled within sixty days after the public notice of the hearing has been issued. The purpose of the conference is to establish the agenda for the proceedings, to define the issues to be considered, and to identify the parties that shall participate.47 It might be added that if the AEC feels a petition is based on issues considered "unrelated" to safety and radiation questions, an intervener may be denied access to the hearing.

At this point, the discovery process commences whereupon intervener groups are allowed their first real opportunity to examine and evaluate an applicant's materials and documents submitted in support of a request for a construction permit. This is a crucial stage of the process for public interveners, for it provides their primary opportunity for securing the materials necessary to prepare their cases. In addition, at this point the Commission is supposed to make available relevant documents compiled by its regulatory staff, which, it might be added, seems to have been done with some reluctance on the part of the AEC.[48] As a matter of fact, while discovery is generally permitted by means of several techniques--written or oral disposition, the reproduction of documents, inspection of properties and facilities, written interrogatories, and so forth--only in exceptional cases does the AEC permit discovery by disposition or written interrogatories against its staff.[49] Furthermore, the AEC has in the past routinely precluded several categories of data--so-called "privileged information"--from public access. As Keating puts it:[50]

> While a substantial amount of information is made available for public scrutiny, there are several categories of data that are routinely denied to the public. Among these categories of "privileged information" are things such as opinions, evaluations, analyses, deliberations, recommendations, advice, and other internal AEC reports and memorandums; information supplied to the Commission in confidence, along with the names of those giving this information, reports comparing the particular reactor under consideration with other reactors; reports on inspection visits to nuclear manufacturers and suppliers; and proprietary information.

One may add to this a comment made by a prominent intervener lawyer, Myron Cherry:[51]

> The thing they (the AEC) put in the document room is the application, an ACRS letter, correspondence which says, "Dear Mr. Morris: There is my application," and one from Peter Morris saying, "Dear Mr. Utility, Thanks."

> I am concerned that every other third memorandum in the Commission gets stamped "Confidential" because somebody is stamp happy. The hard facts are not coming out. I can submit to you almost unequivocally that 40 percent of the time in every licensing hearing has been spent in wrangling over documents which the Commission ultimately released.

It is apparent, therefore, that production of, and access to, important AEC documents was a serious problem for intervener groups. And since the preparation of their case often depended on these rights of discovery, their efforts were hampered, if not stymied altogether.

To this one should add that in procuring information intervener groups work under severe time pressures. For the most part, interveners have about sixty days from the time the hearing is announced to prepare their cases for the prehearing conference, during which time they have the opportunity to examine such documents as are made public at that point--documents, it should be emphasized, which are rather complex, often highly technical, and which have required several months or years of work to prepare. While it cannot be covered here, the AEC's own release schedule for various documents further hampers intervener efforts.[52] Thus even before the discovery process ensues, intervener groups are faced with severe obstacles in procuring important information.

Once the complex discovery process has been completed, a second prehearing conference is scheduled to occur within sixty days. This conference is held primarily as final preparation for the public hearing at the construction permit proceedings. The conference schedules witnesses, specifies, clarifies, and where possible, simplifies issues, considers additions of new facts or documents and authenticates existing ones, and performs other related tasks.[53]

After the second prehearing conference finishes its work, a public hearing is scheduled shortly thereafter at a suitable meeting place, close to the proposed construction site. Unless a hearing is uncontested, which is now rare, the hearing usually continues for many weeks, during which time extensive, exhaustive testimony is taken from the parties (and their representatives) involved. In the most simple case, the parties involved are the Commission's regulatory staff and the applicant;

but now, of course, one or more intervener groups often participate in the hearings as well.[54]

The hearings are presided over by the ASLBs and are divided into two parts: one that deals with plant construction and safety issues, and the other concerning environmental impact review of the Final Environmental Statement. The procedures are the same for all parties: all are entitled to present evidence, oral and written, that aids in disclosure of the relevant facts; rights of cross-examination and rebuttal are provided to all parties; and all parties generally exercise the right of presenting an opening oral statement which briefly describes their position at the present hearings and articulates their concerns.[55] The evidence submitted by the parties consists of:[56]

> The applicant's evidence at the construction permit hearing consists primarily of the application as amended, including the preliminary safety report. Other evidence is served and filed in advance of the hearing in the form of prepared written testimony. The applicant makes available a group of witnesses whose oral testimony largely amounts to submission to cross examination by the staff and other parties, and by the board itself, on the subject matter of the written evidence.
>
> The staff's safety evaluation, which is adopted orally by staff witnesses, constitutes the core of the evidence on behalf of the staff, supplemented by such oral testimony as may be offered or elicited by the board.

As for interveners' evidence, it consists of oral and written testimony, submission of documents and materials procured during the discovery procedure, and testimony from expert witnesses called in to represent a particular group.

At this point it should be mentioned that only the exhibits, the official transcript of testimony, and the materials presented during the proceedings form the basis on which a decision is made.[57] In other words, interveners are required to limit their attention solely to the materials submitted during the hearings, and whether these materials adequately demonstrate that the proposed plant will not violate the health and safety standards set by the AEC. Nowhere are the interveners permitted the opportunity to challenge the validity of either the rules, regulations, or the health and safety standards already set by the AEC.[58] Rather, interveners are limited to highly technical issues such as will this or that piece of hardware perform as advertised, will safety system X come into play at the appropriate time, and so on. As Harold Green summarizes:[59]

> It is anomalous that the AEC compels the case to be contested on narrow technical grounds, since the interveners are really not concerned about the technical features inside the plant; rather, their concern relates to the more fundamental questions as to what harmful materials will come out of the plant in normal operation and in the event of an accident... Most public interveners ... have sought to challenge the validity of the AEC's (radiation protection) standards, claiming that radiation exposures at these levels are not without risk to the public health and safety and the environment generally ... the AEC, however, (has) steadfastly refused to permit challenge of (their radiation protection) standards in licensing cases...(interveners) have very little effective opportunity to articulate within the framework of the hearing process their real concern--that, reviewing the plant as a totality, there is a significant possibility of a catastrophic accident.

It is apparent, therefore, that the AEC's restriction of materials on which a decision for issuing a construction permit is based predisposes the nature of the hearing and seems to beg the very questions one would think the hearing should address.

While the ASLB may request further testimony if uncertainties develop, the board eventually renders a decision--called an "initial decision"--based on the evidence brought before it. The initial decision usually results in the AEC granting a so-called "provisional construction permit" to the applicant.[60] Unless a party objects, issuance of the provisional permit constitutes the basis on which a final AEC decision will be made within forty-five days of such issuance. Objections are referred back to the ASLB for review, and further opportunities for appeal are provided by both the Commission or a federal Court of Appeals. However, notwithstanding such objections, and somewhat contrary to the term "provisional," the provisional permit usually results in substantial construction activity --such as site excavation and clearing, building of access roads and power lines, manufacturing of various components (nuclear and non-nuclear), and construction of various facilities and outbuildings. In short, setting construction into motion seems to imply that an eventual favorable ruling for the applicant is forthcoming.[61]

Once the construction permit has been issued, full-scale construction commences. However, before an operating license can be issued and a nuclear power reactor put into operation, a review process similar to that involved with the issuance of the construction permit must be conducted. The process includes further technical review; description of facilities and equipment; estimates of radioactive effluents to be released into the environment and methods for controlling such releases; specification of various safety features of the plant; and inclusion of an updated environment impact statement--called The Final Environmental Statement--that is basically a revision of the environmental report filed at the construction permit stage.[62] Moreover, as will be recalled, a public hearing is not obligatory at the operating license stage, as per the 1962 amendment to the Atomic Energy Act. However, should a party request such a hearing, the AEC is required to conduct one. The proceedings follow the same general pattern and format of the construction permit hearings, allowing for additional technical review, submission of new evidence, stressing areas for additional consideration, and so forth. Although such a hearing may occur, it should be noted that this hearing does not re-do the proceedings of the construction permit hearing; rather, it is limited only to those issues set forth by the parties in controversy. Opportunities for Commission and judicial review are also available, as above, once a decision has been handed down by the ASLB.[63] Once the applicant has proceeded through these steps, he is granted an operating license which authorizes the start-up of the facility and eventual full power operation sometime thereafter.

WAS THE PUBLIC HEARING EFFECTIVE?

With this overview of the AEC licensing and hearing procedures, we are able to locate public participation in its actual relation to nuclear reactor licensing and regulation. As set forth by the Atomic Energy Act of 1954 and its amendments, the public hearing represented an additional element in nuclear energy regulation and control, that would presumably supplement and widen presently existing regulatory efforts, rather hazily lumped under the general heading of "government control." Public participation had been added to an already stringent regulatory and licensing process which, in most cases, had already piled up several months, even years, of comment, criticism, review, and evaluation of an applicant's proposal to build a nuclear power plant. The intent of this strategy, of course, was to eliminate any possibility of a major design flaw or other problem escaping notice in terms of currently employed standards of evaluation, as well as inform the public of how thorough the AEC had already been with their review.

Yet the latent or unintended consequence was that the very comprehensiveness and complexity of the process seemed to predispose the nature of public participation such that the public intervener played a minor, indeed almost a perfunctory, role in the assessment process. In fact, up until the time the public hearing was actually conducted, interveners were accorded almost no input. But by this time, the process was well under way and the momentum was already in favor of the applicant. Except for some transactions and documents which were included in the public record, the regulation process occured almost totally between the applicant, the various governmental agencies, and the experts called in to assist with technical, environmental, and legal details. To be sure, considerable effort was expended well before the public hearing to demonstrate that the proposed facility was "in fact" sound and would not endanger the health and safety of the public. Thus, once the AEC's regulatory staff and the ACRS approved an application, it seemed that the eventual issuance of a construction permit remained but a formality.[64]

To this is added the fact the public interveners were not only severely handicapped in their efforts to obtain relevant information, but also, the extent of technical expertise required to evaluate such information was often considerable. Since the typical intervener group did not generally possess this technical expertise they had to hire qualified experts, often at great time and expense, in order to adequately represent their positions. Finally, substantial legal and administrative expertise was required if an intervener was to be effective. As Green sums it up:[65]

The entire proceeding is reminiscent of David versus Goliath. The intervener's council sitting alone, usually without adequate technical assistance, faces two or three AEC attorneys, two or three attorneys for the applicant, and large teams of experts who support the AEC and applicant's attorneys. And, in the reality of the situation, the intervener is pitted against both the AEC staff and the applicant.

In view of this situation there was little doubt that when an intervener entered a hearing, the deck was already stacked against him. Consequently, one must ask exactly what was the hearing supposed to accomplish? As mentioned above, the hearing was originally instituted for the explicit purpose of permitting additional monitoring of the health and safety issues by public groups, ostensibly creating a major opportunity for members of the public to state whatever concerns they may harbor. Yet what resulted, as Keating confers, was:[66]

> the mandatory public hearing (was) a charade, in which the only parties were the applicant and the AEC Regulatory Staff, cooperating to expedite issuance of the license. Accordingly, the public hearing came to be regarded as an educational or propaganda exercise, performed primarily to show how safe the plant was and how conscientious the AEC safety review had been.

In other words, the hearing seemed designed more to introduce and reaffirm decisions that had already been made rather than to allow the public a real voice in these decisions, and, hence, the appearance and not the reality of public participation was what was actually demonstrated.[67]

Finally, and perhaps most importantly, was the procedural and substantive context in which the entire licensing-regulation-hearing process occurred seemed largely misguided. It is inappropriate to attempt to resolve questions such as will emergency core-cooling systems come into play in the event of an accident, or do scrubbing systems work as advertised, when the real issues being raised by interveners concerned determinations already made by the AEC regarding matters like: X levels of radiation are *safe*; X benefits are *worth* Y costs; or X levels of probability of a large accident occuring are *acceptable*. It is largely irrelevant to deal with such questions in only technical and scientific terms--much less debating them in an adversary context where the "facts" can be stretched to adhere to one's own view--when the real issues concerned essentially matters of public choice, acceptability, or establishing safety standards--none of which are mainly scientific or technical questions.[68] And, by the same token, when some of the parties to the proceedings lacked necessary information, technical expertise and sophistication, and adequate legal and administrative skills--as the interveners often did--one must question whether these parties could realistically contribute anything to the assessment process other than additional delay and disagreement.

SUMMARY AND CONCLUSIONS

In retrospect, it is plain how the public's experience *vis-a-vis* AEC procedure was bound to be a source of dissatisfaction and alienation. The so-called "open door" policy advocated by Senator Clinton P. Anderson in the 1950s was little more than pretense since the public hearing did not transcend the goals and purposes of the regulatory subsystem. Conducted in these terms, the hearings were destined to become a major source of distrust and criticism of the government's policies of nuclear energy development. The public was forced to conclude that the government had something to hide, thereby opening to question the entire safety and regulatory program.

While the public participation "experiment" had endeavored to expand the bases of public support for nuclear power, it actually had the opposite effect. Naturally, the interveners in time came to realize that the hearing was nothing more than show, but it was about the only participatory vehicle available and had to be used irrespective of the outcome. As one observer describes the situation:[69]

> If the licensed project will damage the environment, it must be opposed irrespective of the prospects for victory or defeat. The administrative arena must be used as an educational forum to alert the public to the project's adverse effects on environmental quality. The environmental stakes must be vividly dramatized as a prelude to organized political action to block the project or correct its deficiencies. Viewed in this perspective, a losing environmental cause is worth fighting for because *it adds to the ecological enlightenment of the public.*

As the interveners became ever more technically and legally sophisticated, they indeed brought the issues into the public arena, and forced costly construction delays for several years while the legal and technical maneuverings were ironed out. Perhaps more than any single factor, public participation served notice that the politics of nuclear energy appeared hopelessly mired in the regulatory subsystem of the atom. The aggravation of controversy and the expansion of the debate into other public forums could be the only outcome: as nuclear plants proliferated, so would public opposition.

NOTES

1. See Public Law 703, "Atomic Energy Act of 1954," in *United States Statutes at Large 1954*, V. 68, Part 1 (Washington, D.C.: U.S. Government Printing Office, 1955), pp. 936-39. For an excellent summary of the legislative history of the 1954 Act, including its role in facilitating industry involvement in nuclear energy development, see Frank G. Dawson, *Nuclear Power: Development and Management of a Technology* (Seattle: University of Washington Press, 1976), pp. 58-75.

2. Harold P. Green, "Nuclear Power Licensing and Regulation," *The Annals* 400 (March 1972): 117. See also Arthur W. Murphy, "Nuclear Power Plant Regulation," in Arthur W. Murphy (ed.), *The Nuclear Power Controversy* (Englewood Cliffs: Prentice-Hall, 1976), pp. 108-28.

3. See Public Law 703, "Atomic Energy Act of 1954," pp. 955-56.

4. Ibid., p. 921; emphasis added.

5. Cited in Arthur W. Murphy, "Atomic Safety and Licensing Boards: An Experiment in Administrative Decision Making on Safety Questions," *Law and Contemporary Problems* 33 (Summer 1968): 574, note 37.

6. Public Law 85-256, "An Amendment to the Atomic Energy Act of 1954," in *United States Statutes at Large 1957*, V. 77 (Washington, D.C.: U.S. Government Printing Office, 1958), p. 579.

7. Cited in Murphy, "Atomic Safety and Licensing Boards," p. 574, note 37.

8. See Public Law 87-615, "An Act to Amend the Atomic Energy Act of 1954," in *United States Statutes at Large, 1962*, V. 76 (Washington, D.C.: U.S. Government Printing Office, 1963), p. 409. For an excellent discussion of licensing procedures and hearing requirements see Sidney G. Kingsley, "The Licensing of Nuclear Power Reactors in the United States," *Atomic Energy Law Journal* 7 (Fall 1965): 316-18.

9. Ibid.; see also Murphy, "Atomic Safety and Licensing Boards," pp. 575-76, and Dawson, *Nuclear Power*, pp. 176-79.

10. United States Congress, Joint Committee on Atomic Energy, *A Study of AEC Licensing Procedures and Organization in Licensing Reactor Facilities*, 85th Congress, 1st Session, 1957 (Washington, D.C.:

U.S. Government Printing Office, 1957), p. 17; cited in Kingsley, "The Licensing of Nuclear Power Reactors in the United States," p. 317.

11. See the National Academy of Sciences, *Technology: Processes of Assessment and Choice* (Washington, D.C.: U.S. Government Printing Office, 1969), p. 76. See also Thomas Keating, "Politics, Energy and the Environment: The Role of Technology Assessment," *American Behavioral Scientist* 19 (September-October 1975): 50.

12. L.D. Smith, "Evolution of Opposition to the Peaceful Uses of Nuclear Energy," *Nuclear Engineering International* 17 (June 1972): 462.

13. United States Atomic Energy Commission, *Civilian Nuclear Power: A Report to the President--1962* (Washington, D.C.: United States Atomic Energy Commission, 1962), p. 8.

14. United States Atomic Energy Commission, *Civilian Nuclear Power: The 1967 Supplement to the 1962 Report to the President* (Washington, D.C.: United States Atomic Energy Commission, 1967), p. 6.

15. President's Office of Science and Technology, *Report on Considerations Affecting Steam Power Plant Site Selection* (Washington, D.C.: U.S. Government Printing Office, 1968), Chapter 1.

16. United States Atomic Energy Commission, *Annual Report to Congress 1968* (Washington, D.C.: U.S. Government Printing Office, 1969). For informative reviews see also Alvin Weinberg and Gale Young, "The Nuclear Energy Revolution," *Proceedings of the National Academy of Sciences* 57 (January 1967): 1-15 and John F. Hogerton, "The Arrival of Nuclear Power," *Scientific American* 218 (February 1968): 21-31.

17. These estimates are based on United States Atomic Energy Commission, *Civilian Nuclear Power: The 1967 Supplement to the 1962 Report to the President.*

18. See Public Law 89-210, "An Act to Amend the Atomic Energy Act of 1954," in *United States Statutes at Large 1965*, V. 79 (Washington, D.C.: U.S. Government Printing Office, 1966), pp. 855-57.

19. For a discussion see Harold P. Green, "Nuclear Safety and the Public Interest," *Nuclear News* 15 (September 1972): 75-77.

20. Ibid., pp. 76-77.

21. Green, "Nuclear Power Licensing and Regulation," p. 124.

22. Thomas Keating, "Politics, Energy, and the Environment, pp. 52 ff. for further discussion of this point.

23. Ibid., p. 59.

24. The most informative discussions of AEC procedures are those of Kingsley, "The Licensing of Nuclear Power Reactors in the United States," pp. 309-52 and Steven Ebbin and Raphael Kasper, *Citizen Groups and the Nuclear Power Controversy: Uses of Scientific and Technological Information* (Cambridge, Mass.: MIT Press, 1974), pp. 33-58, which draws heavily upon Kingsley's treatment and the relevant AEC materials. Also, the following discussion uses the present tense, although it emphasized that the discussion of procedures refers only to pre-1974 practices.

25. Ebbin and Kasper, *Citizen Groups and the Nuclear Power Controversy*, p. 33. See also Murphy, "Nuclear Power Plant Regulation."

26. Kingsley, "The Licensing of Nuclear Power Reactors in the United States," p. 319.

27. Ebbin and Kasper, *Citizen Groups and the Nuclear Power Controversy*, p. 36.

28. Kingsley, "The Licensing of Nuclear Power Reactors in the United States," p. 320.

29. Ibid., Ebbin and Kasper, *Citizen Groups and the Nuclear Power Controversy*, p. 36.

30. Kingsley, "The Licensing of Nuclear Power Reactors in the United States," p. 321.

31. See Public Law 85-256, "An Amendment to the Atomic Energy Act of 1954," p. 579, and Murphy, "Atomic Safety and Licensing Boards," p. 569.

32. The duties of the ACRS were stated in the 1957 amendment as follows: "The Committee shall review safety studies and facility license applications referred to it and shall make reports thereon, shall advise the Commission with regard to the hazards of proposed or existing reactor facilities and the adequacy of proposed reactor safety standards, and shall perform such other duties as the Commission may request." See Public Law 85-256, "An Amendment to the Atomic Energy Act of 1954," p. 579.

33. See United States Congress, Hearings before the Joint Committee on Atomic Energy, *AEC Licensing Procedure and Related Legislation*, 92nd Congress, 1st Session, 1971 (Washington, D.C.: U.S. Government Printing Office, 1972) Part 1, pp. 95 ff. See also Kingsley, "The Licensing of Nuclear Power Reactors in the United States," pp. 322-23 and Ebbin and Kasper, *Citizen Groups and the Nuclear Power Controversy*, p. 37.

34. Kingsley, "The Licensing of Nuclear Power Reactors in the United States," pp. 322-23, and Murphy, "Atomic Safety and Licensing Boards," p. 569. It might be added that by March 1973, the newly enacted Federal Advisory Committee Act required that some portion of the ACRS Committee proceedings be opened up to the public. See Ebbin and Kasper, *Citizen Groups and the Nuclear Power Controversy*, pp. 37-38.

35. Kingsley, "The Licensing of Nuclear Power Reactors in the United States," p. 323, and Ebbin and Kasper, *Citizen Groups and the Nuclear Power Controversy*, pp. 37-38.

36. Murphy, "Atomic Safety and Licensing Boards," p. 569. Probably the most well-known and controversial instance of disagreement in this regard is when the ACRS report was favorable on the Pacific Gas and Electric nuclear facility planned for Bodega Bay, California and yet a construction permit was denied by the AEC. See Joel Hedgepath, "Bodega Head--A Partisan View," *Bulletin of the Atomic Scientists* 21 (March 1965): 2-7.

37. See United States Atomic Energy Commission, Directorate of Regulatory Standards, *Guide to the Preparation of Environmental Reports for Nuclear Power Plants 1972* (Washington, D.C.: U.S. Government Printing Office, 1972), pp. 1-2.

38. Ibid., p. 3.

39. Ibid., and Ebbin and Kasper, *Citizen Groups and the Nuclear Power Controversy*, pp. 39-40.

40. Ebbin and Kasper, *Citizen Groups and the Nuclear Power Controversy*, p. 41.

41. Murphy, "Atomic Safety and Licensing Boards," pp. 574-75.

42. See Public Law 87-615, "An Act to Amend the Atomic Energy Act of 1954," pp. 409-11.

43. Ibid.

44. Harold P. Green, "Safety Determinations in Nuclear Power Licensing: A Critical View," *Notre Dame Lawyer* 42 (1968): 641 ff.; Ebbin and Kasper, *Citizen Groups and the Nuclear Power Controversy*, pp. 32-42; and Murphy, "Atomic Safety and Licensing Boards," pp. 577 ff.

45. Ebbin and Kasper, *Citizen Groups and the Nuclear Power Controversy*, p. 43.

46. For a good discussion of this problem see Murphy, "Atomic Safety and Licensing Boards," pp. 578 ff.

47. Ebbin and Kasper, *Citizen Groups and the Nuclear Power Controversy*, p. 43.

48. Ibid., p. 44. See also Daniel F. Ford and Henry W. Kendall, "Nuclear Misinformation," *Environment* 17 (July-August 1975): 25.

49. Ebbin and Kasper, *Citizen Groups and the Nuclear Power Controversy*, p. 44.

50. Keating, "Politics, Energy and the Environment," p. 57 .

51. Cited in Ebbin and Kasper, *Citizen Groups and the Nuclear Power Controversy*, p. 46.

52. See for example the report, United States Atomic Energy Commission, *AEC Considers Amendments to Regulations and Revised Policy Statement on Reactor Licensing Procedures* (Washington, D.C.: U.S. Government Printing Office, 1967).

53. Ebbin and Kasper, *Citizen Groups and the Nuclear Power Controversy*, p. 46.

54. Kingsley, "The Licensing of Nuclear Power Reactors in the United States," p. 325 and Ibid., pp. 46-47.

55. Ebbin and Kasper, *Citizen Groups and the Nuclear Power Controversy*, p. 47. Note also that the applicant is responsible for the burden of proof on all issues.

56. Kingsley, "The Licensing of Nuclear Power Reactors in the United States," pp. 326-27.

57. Ibid., p. 326.

58. Keating, "Politics, Energy, and the Environment," p. 56.

59. Green, "Nuclear Power Licensing and Regulation," pp. 121-122.

60. Kingsley, "The Licensing of Nuclear Power Reactors in the United States," pp. 327-28.

61. Keating, "Politics, Energy, and the Environment," pp. 56-57. See also, United States Atomic Energy Commission, Office of the Director of Regulation, *Step-by-Step Procedure in Licensing Nuclear Power Reactors* (Washington, D.C.: U.S. Government Printing Office, 1972).

62. Ebbin and Kasper, *Citizen Groups and the Nuclear Power Controversy*, pp. 51 ff.

63. For a good discussion of the operating license procedures see Kingsley, "The Licensing of Nuclear Power Reactors in the United States," pp. 332 ff.

64. See Harold P. Green, "The Risk-Benefit Calculus in Nuclear Power Licensing," in Harry Foreman (ed.), *Nuclear Power and the Public* Minneapolis: University of Minnesota Press, 1970), pp. 131 ff. See also Green, "Nuclear Power Licensing and Regulation."

65. Green,"The Risk Benefit Calculus in Nuclear Power Licensing," p. 120.

66. Green, "Nuclear Power Licensing and Regulation," p. 120.

67. See Harold P. Green, "Nuclear Safety and the Public Interest," pp. 75-78; Ebbin and Kasper, *Citizen Groups and the Nuclear Power Controversy*, pp. 140-41, and Ford and Kendall, "Nuclear Misinformation," p. 25.

68. For a good discussion of these problems see William W. Lowrance, *Of Acceptable Risk: Science and the Determination of Safety* (Los Altos, Calif.: William Kaufmann, 1976).

69. See I. Like, "Multi-Media Confrontation--The Environmentalists' Strategy for a 'No-Win' Agency Proceeding," in United States Congress, Hearings before the Joint Committee on Atomic Energy, *AEC Licensing Procedure and Related Legislation*, 92nd Congress, 1st Session, 1971 (Washington, D.C.: U.S. Government Printing Office, 1971). Cited in Keating, "Politics, Energy, and the Environment," p. 60; emphasis added.

6
The Evolution of Opposition to Nuclear Power in the United States (II): Transcending Subsystem Politics

> The growing success of the (anti-nuclear) movement gives considerable hope that the barrier between the atomic energy program and the general public is being breached, and that more than one voice will be heard when atomic energy is talked of; that the moral and political decisions regarding reactors will be made, at least in part, by those who will bear the consequences of the decisions. In short, we can hope that advancing science has not left democracy behind.
>
> -Sheldon Novick

INTRODUCTION

Even before the first atomic blast rocked the Alamogordo test site in New Mexico in 1945, those connected with the Manhattan Project already realized that nuclear energy's unique and powerful nature would require intensive regulation and control. Nuclear energy posed a unique challenge for the democratic control of science and technology; the standard methods were clearly outmoded. Leo Szilard knew this in 1939, when he prompted Albert Einstein to write to President Roosevelt concerning the possibility of using nuclear chain reaction for producing a powerful bomb.[1]

From the vantage point of the government and the nuclear industry, this post-War challenge appeared to have been met: cost-competitive nuclear power had been achieved without compromising the health and safety of the public. Yet as the events unfolded in the late 1960s and early 1970s, opposition to nuclear power increased in numbers and strength. As shown in the previous chapter, much of this opposition was engendered by the AEC's own licensing and regulation procedures, which seemed overly promotional and did little more than thwart public groups participating in the regulatory process.

However, such an explanation is not sufficient to account for the magnitude of controversy, nor for the nature and diversity of additional interest groups which entered the debate over the years by means of different political and administrative forums. The task of the present chapter, therefore, is to trace the involvement of additional political groups in nuclear energy policy-making--i.e., the macropolitical sector--and to show how subsystem procedures were eventually overcome.

THE NUCLEAR POWER DEBATE: THE DEVELOPMENT OF THE CONTROVERSY

The Labor Unions

To some, the current debate over nuclear power seems a relatively recent phenomenon. But in actuality, nuclear energy has almost always been surrounded by controversy. Many assume that environmentalists have led the assault on nuclear power; however, they are relative newcomers to the debate. The first interveners in nuclear power cases were actually the labor unions. As early as 1949, Leo Goodman, the secretary of the CIO housing committee, had accused the AEC of providing substandard housing for workers employed at the Oak Ridge National Laboratory, as well as charged that the Commission's radiation protection standards for workers were completely inadequate.[2] Goodman soon became a leading spokesman in a number of disputed cases between organized labor and the AEC in the late 1950s and early 1960s. In addition, labor unions had been the primary disputants in controversies at several nuclear sites, including Monroe, Michigan, Fort St. Vrain, Colorado, and Consolidated Edison's facilities at Indian Point, New York, to name a few.[3]

However, perhaps the most famous case of union involvement was the dispute over the safety of the Enrico Fermi experimental fast breeder plant, located at Lagoona Beach, Michigan, only thirty miles from downtown Detroit. After learning of an unfavorable report from the AEC's Advisory Committee on Reactor Safeguards, which the Commission apparently "suppressed," to use the words of Congressman and member of the Joint Committee, Chet Holifield, AFL-CIO members and the Governor of Michigan were asked by Joint Committee Chairman, Senator Clinton P. Anderson, to intervene in the fall of 1956. After a number of legal battles with the AEC, the union finally won a victory in the United States Court of Appeals, only to have it overturned in 1959 by the United States Supreme Court. The high Court held that the AEC could issue a construction permit while remaining technical difficulties were being worked out. Despite its eventual defeat in the Supreme Court, the AFL-CIO fight marked the union's stand on the construction and operation of the Fermi plant.[4]

In addition to the Fermi dispute, it was the labor unions--in this case the Oil, Chemical and Atomic Workers Local--which brought to public attention the SL-1 test reactor accident at the National Reactor Testing Station in Idaho. On January 3, 1961 the SL-1 reactor exploded, killing three workers. Since the workers were the only ones present at the time, the AEC could never entirely explain the mishap satisfactorily, and the Oil, Chemical, and Atomic Workers Local charged that the AEC had "whitewashed" the entire incident. Further, the union claimed that:[5]

> highly radioactive parts of the (victim's) bodies were removed; heads, arms, and what have you were removed and unceremoniously buried at the hot waste dump at the site. The remainder was put in small lead boxes and placed in caskets for burial.

Throughout the incident, the AEC mentioned little about the radiation which had covered and burned the three victims' bodies. Indeed, some seven years later in a report entitled *Operational Accidents and Radiation Exposure Experience within the United States Atomic Energy Commission, 1943-1967*, the AEC's Division of Operational Safety said that the SL-1 workers had died of "skeletal and internal injuries."[6]

These are only a few of the incidents which organized labor attempted to reveal. By 1961, the omnipresent Leo Goodman, working in behalf of the United Automobile Workers and the AFL-CIO, presented a partial list of the nuclear reactor accidents to the Joint Committee on Atomic Energy,[7] completing a larger list six years later in 1967. Goodman's listing contained 139 incidents which had resulted from "atomic science fatalities" during the period between 1944 and 1967.[8] As expected, the AEC attempted to refute most of Goodman's claims, including some fifty-four cancer cases which Goodman said occurred to workers on the job.[9]

While these are only a few examples of the labor unions' involvement in nuclear power disputes, they are enough to show that organized labor was one of the first groups to enter the nuclear power controversy. Indeed, Goodman and others tireless efforts were a constant thorn in the side of the AEC throughout the 1950s and 1960s, even though we tend to think of organized labor as a stanch supporter of nuclear power development.

The Monticello Intervention: States Versus the Federal Government

Perhaps one of the prime examples of the first significantly organized citizen opposition to nuclear power concerned the dispute over the nuclear facility planned for Monticello, Minnesota in 1966. We single out the Monticello case because it not only represents a well-organized citizen intervention, but also, it raises some crucial social and legal issues fundamental to the use of nuclear fission for generating electricity, particularly the limits of state authority in regulating nuclear power.

In 1966 the Northern States Power Company (NSP) which sells electric power in Minnesota, South Dakota, and Wisconsin, requested permission from the AEC to construct a 545,000 kilowatt facility at the Monticello site, approximately forty miles upstream on the Mississippi River from St. Paul and Minneapolis. Construction of the $115 million plant began in 1967. On January 8, 1969, NSP appeared before the Minnesota Pollution Control Agency (MPCA) to request a permit to discharge industrial waste into the Mississippi River. The utility was seeking a permit to discharge significant amounts of heated water which the plant would use in normal operation, as well as a permit to discharge small amounts of radioactive waste into the atmosphere via smokestack. Perhaps because the St. Paul-Minneapolis water supply was drawn down-river from the proposed plant, the MPCA decided to hold a public hearing on the matter on February 13, 1968. As soon as the meeting opened, substantial resistance surfaced.[10]

The opponents, led by a group of University of

Minnesota scientists, argued that an altered design of the plant's cooling system could significantly reduce the amount of thermal and radioactive pollution emitted from the plant. NSP, however, claimed that such alteration would be overly time-consuming and expensive; and besides, argued NSP, the plant's design characteristics and the amounts of thermal and radioactive waste to be discharged were well within the guidelines set by the AEC. Caught between opposing camps, the MPCA decided to defer issuance of a permit until it could retain outside consultation for recommendations on the more controversial questions.[11]

After considering several proposals, Dr. Ernest C. Tsivoglou, Professor of Engineering at Georgia Institute of Technology, was hired as a consultant. Meanwhile, the Minnesota Committee for Environmental Information (MCEI), a group whose membership was mostly scientific and technical, had formed and entered the dispute. Tsivoglou suggested that it might be helpful if the MCEI also submitted a statement of their concerns to the MPCA.[12]

The MCEI took up Tsivoglou's suggestion, and in its report argued that a general lack of experience prevented a rigorous and precise statement of the benefits and risks of nuclear power reactors: "the clearest fact which emerges from this discussion is the uncertainty, the experimental nature, of the nuclear program, which makes it difficult to make any but the most general guesses about the program's future."[13] The report went on to state some rather serious concerns about radioactive and thermal discharges, indicating that in certain situations, especially accidental releases, the general well-being of the public could be significantly endangered. The report urged the MPCA's continued deliberations on the question of nuclear reactor safety and stressed the importance of making relevant information available to the public and other interested parties, such that the Agency would be assured of the "greatest possible assistance and support in this difficult task."[14]

It was Tsivoglou himself, however, who raised the most important questions. According to Tsivoglou, the crucial issues to be decided were:[15]

> Whether the State of Minnesota has the legal right to set pollution control standards which are more restrictive than the radiation standards established by the AEC,

and:

> Whether, as demanded by the NSP, the state's Pollution Control Agency must "prove" that such restrictive standards are needed.

Tsivoglou argued that these were fundamental questions to all pollution control issues throughout the nation, nuclear or otherwise. It was his opinion that the MPCA, since its task was to protect the public from environmental danger and pollution, had a right to demand the lowest possible pollution of the environment. Therefore, asserted Tsivoglou, it was the proper duty of the utility and *not* the MPCA to "explain and defend its desire to pollute beyond levels that the MPCA regards as practical and reasonable."[16]

On the question of whether the MPCA had the right to set pollution standards lower than those already established by the AEC, Tsivoglou admitted that this was essentially a legal issue which had not been resolved, and in practice outcomes depended largely on how existing rules were interpreted. Tsivoglou did say, however, that the Federal Radiation Council, of which the AEC was a member, adhered to the policy of reducing radiation as much as possible and that allowable levels of radiation exposure depended upon the *reasons* such exposures should be permitted. Thus, Tsivoglou seemed to argue that radiation exposure ought to be reduced to the lowest possible levels. He made the following four recommendations to the MPCA:[17]

> (1) That the MPCA should pursue this case to clear conclusion regarding the very basic issue of the old negative practice of maximum pollution of the environment as against the modern approach of minimizing and reducing pollution to the full extent that is practical and reasonable.
>
> (2) The MPCA should pursue the issue of the right of the State of Minnesota to set pollution control standards that are more strict than the AEC's own radiation control standards.
>
> (3) The MPCA should pursue, by way of permit, the fullest possible control and minimization of radioactive effluents from the Monticello nuclear power plant.

(4) The MPCA should plan for the fullest feasible control and minimization of radioactive pollution of the environment from all nuclear plants which are planned in Minnesota.

There seemed little doubt that Tsivoglou's recommendations would raise some important issues for debate.

The Northern States Power Company, however, was not without its own view of the matter. In a statement submitted to the MPCA, the utility claimed that Tsivoglou's standards were unduly strict, stating that "we believe that the standards established by the Atomic Energy Commission after years of research by highly competent and respected scientists and the expenditure of hundreds of millions of dollars in research on the subject of radiation should be the standards adopted in Minnesota as they have been in other states where the question has been raised."[18] The utility felt that AEC standards preempted whatever radiation standards the individual states might establish. The utility further stated that if the state of Minnesota wished to establish standards stricter than those already set by the AEC, "then the Minnesota Pollution Control Agency should prove the need for such restrictive standards."[19] The utility was forced to assume such a position, for if the state of Minnesota could enforce radiation standards one hundred times more strict than the AEC's, what would prevent the other forty-nine states from doing the same thing? Thus, the power industry could be faced with fifty different radiation codes, a situation which clearly worked against their best interests.

Apparently sensing the gravity of the issue, Northern States Power Company opted for legal action, and on August 26, 1969 they filed suit in United States District Court at St. Paul. NSP said that the state of Minnesota was without authority to supersede AEC radiation standards with their own, more highly restrictive measures. Basic to the entire issue, of course, was how far could the states go to protect the life and property of their own citizens, and to what extent did federal regulations preempt the states' rights to undertake such actions? The case was an important one and aroused immediate national attention.[20]

Basically, NSP's entire case seemed rooted in an economic argument: lower levels of radioactive discharge were certainly possible, but the added cost of modification of plant design and operating procedures did not "justify" such expenditures. In fact, the situation seemed so intolerable that NSP concluded: "It is impossible to comply fully with all requirements of the MPCA permit regarding radioactive waste discharges, although the plaintiff could operate well within the standards promulgated by the AEC."[21] So in addition to questioning the extent to which states could require pollution control standards stricter than those already set by the AEC, NSP had actually posed a second issue: how much should public health standards be compromised for the economical production of electric power?

The court delivered its opinion on the matter on March 17, 1971. Chief Judge Edward J. Devitt ruled the state of Minnesota was without authority to set its own radiation release standards since "Congress has preempted the field of regulation of radioactive releases by nuclear power plants ... and Minnesota is without authority to enforce its regulations in this field."[22] Judge Devitt's decision was subsequently appealed, but it was upheld by both the Eighth Circuit Court of Appeals at St. Louis and by the United States Supreme Court.

Thus, Minnesota and the anti-nuclear groups had lost an important decision, as Northern States Power Company's Monticello nuclear plant was phased into their electrical grid in 1972. But not all was lost; the case lasted nearly six years, delaying construction of the proposed facility and raising public consciousness of the hazards of nuclear power plants. The interveners had succeeded in recruiting the Minnesota Pollution Control Agency, the Minnesota Academy of Science, and other interested groups. In addition, the Minnesota Committee for Environmental Information had been established and promised to seek public education and understanding of other important environmental issues. If nothing else, the Monticello case indicated that some rather crucial problems had not been adequately addressed by the nuclear power establishment. As Monticello swelled the tide of public awareness, it seemed the nuclear power programs were destined for a new round of conflict and debate as the last years of the 1960s ticked away.

The Radiation Issue

Perhaps most important in raising public awareness of the hazards of nuclear power was the radiation controversy which emerged in the late 1950s and burst fully onto the scene by 1969. The effects of low-level radiation had long since been postulated. Nobel laureate Herman J. Muller showed in 1946 that radiation exposure could produce genetic mutations in fruit flies. Linus Pauling, another Nobel laureate, echoed similar warnings in the early 1960s; while Dr. Brien McMahon of the Harvard School of Public Health offered evidence to support a study by Dr. Alice Stewart showing that increased exposure to x-rays to children *in utero* increased their chances of contacting leukemia, a finding further corroborated by Stewart and Kneal in a 1968 study. Meanwhile, Professor Ernest J. Sternglass reported in *Science* magazine in 1963 that increased radioactive fallout from atmospheric nuclear testing seemed to increase the incidence of cancer in young children.[23]

Much of the public's concern had been exacerbated by the AEC's own handling of standards for radioactive fallout from atmospheric nuclear testing in the late 1950s and early 1960s. The AEC consistently downplayed the harmful effects of radiation throughout this period, with the public learning only sometime later that many grossly irresponsible blunders had been committed in setting radiation protection standards.[24] In addition, many of the AEC's deliberations on this matter seem to have been purposely concealed from public view so that the AEC's research programs would not be held back. Representative Chet Holifield, member of the Joint Committee on Atomic Energy, accused the Commission of being "grossly tardy and negligent" about the dangers of radioactive fallout and said, further:[25]

> I believe from our hearings that the AEC approach to the hazards from bomb test fallout seems to add up to a party line--"play it down." As custodian of official information, the AEC has an urgent responsibility to communicate the facts to the public. Yet time after time there has been a long delay in issuance of the facts, and oftentimes the facts have to be dragged out of the agency by the Congress. Certainly it took our investigation to enable some of the Commission's

own experts to break through the party line on fallout.

The radiation issue was finally brought to a head, however, by Drs. Arthur R. Tamplin and John W. Gofman, both on the staff of the AEC's highly respected Lawrence Radiation Laboratory in Berkeley, California. Tamplin was ironically led to what later turned out to be a highly critical position of the AEC's official stance on radiation. While his original intent was to critique and discredit the Sternglass report, Tamplin concluded that Sternglass' claim was wrong only in so far as it had overestimated the number of deaths that could result from radiation exposure. He and Sternglass both agreed that fallout radiation could indeed harm infants and fetuses; the two scientists disagreed only over the *number* of deaths fallout radiation might induce.[26]

Eventually, Tamplin was joined by his colleague at the Lawrence Radiation Laboratory, John Gofman. Together, the two scientists formally charged the AEC with lax radiation protection standards in the fall of 1969. In a paper delivered before the Nuclear Science Symposium of the Institute of Electrical and Electronic Engineers in October 1969 at San Francisco, California, Tamplin and Gofman argued that at least a tenfold reduction in allowable levels of radiation exposure was necessary to avert thousands of yearly cancer deaths.[27]

By the middle of 1970 and several appearances before Congressional investigating committees, including the Joint Committee on Atomic Energy, Gofman and Tamplin began to feel the heat from the AEC. The AEC began to fight back, using a number of suppression and censorship tactics to silence the two critics.[28] But it was too late; Gofman and Tamplin had already sounded the alarm, and it had become public knowledge that the AEC's radiation standards were inadequate and had to be revised in a more conservative direction. Thus the work of two of the AEC's own highly respected radiation experts now supported claims which only a few years before had been considered the work of cranks and charlatans.

By the late 1960s and the early 1970s, the radiation hazard had been further emphasized in a skirmish between citizen groups and the Long Island Lighting Company (LILCO), which had proposed building a 820,000 kilowatt nuclear plant at Shoreham, New York, on the north shore of Long

Island. The interveners, who called themselves the Lloyd Harbor Study Group (LHSG), objected to the plant on a number of grounds, including the possibility of an aircraft collision with the plant, which was being built only 4.5 miles away from a busy airport and less than 7,000 feet from an active Nike base.[29] In addition to these considerations, the LHSG remained opposed to the plant for several other reasons, described by the group's Research Director, Mrs. Ann Carl:[30]

> (1) AEC conflict of interest as both promoter and regulator of nuclear energy;
> (2) credibility of the AEC;
> (3) non-compliance with NEPA (National Environmental Policy Act);
> (4) engineering deficiencies, including the accident potential;
> (5) environmental unknowns, including storage of radioactive wastes;
> (6) radiation emission controversy;
> (7) lack of full financial responsibility; and
> (8) specific site questions at Shoreham.

It was the radiation issue, however, that received most of the attention throughout the intervention proceedings, which wound up lasting nearly two years.

Throughout the winter and spring of 1971 the radiation issue generated a heated debate between the AEC, LILCO, the LHSG, and another intervener, an organization that called itself the Suffolk County Scientists for Cleaner Power and a Safer Environment (SCS). The SCS group was composed mainly of employees of the Brookhaven National Laboratory, one of the Commission's primary research laboratories located a short distance away in Upton, New York. Naturally, the SCS favored construction of the plant, and argued that it represented a far cleaner source of power than the conventional fossil fuel installations that would have to be build in order to cope with the increased electrical demand anticipated for Long Island in the coming years.[31] LHSG, however, insisted that the plant would emit unacceptable levels of radioactivity and was not the "clean" source of power that the SCS said it was. LHSG called in several expert witnesses to support their contentions throughout the hearing period, among them, British physician Dr. Alice Stewart; Dr. James D. Watson, Nobel Laureate and Director of the Cold

Spring Harbor Research Laboratory on Long Island, where he was studying the relationships between cancer and viruses; and Dr. Ernest J. Sternglass, Professor of Radiation Physics at the University of Pittsburgh.

The first witness called in to support the LHSG position was Dr. Alice Stewart, Director of the Department of Social Medicine at Oxford University. Stewart offered epidemiological evidence which showed that "medical x-ray doses to the fetus in the range of less than one rad have produced measurable excess cancer in English children under 10 years of age."[32] However, the SCS was quick to point out that Stewart and her colleagues had not related these effects specifically to nuclear power plant effluents, and that their studies, which relied heavily on extrapolations, actually demonstrated the existence of certain "high risk groups" more than anything else.[33] Thus, the SCS argued that Stewart's findings were neither applicable nor detrimental to the proposed Shoreham plant.

As for Watson's testimony, he admitted that the fundamental relationships between radiation and cancer were still largely unknown, but that enough cancer research had been conducted, he asserted, to show that the proliferation of nuclear plants in highly populated areas was a questionable strategy.[34] Not only was the AEC's maximum allowable radiation dose not "the great figure" it was claimed to be, but Watson asked why more money was not being spent on cancer research and for the much "cleaner" fusion reactor which had been on AEC drawing boards for years. Watson also said that even if the area immediately surrounding the proposed Shoreham plant could be protected satisfactorily from emissions, it would only mean more emissions for the people who resided in the areas of the fuel reprocessing installations. How could the proponents of the plant, then, justify such an arrangement?[35]

The SCS countered by claiming that:[36]

> Watson's testimony was philosophical and general in nature and did not include any data to support his conclusions. Cross-examination revealed he had not studied the Preliminary Safety Analysis Report, and did not know the magnitude of natural radiation background at the site of his own laboratory at Cold Spring Harbor.

The SCS went on to call Watson's remarks a "disappointment," and to indicate their general dismay with the fact that a man of Watson's undeniable stature in the scientific community had presented no scientific evidence to support his contentions and had appeared to have made no "serious study (of) the problem before testimony."[37] The SCS said it had no alternative but to dismiss Watson's remarks as little more than off-the-cuff, and hardly a serious consideration in terms of evaluating the proposed plant.

Finally, the LHSG called Professor Sternglass to support their position on radioactivity. When Sternglass took the witness stand, he alleged that there was a direct correlation between start-up and use of the AEC's experimental reactor at Brookhaven Laboratory and the rise of infant mortality in Suffolk County during the same time period. The Sternglass argument ran like this:[38]

> From 1953 to 1955, the infant mortality rate in Suffolk County rose from 19.5 to 23.5 deaths per 1,000 births. In this period, radioactivity emitted by the Brookhaven reactor in liquid wastes increased from 35.8 microcuries in 1953 to 75 microcuries in 1955. Again, as radioactive emissions rose from 106 to 219.1 microcuries between 1958 and 1961, the infant mortality rate in the county jumped from 21.1 to 24.1 deaths per 1,000 live births from 1960 to 1961. The infant death rate then declined to 19 per 1,000 in 1964 when radioactivity in liquid wastes dropped to 76.4 millicuries per year. It reached a low of 13.1 per 1,000 births in 1969, in parallel with a drop in radioactive emissions from Brookhaven to a level of 16.2 microcuries by 1968.

A similar correlation, alleged Sternglass, also could be made in Westchester County, New York, in the vicinity of the Indian Point nuclear installation. Yet in nearby Fairfield County (Connecticut), New York City, and Nassau County, where no nuclear plants were operating, no fluctuations in the infant mortality rate had been observed. Sternglass therefore concluded that the operation of nuclear plants seemed at least partially responsible for these fluctuations in the infant mortality rates.[39]

As expected, the SCS attempted to demolish the Sternglass findings. They immediately claimed that the rise of infant mortality rates in Suffolk County in the period indicated by Sternglass was due to rapid population growth there, and not the operation of the Brookhaven reactor. Moreover, the Brookhaven reactor, said the SCS, was well east--not to mention downwind and downstream on the Peconic River (into which liquid wastes were dumped)--away from ninety percent of the population of Suffolk County. In other words, only ten percent of the residents of Suffolk County possibly could have been affected by the Brookhaven reactor. The debate between Sternglass and the SCS see-sawed in this fashion point-by-point, with Sternglass offering a finding and the SCS refuting it.[40]

By the time the public hearings had been terminated, a transcript of some 13,000 pages had been compiled, scores of technical witnesses had appeared for both sides, and nearly two years had elapsed. The LHSG maintained the whole thing was a valuable source of public enlightenment about the pros and cons of nuclear power, while the SCS concluded that the LHSG intervention had only succeeded in arousing "irrational emotional fears and had not served to enlighten the public on the real facts," but only "muddied the waters (with) public presentations filled with erroneous information and sensationalism which served only to create hysteria and unreasoning fear."[41]

But perhaps most important is the fact that the apparent polarization of experts pro and con seemed only to further cloud the issues and increase public apprehension of nuclear power, for now it was plain that the experts themselves did not agree on the facts. Meanwhile, the public was left in the unenviable position of deciding whom to believe, as the radiation issues addressed throughout the Shoreham controversy seemed to raise many more questions than they had answered. After more than twenty-four months of hearings at Shoreham, it seemed that little had been accomplished, as both the radiation issue and the nuclear controversy raged more intense than ever.

The National Environmental Policy Act of 1969: The Calvert Cliffs Test

It now seemed as if the roof was caving in on nuclear power programs, for by the mid-1960s the environmental movement was picking up momentum as well. All forms of science and technology were being critically assailed for their adverse effects on the environment. As the environmental movement swelled, the original conservationists at long last had carried the day. Naturally, as far as the environmentalists were concerned, nuclear power was without question high on the list of environmental horrors and was probably the prime candidate for environmental public enemy number one.

Yet the environmentalists lacked "teeth." Irrespective of the tremendous awareness they had generated among the public concerning the hazards of technology to the environment, there was little the environmentalists could do to gain substantive political input. All this changed in 1969 when President Nixon signed into law the nation's first systematic national environmental policy, the National Environmental Policy Act of 1969 (NEPA).[42] The Act not only set up the Environmental Protection Agency to oversee and direct national environmental policies and monitor the activities of all agencies whose activities might affect the environment, but also provided a mechanism enabling environmental groups and other concerned citizens to take legal action in contesting nuclear power licensing cases. Consequently, it wasn't long before opponents to nuclear energy began taking advantage of the new law.

Section 102 of the Act[43] required all federal agencies, including the AEC, to evaluate and assess the full environmental impact of all agency sponsored programs. It was further stipulated that all federal agencies shall prepare and disseminate an environmental impact statement on activities that may adversely affect the environment. In response to NEPA, the AEC claimed its own role required no more than to insure that proposed reactors were safe and that radioactive particle emissions were kept at currently acceptable levels.[44] In holding the line at this position, the Commission obviously opted for a narrow interpretation of NEPA.

The Commission's position on NEPA, however, was tested in the Calvert Cliffs case in 1970-1971. In this case the AEC issued a construction permit to Baltimore Gas and Electric Company to build a nuclear reactor at Calvert Cliffs, Maryland, some thirty miles from Washington, D.C. Concerned citizens, environmentalists, and public interveners were worried about the effects of thermal pollution on Chesapeake Bay. When they confronted the Commission with this matter, the AEC responded by saying they would not deal with nonradiological issues, thus, in effect, exempting Calvert Cliffs from NEPA. The anti-nuclear group, Chesapeake Environmental Protection Association (CEPA), argued that NEPA required the utility to conduct a comprehensive study of *all* environmental impacts of the proposed facility, and that an environmental impact statement should be issued for public examination. When CEPA petitioned the AEC to enforce what they presumed were the requirements of NEPA, the Commission stalled until interveners filed a petition in the United States Court of Appeals for the District of Columbia Circuit in November of 1970.[45]

Under pressure of litigation the AEC finally responded and issued the following guidelines on December 3, 1970:[46]

> The rules, formulated as Appendix D to Part 50 of the AEC's governing regulations, provided in part that:
>
> 1. Environmental factors need not be considered by the hearing board unless affirmatively raised by outside parties or staff members.
>
> 2. No party to a hearing could raise non-radiological environmental issues if the hearing notice appeared in the Federal Register before March 4, 1971. This rule exempted Calvert Cliffs, along with other plants in construction, from NEPA.
>
> 3. The hearing board is prohibited from conducting an independent evaluation and balancing of certain environmental factors if other responsible agencies--state, regional, or federal--already have certified that their own environmental standards are satisfied.
>
> 4. When a construction permit has been issued before the NEPA compliance was required, and when an operating license has yet to be issued, the agency will not formally consider environmental factors or require modifications (backfitting) in the proposed facility until the time of the operating license.

But this was still unsatisfactory. The petitioners registered a second complaint with the Court of Appeals, calling for a *complete* application of NEPA standards to the Calvert Cliffs plant.

The decision was handed down from the court on July 23, 1971 by Judge James Skelly Wright. In a strongly worded opinion, Judge Wright declared that it was the duty of the AEC, like all federal agencies, to take environmental values fully into account, and that attention should be given to *all non-radiological effects* of the proposed plant. Judge Wright noted further that the AEC had been reluctant in fulfilling its obligations under NEPA and that "the Commission's crabbed interpretation of NEPA makes a mockery of the Act."[47] Judge Wright added that the Commission was responsible for conducting a *complete* assessment of every reactor proposal and that all recommendations and findings be made available and completely open to challenge at the licensing hearing.[48] Thus, Judge Wright asserted, the very purpose of NEPA "was to tell federal agencies that environmental protection is as much a part of their responsibility as is protection and promotion of the industries they regulate."[49]

The Wright decision was clearly a milestone for concerned citizens and environmentalists. Not only was the AEC forced to reassess its regulatory role, but the battle between nuclear technology and the environment was now thrust squarely in the forefront of the public view. Now more than ever the question of nuclear reactor safety was being hotly debated, as the Calvert Cliffs case had split the issue open at its seams.

The Question of Radioactive Wastes

At about the same time the Calvert Cliffs controversy was making the headlines, the nuclear power programs were finding themselves in hot water from yet another source of disagreement and controversy: the question of the disposal of high-level nuclear waste. The proliferation of commercial nuclear plants--twenty-nine were operating by the end of 1971--meant the problem of long-term storage of the wastes had to be solved. The twenty-nine operating plants would produce some 58,000 cubic feet per year of lethal waste by the year 2000.[50] Naturally, every time another plant was brought on-line the problem worsened. Hence, unless a feasible method of disposing waste was found, a large-scale nuclear energy program would ultimately have to be scuttled. Settling the problem of radioactive waste disposal was rapidly becoming one of the most important issues of the entire nuclear controversy.

Yet the problem of what to do with nuclear waste wasn't really all that new. The nation's military and research and development programs had by the mid-1950s already accumulated significant amounts of high-level waste. The problem was that no one knew how to dispose of the wastes *permanently*. Since the AEC was anticipating the expansion of the civilian power programs, as the Atomic Energy Act of 1954 seemed to indicate, it decided to approach the National Academy of Sciences--National Research Council with a proposal to study what to do about the waste problem. Thus, in 1955 the National Academy of Sciences--National Research Council, at the request of the AEC, established a committee of geophysicists and geologists to study the problem. The responsibilities of the committee would include:[51]

> assembling the existing geologic information pertinent to disposal, delineating the unanswered problems associated with the disposal schemes proposed, and point out areas of research and development meriting first attention; the committee is to serve as continuing advisor on the geological aspects of disposal and the research and development program.

With the assistance of the Johns Hopkins University, the committee first assembled in September 1955 at Princeton University. The conference included members of the United States Geological Survey, representatives of the AEC, members of the Department of Sanitary Engineering of Johns Hopkins, and representatives from industry and other competent scientists working in relevant areas of research. At the conference, the AEC asked these experts for informed opinions about the various problems involved with disposal of high-level waste. The conference resulted in several broad areas of study and discussion, with the committee members subsequently inspecting all AEC waste disposal sites. The outcome of these studies was published in a 1957 report, *The Disposal of Radioactive Waste on Land*.[52] Some of its main conclusions may be summarized as follows.

First of all, the report stressed the significant hazards posed by the problem of nuclear waste: "Unlike the disposal of any other type of waste, the hazard related to radioactive waste is so great that no element of doubt should be allowed to exist regarding safety. Stringent rules must be set up and a system of inspection and monitoring instituted" (p. 3). This statement was made in view of the fact that radioactive waste was so dangerous and lethal that it had to be kept out of the biosphere for 500,000 to 1 million years. The final decision of what to do with the waste, then, would be among the most significant and far-reaching scientific and technological decisions ever made; for what would happen if some unforeseen mistake were made which allowed large quantities of dangerous radiation to leak into the environment say, 50, 500, or even 5,000 years later? The report's serious tone was indeed an understatement.

Due to the gravity of the hazard, the report emphasized that the wastes simply couldn't be stored anywhere that nuclear power plants and research and development activities happened to exist. The Atlantic Seaboard, for example, was completely out of the question. The committee was convinced, however, "that radioactive waste can be disposed of safely in a variety of ways and at a large number of sites in the United States" (p. 3). While admitting that a good deal of research and development was still required, the committee concluded:

> The most promising method of disposal of high-level waste at the present time seems to be in salt deposits. The great advantage here is that no water can pass through salt. Fractures are self-sealing. Abandoned salt mines or cavities especially mined to hold waste are, in essence, long-enduring tanks. (p. 4)

But until the necessary studies could be conducted to perfect methods of disposal in salt deposits, the committee further recommended that "storage in tanks is *at present* the safest and possibly the most economical method of containing waste." (p. 6). Lastly, the committee recommended that "continuing disposal of certain (large volume) low-level waste in the vadose water zone, above the water table, is of limited application and probably involves unacceptable long term risks" (p. 7). Thus, the National Academy of Sciences--National Research Council report set into motion a search for suitable salt deposits for the nation's first permanent disposal of radioactive waste. It now seemed only a matter of where the new atomic graveyard would be located.

By 1968 several events reemphasized the importance of getting on with some sort of permanent waste disposal project. Since the days of the Manhattan Project, the nuclear energy programs had already accumulated some 90 million gallons of high-level waste which over the years had been stored in liquid form in several concrete-encased, million-gallon stainless steel tanks at AEC defense laboratories in Richland, Washington; on the Savannah River near Aiken, South Carolina; and at a location near Idaho Falls, Idaho. In its 1968 report, the General Accounting Office indicated that some 227,000 gallons of high-level waste had already leaked from the storage tanks, a highly critical situation in view of the lack of back-up containment procedures. The radioactivity simply seeped into the ground where it would eventually work its way into the underground water supply, perhaps contaminating underground aquifers for generations to come.[54]

In 1970 the AEC therefore announced the selection of the Lyons, Kansas site for immediate development of the nation's first radioactive disposal center. Oak Ridge had worked out an elaborate procedure for developing the site and disposing the wastes and their plan had apparently satisfied the AEC and the Joint Committee. The AEC then requested from the Joint Committee in March 1971 an immediate appropriation of $3.5 million to purchase the site, with an additional $25 million being seen as the estimated cost for final completion of the facility.[55] With the money from Congress forthcoming, it seemed as if the AEC had at last found a solution to the nagging problem of radioactive waste disposal.

William H. Hambleton, Director of the Kansas Geological Survey, Representative Joe Skubitz (D-Kansas), and Kansas Governor Robert Docking, however, were of a different opinion. Hambleton insisted that Oak Ridge's basic assumptions were open to question, and that the final experimental results were at best misleading. Hambleton said that Oak Ridge's heat-flow studies were inadequate and he was convinced that the possibility of thermal expansion of the salt deposits had not been adequately considered. He argued that disintegration of the waste canisters could possibly result in enough heat to crack the overlying rock formations such that ground water could seep into the huge nuclear tomb. The water would be heated by the wastes and turned into steam. It was not inconceivable that the pressure created by the steam could result in the eruption of radioactive geysers. As Richard Lewis describes the scenario:[56]

> One could imagine a Kansas version of Old Faithful, blowing alpha particles and gamma rays into the biosphere, and leaving the ground

covered with a film of radioactive salt. Could it happen? No one knew. That was the point. No one knew--not on the basis of the AEC's testing program.

In addition, Representative Skubitz, citing the Kansas Geological Survey's report, claimed that the AEC's transportation plans were "completely inadequate," and that no firm plan existed in case the wastes had to be retrieved in an emergency. Not only that, said Skubitz, but what about the residents of Kansas? Were they without rights, without a voice in the matter? He alleged that the AEC had paid no attention to how the residents of Kansas felt about having a radioactive dump in their backyards.[57]

The entire dispute was exacerbated when Assistant Secretary of the Department of the Interior, Hollis Dole, sent a letter to the AEC which shared the concerns of the Kansas Geological Survey and Representative Skubitz. Dole said that existing studies of the Lyons facility did not "demonstrate conclusively, beyond a reasonable doubt, that these deposits were indeed suitable for the final repository."[58] He was further concerned about the stability of the salt deposits once the thermally active radioactive wastes were implanted there and, thus, with the lack of adequate retrieval methods if the wastes had to be recovered in the event of some unforeseen circumstance. In short, Dole was not convinced by the AEC's environmental statement that the salt deposits would in fact remain stable for the many millenia during which the wastes would be radioactively hot. The evidence simply wasn't there.

By the spring of 1971 the AEC agreed to address the criticisms of the Kansas Geological Survey's report before going ahead with the facility. But the Commission had acted too late; the continued political pressure applied by Governor Docking, Representative Skubitz, and other Kansas Congressmen, including Senators Dole and Pearson, had forced a halt to the project by the end of 1971. By May of 1972 the new AEC Chairman, James R. Schlesinger, announced an alternate plan for the storage of high-level radioactive waste that called for above-ground storage facilities, or "engineered surface facilities," as the AEC called them. Such facilities would serve the nuclear power industry on an "interim basis"; they were expected to last "only" a few centuries.[59]

Apparently, the idea of storing wastes in salt deposits was now dead; and Lyons, Kansas no longer worried about the dubious distinction of sitting atop the world's first radioactive dump.

Besides creating increased public awareness of the hazards of nuclear power, the waste disposal controversy posed some serious questions: Could the nation afford a full-scale civilian power program without first devising some reliable method of handling the huge amounts of radioactive waste produced by the reactors? And didn't the civilian power program make some rather questionable assumptions about the stability of man's social institutions? What kind of stability would be required to insure constant, long-term vigilance over the tons of lethal waste created by the power programs? And did society have the moral right to thrust this long-term hazard on posterity? It is not surprising therefore that the anti-nuclear forces were up-in-arms over the waste disposal issue; perhaps the technological quotient had finally been taken too far. But ironically, it was Representative Craig Hosmer of California, an ardent supporter of AEC programs throughout his many years on the Joint Committee, who summarized the anti-technology attitude best: "I get the impression that we should have never invented the wheel if we had thought about it beforehand."[60]

The Experts Disagree: The Stance of the Scientists Institute for Public Information and the Union of Concerned Scientists

The Breeder Reactor Controversy. Yet perhaps the most important factor in solidifying the debate and propelling it to its current level of intensity concerned the involvement of scientists in the controversy. As we have shown above, a significant number of scientists and engineers had always been skeptical of the nuclear programs and of the dangers of radioactivity. But as the years progressed, and knowledge of the atom and nuclear physics increased, greater numbers of scientists began to join the controversy, including some of the AEC's own highly respected scientific experts. But perhaps most significant, none of the outcries were coming from one or two isolated scientists, seemingly crying "wolf" from the periphery of the nuclear science community. Rather, criticisms were now being made by reputable scientists and engineers who had organized themselves into effective pressure groups. Certainly notable among these groups were the efforts of the Scientists Institute for Public Information (SIPI) and the Union of Concerned Scientists (UCS). Nothing serves to escalate the conflict and debate among the public more than a scientific and technical debate among the experts; for if the experts can't agree, how can the public decide? Thus, the indefatigable efforts of groups such as SIPI and UCS became important elements in generating increased public awareness and controversy over nuclear power.

As for SIPI,[61] they have been instrumental in revealing to the public the inherent dangers of the fast breeder reactor, a project which had been on the AEC's top priority drawing boards for many years. As the reader will recall from the discussion of the development of the civilian power reactor programs above, the world's first breeder reactor was the experimental reactor located at Los Alamos, New Mexico and known as "Clementine." Also, in December 1951 the National Reactor Testing Station in Idaho had completed the world's first breeder reactor to produce electricity. By the mid-1960s, the AEC had at least two other breeder reactors in service for testing and demonstration purposes: A second experimental breeder located at the Idaho site, and the Enrico Fermi I reactor located in Lagoona Beach, Michigan.[62]

Even though breeder technology was relatively undeveloped as far as commercial application was concerned, Glenn Seaborg, the Chairman of the AEC, seemed confident enough about the prospects of the breeder reactor to state in the Commission's 1962 report to the President that:[63]

> for the long-term benefit of the country, and indeed for the whole world, it was time we placed relatively more emphasis on the longer-range and more difficult problem of breeder reactors, which can make use of *nearly all* of our uranium and thorium reserves, instead of the less than one percent of the uranium and very little of the thorium utilized in the present types of reactors. Only by use of breeders would we really solve the problem of adequate energy supply for future generations.

Actually, it wasn't surprising that Seaborg assumed such an enthusiastic stance on the future of the breeder. The breeder, after all, utilizes plutonium as fuel, an element which Seaborg and Edwin

M. McMillan discovered and for which they shared the 1951 Nobel Prize in Chemistry. As far as Seaborg was concerned, the year 2000 would find seventy percent of the nation's electricity being generated from breeder reactors using plutonium. It must have been gratifying to think that one's own discovery would be the great energy reserve of the American future. Moreover, other scientists such as Massachusetts Institute of Technology's Mason Benedict, shared Seaborg's rosy optimism for the breeder. In a presentation before the National Academy of Sciences in April of 1971, Benedict estimated that fast breeder reactors could produce electricity in the United States for the next 64,000 years at 1971 levels of production.[64] Seen from this perspective, a future of unlimited energy seemed on the horizon with the development of the breeder reactor.

All-out development of the breeder appeared a foregone conclusion by the summer of 1971. In a special message to Congress on June 4, 1971, President Nixon said:[65]

> Our best hope today for meeting the Nation's growing demand for economical clean energy lies with the fast breeder reactor. Because of its highly efficient use of nuclear fuel, the breeder reactor could extend the life of our natural uranium fuel supply from decades to centuries, with far less impact on the environment than the power plants which are operating today.
>
> We have very high hopes that the breeder reactor will soon become a key element in the national fight against air and water pollution.
>
> I believe it important to the Nation that the commercial demonstration of a breeder reactor be completed by 1980.

Having received President Nixon's hardy endorsement, the AEC billed the breeder demonstration project as top priority. As the project took shape, two demonstration breeder reactors would be constructed.

Not all scientists, however, shared this unbridled optimism for the prospects of the breeder. In fact, even before President Nixon had delivered his special message to Congress, SIPI had disagreed with the official proclamations of the bright new future which the breeder promised. In May of 1971 SIPI filed suit in United States District Court charging the AEC's development of the breeder reactor was in violation of the requirements of NEPA. Specifically, the St. Louis-based organization of scientists charged that the AEC was attempting to introduce a new technology without adequately considering its environmental impacts and side effects. In addition, the breeder was being developed in view of a number of questionable assumptions: that power demands would continue to accelerate at present rates, and that such demands should be met with power generated by *nuclear* technology. SIPI was concerned that the breeder was not so much filling a need that was likely to develop but that it was actually creating such a need itself. And as if this weren't already enough, SIPI stressed that since breeders use and produce plutonium, the most toxic material known to man, it was likely that severe problems would develop concerning waste disposal, diversion of plutonium by terrorists, and other problems which inevitably accompany a plutonium-based energy dependency, including human judgmental errors, acts of God, demands of stability on man's social institutions for centuries to come, and the creation of a "nuclear priesthood" to maintain constant surveillance over the new plutonium society. Although the suit was dismissed a year later, there could be little question that SIPI had raised some crucial and important issues for public consideration.

By mid-June 1971, the AEC issued a response to the SIPI charges in the form of a Draft Environmental Statement on the breeder project which it proposed to construct in cooperation with private industry. The AEC claimed that NEPA required it to submit an environmental statement on *each separate facility* and not on the entire breeder program as SIPI had insisted in their suit in District Court. Since the AEC would be in partnership with private industry in the development of the breeder, the AEC was in effect judging its own program. One could of course predict the content of the environmental statement: it was filled with assurances that the breeder project was essential for the future energy well-being of the nation and that safety problems had been adequately assessed. In fact, the statement went so far as to assert that the successful introduction of the breeder would actually *lessen* the impact of nuclear power on the environment.[66]

Working in behalf of SIPI, Dean E. Abrahamson of the University of Minnesota and Arthur R. Tamplin of the Lawrence Radiation Laboratory were not convinced by the AEC's environmental statement. The two scientists charged that the statement was "worthless," "inadequate," "superficial," and "inaccurate and misleading." Not only was the need for the breeder reactor unjustified, charged the scientists, but feasible alternatives to the breeder had not been explored and analyzed. Furthermore, the AEC had invoked its safety record in support of the new program. Abrahamson and Tamplin insisted, however, that the AEC's safety record was far from perfect throughout the nuclear reactor programs: What about the blunders committed in setting radiation protection standards? And the plutonium fires at Rocky Flats, Colorado, where plutonium had leaked into the environment? Or the radiation leaks from nuclear testing at the AEC's Nevada test site? Finally, the scientists contended that the AEC had given no details about the disposal of extremely toxic wastes; nor had it adequately discussed the possibility of various accidents which theoretically could occur. At the very least, asserted the scientists, the public should be informed about:[67]

> (1) The projected number of commercial LMFBRs (Liquid Metal Fast Breeder Reactors) and the fuel reprocessing plants that the new technology would have to provide; (2) where these would be located; (3) the amount of uranium ore the program would need; (4) the volume of radioactive wastes and plutonium that would ultimately be produced in the new generation of reactors; (5) how the wastes and the plutonium would be shipped; (6) how the wastes would be stored--and where--in Kansas; and (7) what the problems might be of safeguarding these materials, of preventing hijacking and the development of a plutonium black market.

Despite these criticisms, the AEC went ahead with the project. The AEC's January 1972 announcement of the new $500 million demonstration breeder reactor seemed to reaffirm what critics had long cited as the AEC's basic ignorance of some fundamental and far-reaching environmental and safety questions. Once again the AEC had chosen to emphasize its promotional role over its regulatory responsibilities. Was the United States moving to the plutonium-based society which Seaborg had so enthusiastically predicted some ten years before? It was hard to say. But one thing was certain: the Scientists Institute for Public Information had brought the weaknesses of the breeder program into full public view. Hence, the development of the breeder would at least have to proceed in the face of these perplexing difficulties and criticisms.[68]

The Emergency Core-Cooling Dispute. Turning to the Union of Concerned Scientists (UCS), they too have been instrumental in generating public awareness of the hazards of nuclear power.[69] The UCS group has perhaps done most by revealing that emergency core-cooling systems could malfunction in the event of a loss-of-coolant accident. In a report published in *Nuclear News* in 1971 the USC authors studied "the technical nature of a loss-of-coolant accident and the emergency core-cooling systems designed to prevent meltdown."[70] The authors also evaluated the consequences of a major accident in which lethal radioactivity would be released into the environment surrounding the plant.

The most remarkable thing about the UCS study is that they used many of the AEC's own technical reports to show that basic engineering data on the reliability of emergency core-cooling systems was deficient, and that surprisingly few actual tests had been conducted during the some fourteen years since the AEC's first major safety study (WASH-740) had been published. This was all the more astonishing, the authors pointed out, in view of the fact that twenty-one currently operating nuclear plants and fifty-three under construction appeared to have deficient cooling systems.[71] To remedy this situation, the authors offered two major recommendations:[72]

> (1) A total halt to the issuance of operating licenses for nuclear power reactors presently under construction, until safeguards of assured performance can be provided.
>
> (2) A thorough technical and engineering review, by a qualified, independent group, of the expected performance of emergency core-cooling systems, installed in operating power reactors to determine whether these reactors now constitute an unacceptable hazard to the population.

In a second, follow-up report published again in *Nuclear News*,[73] the UCS authors criticized the AEC's interim policy statement called "Interim Acceptance Criteria for Light-Water Power Plants" that appeared in the *Federal Register* in June of 1971. The AEC had adopted these Interim Criteria under the pressure of outside criticism and while its regulatory staff was conducting a comprehensive task force study and evaluation of presently operating emergency core-cooling systems. The UCS article, however, not only charged that the AEC had continued to issue reactor licenses even though the results of the task force study were not yet in, but also stressed "abundant evidence of weaknesses in the interim criteria,"[74] adding that they "cannot add even marginally to the presently narrow or possibly nonexistent margins of safety in a loss-of-coolant accident."[75] The authors also demonstrated the inadequacy of the mathematical models and computer codes on which the criteria were based.[76] As they did in their first article, the UCS authors concluded with two specific recommendations:[77]

> 1. An immediate separation from the Atomic Energy Commission of the responsibility for determining criteria for all aspects of nuclear power reactor safety and for overseeing compliance with the criteria, including understanding and control both of planned and unplanned releases of radioactive material. The responsibility must be assumed by an agency independent of the AEC
> 2. Prompt initiation of a thorough technical and engineering study, by a qualified group, independent of the AEC, whose objective will be:
>   (a) To review the expected performance of emergency core-cooling systems installed in operating power reactors...;
>   (b) To determine the hazard to the public expected from the reactors now under construction and planned; and
>   (c) To develop the outline of an adequate program of engineering research and development that would clarify the nature and means of mitigating loss-of-coolant accidents, a program to have national support.

By January of 1972, the emergency core-cooling system and loss-of-fluid issues were being raised by public interveners at most of the licensing hearings for new reactors. No doubt, the UCS had been important in bringing these and other safety issues to the attention of interveners.[78] However, January of 1972 also marked the opening of AEC hearings on the adequacy of the Interim Criteria for reactor emergency systems, and in which the UCS participated heavily.[79] Throughout the hearings UCS spokesmen hammered away at AEC and industry witnesses, disclosing some rather substantive disagreements within the AEC over the adequacy of the Interim Criteria. Even though the Commission was allowed additional time for rebuttal, the hearings ended with the parties hopelessly deadlocked. The AEC and the nuclear industry, as expected, maintained that the Interim Criteria were too *conservative* and ought to be relaxed instead of strengthened. The UCS witnesses, on the other hand, argued that the AEC's own technical staff were far from agreement over the adequacy of the Interim Criteria; hence, if the Commission's own experts disagreed, on what basis could the AEC continue licensing water-cooled power reactors?[80] In spite of the way things turned out, the UCS group had raised some important questions concerning the status of nuclear reactor safety and the credibility of the AEC's regulatory policies.

Thus by the end of 1972 the question of nuclear reactor safety was firmly planted in the public mind. From the opposition initially posed by labor unions in the early years of the reactor programs, through the radiation controversy, the increased use of hearings by dissenting public groups, the controversies over the National Environmental Policy Act of 1969, the waste disposal issue and, finally, to the efforts of the Scientists Institute for Public Information and the Union of Concerned Scientists, the question of nuclear reactor safety had become one of the most debated technological issues of the times. And, to top it off, these questions reached the public arena nearly the same time as OPEC announced a seventy percent increase in the price of oil in 1973.

SUMMARY AND CONCLUSIONS

The preceding pages attempted to trace some of the factors which contributed to the expansion of the nuclear power controversy. In actuality, the controversy had already begun when the utilities brought the first commercial nuclear stations on-line in the late 1950s. Labor unions had taken the AEC to court, disputing the safety of the Enrico Fermi nuclear plant, one of the nation's first commercial nuclear power plants. Similarly, workers had walked off the job in protest at Monroe, Michigan, alleging that the new plant under construction posed serious hazards to the natural environment and surrounding population. At first, some observers were tempted to dismiss these events as isolated occurrences, as unexpected or freakish. But evidence to the contrary began to mount: the AEC's own safety study compiled by the Brookhaven National Laboratory and published in 1957 admitted that a large reactor accident could rival and perhaps exceed major natural catastrophes such as earthquakes and tornados. Moreover, increasing numbers of experts and scientists began speaking out on the radiation standards set by the AEC, warning of the adverse effects radiation posed for the population. The AEC's own handling of radiation dangers from increased nuclear atmospheric testing had been disastrous, and the Commission's irresponsibility in this matter was finally brought to light when two of its most esteemed radiation experts, Drs. Arthur Tamplin and John Gofman, charged that the AEC's radiation standards were far too lenient and should be increased tenfold.

But the criticism did not come only from those who worked primarily within the nuclear energy programs. Realizing that AEC licensing procedures were predisposed in favor of expediting the proliferation of nuclear power, concerned citizens and environmentalists began using the public hearing and other forums as stall and public enlightenment mechanisms to delay construction of new facilities, as AEC and utility attorneys began finding themselves confronted with a maze of legal obstacles to hurdle. The anti-nuclear forces finally gained welcomed political clout in 1969 when President Nixon signed the National Environmental Policy Act into law. The first test of nuclear power under the new environmental laws came in 1970-1971, with the AEC being charged with having miserably failed in its environmental protection responsibilities. Coupled with the waste disposal controversy which emerged in the late 1960s and early 1970s, significant numbers of outside scientists had organized themselves into effective pressure groups and independently studied the manifold aspects of the nuclear power programs. Two of these groups, the Scientists Institute for Public Information and the Union of Concerned Scientists, forcefully challenged the Commission's views on the feasibility of the breeder reactor and the adequacy of Commission-approved emergency core-cooling systems for light-water power reactors, the predominant type of nuclear reactor now in service in the United States.

By 1973 the Joint Committee on Atomic Energy decided to do something about this growing public uproar over nuclear power, and they scheduled public hearings on the safety of nuclear power reactors. As Senator John O. Pastore opened the first session of the hearings on *The Status of Nuclear Safety* on Tuesday, January 23, 1973--almost exactly twenty-seven years after Senator Brien McMahon had gavelled to order the very first meeting of the Senate's Special Committee on Atomic Energy on January 22, 1946--he projected a serious tone, strangely reminiscent of Senator McMahon's original remarks. Senator Pastore said in part:[81]

> The public today is absolutely confused. The public is not being told in categorical terms "Yes" and "No." We are imagining in many instances a catastrophe that might have a probability of occurrence of one in a billion years or may never happen. We are being told that the electricity generating capacity has to be cut down. We are being told by the environmentalists that we are going too far.
>
> And, what is even worse is the fact that right within the agency (the AEC), itself, you haven't made up your minds whether it is or it isn't. You have people who are being payed to do a job who are saying that it is good and other people who are being paid to do the same job who are saying that it isn't good ... (Dr. Schlesinger) I am glad you are here today to tell John Pastore and this committee "yes" or "no"--where are we going and what is the trouble?

There could be little doubt that Pastore's statement adequately reflected the intense polarization of the nuclear issue, and clearly indicated the awesome challenge nuclear energy would face in the future. New interest groups had mobilized their forces, and the regulatory subsystem's firm grip on nuclear policy appeared to be loosening. The atom was once again entangled in controversy--this time, however, the opposition was larger and more organized than ever before. The new challenge would be formidable.

NOTES

1. Albert Einstein, "The Einstein Letter," in Morton Grodzins and Eugene Rabinowitz (eds.), *The Atomic Age; Scientists in National and World Affairs* (New York: Basic Books, 1963), pp. 11-12.

2. See L. D. Smith, "Evolution of Opposition to the Peaceful Uses of Nuclear Energy," *Nuclear Engineering International* 17 (June 1972): 461.

3. Ibid.

4. Ibid. While the Fermi nuclear plant was licensed for operation, it was shut down in 1966 by a core-meltdown accident, caused by what Congressman Chet Holifield called "band-aid technology." See Harold P. Green, "'Reasonable Assurance' of 'No Undue Risk'," *Scientist and Citizen* 10 (June-July 1968): 137. Additional materials on the Fermi dispute can be found in Frank G. Dawson, *Nuclear Power: Development and Management of a Technology* (Seattle: University of Washington Press, 1976), pp. 192-194.

5. Cited in H. Peter Metzger, *The Atomic Establishment* (New York: Simon and Schuster, 1972), p. 116.

6. See United States Atomic Energy Commission, Division of Operational Safety, *Operational Accidents and Radiation Experience within the United States Atomic Energy Commission, 1943-1967* (Washington, D.C.: United States Atomic Energy Commission, 1968).

7. Smith, "Evolution of Opposition to the Peaceful Uses of Nuclear Energy," pp. 461-62; and Metzger, *The Atomic Establishment*, p. 116.

8. Leo Goodman, "Atomic Science Fatalities," Report prepared for Energy and National Resources, United Automobile Workers, 1968.

9. See United States Atomic Energy Commission, *Studies in Workmen's Compensation and Radiation Injury*, V. 5 (Washington, D.C.: United States Atomic Energy Commission, 1969).

10. "Scientists Question Reactor Effects: A Study of the Monticello Generating Plant in Minnesota," *Scientist and Citizen* 10 (August 1968): 154. See also Philip M. Boffey, "Radioactive Pollution: Minnesota Finds AEC Standards Too Lax," *Science* 163 (March 7, 1969):1043-44, and Harry Foreman (ed.), *Nuclear Power and the Public* (Minneapolis: University of Minnesota Press, 1970) for additional materials.

11. Ibid.

12. "Cooling it in Minnesota," *Environment* 11 (May 1969): 29. See also Dawson, *Nuclear Power*, pp. 194-198.

13. "Cooling it in Minnesota," p. 23.

14. Ibid., p. 24.

15. Ibid., p. 25.

16. Ibid.

17. Ibid.

18. Ibid.

19. Ibid.

20. For a good discussion see Richard S. Lewis, *The Nuclear Power Rebellion: Citizens vs. the Atomic Industrial Establishment* (New York: Viking Press, 1972), pp. 123 ff.

21. Cited in Ibid., p. 125.

22. Ibid., p. 126.

23. These examples are drawn primarily from Ibid., pp. 48-80. For further information consult Metzger, *The Atomic Establishment*; John W. Gofman and Arthur Tamplin, *Poisened Power* (Emmanus, Pa.: Rodale Press, 1971); Richard Curtis and Elizabeth Hogan, *Perils of the Peaceful Atom* (Garden City: Doubleday and Company, 1969); and John Holdren and Phillip Herrara, *Energy* (San Francisco: Sierra Club, 1971).

24. See Metzger, *The Atomic Establishment*, pp. 79-113. See also Curtis and Hogan, *Perils of the Peaceful Atom*.

25. Chet Holifield, "Who Should Judge the Atom?" *Saturday Review*, August 3, 1957; cited in Metzger, *The Atomic Establishment*, p. 86.

26. See Metzger, *The Atomic Establishment*, p. 277, note 17. Metzger recounts the story in the following fashion:

> Assigned the task of discrediting Sternglass' work, Dr. Arthur R. Tamplin, of the Lawrence Livermore Laboratory, published "A Criticism of the Sternglass Article on Fetal and Infant Mortality," in 1969. Tamplin found that the excess mortality reported by Sternglass was due to "differing social-economic conditions," but he went on to say, "At the same time, the existing experimental data indicates that fall-out radiation probably did contribute to infant and fetal mortality by way of lethal mutations but nowhere near the effect suggested by Sternglass. The effect is most likely at least a factor of 100 smaller than he proposes."

Since Sternglass predicted that some 400,000 babies had died due to fallout radiation, Tamplin's estimate was 4,000 deaths. While nowhere near the Sternglass figure, 4,000 radiation induced deaths is still significant. For a good review of the polemic see Philip M. Boffey, "Ernest J. Sternglass: Controversial Prophet of Doom," *Science* 166 (October 10, 1969): 195-200.

27. Reported in Lewis, *The Nuclear Power Rebellion*, p. 84.

28. Ibid., pp. 88 ff. See also Metzger, *The Atomic Establishment*, pp. 276-78, note 17.

29. Ann Carl, "The Lloyd Harbor Study Group Intervention--A Response," *Bulletin of the Atomic Scientists* 28 (June 1972): 35.

30. Ibid., p. 32.

31. See Vance L. Sailor, "The Role of the Lloyd Harbor Study Group in the Shoreham Hearings," *Bulletin of the Atomic Scientists* 28 (June 1972): 25-31.

32. Cited in Carl, "The Lloyd Harbor Study Group Intervention," p. 29.

33. See Sailor, "The Role of the Lloyd Harbor Study Group in the Shoreham Hearings," p. 34. For further information on the dispute see Lewis, *The Nuclear Power Rebellion*, pp. 117-18.

34. Lewis, *The Nuclear Power Rebellion*, pp. 116-17.

35. See Carl, "The Lloyd Harbor Study Group Intervention," p. 34.

36. Sailor, "The Role of the Lloyd Harbor Study Group in the Shoreham Hearings," p. 29.

37. Ibid.

38. Cited in Lewis, *The Nuclear Power Rebellion*, p. 118.

39. Ibid., pp. 118-19 and Carl, "The Lloyd Harbor Study Group Intervention," p. 34.

40. See Lewis, *The Nuclear Power Rebellion*, pp. 118-21.

41. Sailor, "The Role of the Lloyd Harbor Study Group in the Shoreham Hearings," pp. 25, 30.

42. See Public Law 91-190, "National Environmental Policy Act of 1969," in *United States Statutes at Large 1969*, V. 82 (Washington, D.C.: U.S. Government Printing Office, 1970), pp. 852-56.

43. Ibid.

44. Harold P. Green, "Nuclear Power Licensing and Regulation," *The Annals* 400 (March 1972): 124-25.

45. For an excellent discussion see Lewis, *The Nuclear Power Rebellion*, pp. 277-78.

46. Cited in Ibid., p. 278.

47. Ibid., p. 283, See also Thomas W, Keating, "Politics, Energy, and the Environment: The Role of Technology Assessment," *American Behavioral Scientist* 19 (September-October 1975): 62-64.

48. Keating, "Politics, Energy, and the Environment," p. 64.

49. Cited in Lewis, *The Nuclear Power Rebellion*, p. 284. For a useful discussion of NEPA and the Calvert Cliffs case see also Dawson, *Nuclear Power*, pp. 198-203.

50. This figure is reported in Constance Holden, "Nuclear Waste: Kansans Riled by AEC Plans for Atom Dump," *Science* 172 (April 16, 1971): 249. For summary discussion and some of the critics' views on waste disposal issues see Sheldon Novick, *The Careless Atom* (Boston: Houghton-Mifflin Co., 1969).

51. See National Academy of Sciences--National Research Council, Publication No. 519, *The Disposal of Radioactive Waste on Land* (Washington, D.C.: National Academy of Sciences-National Research Council, 1957), p. 1.

52. Ibid. References to this report in text hereinafter enclosed in parentheses.

53. See Lewis, *The Nuclear Power Rebellion*, p. 151.

54. Ibid., p. 149; Holden, "Nuclear Waste," p. 249; and Richard S. Lewis, "The Radioactive Saltmine," *Bulletin of the Atomic Scientists* 27 (June 1971): 27.

55. Holden, "Nuclear Waste," p. 249.

56. Lewis, *The Nuclear Power Rebellion*, p. 163.

57. Holden, "Nuclear Waste," p. 249.

58. Lewis, "The Radioactive Saltmine," p. 30.

59. Lewis, *The Nuclear Power Rebellion*, pp. 167-170.

60. Lewis, "The Radioactive Saltmine," p. 30.

61. Lewis, *The Nuclear Power Rebellion*, pp. 250-53.

62. Ibid., p. 244.

63. See Glenn T. Seaborg, Letter to President John F. Kennedy, November 20, 1962. This letter is reprinted in its entirety in United States Atomic Energy Commission, *Civilian Nuclear Power: A Report to the President--1962* (Washington, D.C.: U.S. Government Printing Office, 1962), p. 9.

64. These statistics are reported in Lewis, *The Nuclear Power Rebellion*, p. 304.

65. The entirety of President Nixon's special message is cited in John G. Yevick, "Breeder Reactors," in Leonard A. Sagan (ed.), *Human and*

Ecologic Effects of Nuclear Power Plants (Springfield, Illinois: Charles C. Thomas, 1974), p. 245. Yevick's article, though highly technical, is perhaps the most indepth, compact treatment of the subject available. See also Glenn T. Seaborg and Justin L. Bloom, "Fast Breeder Reactors," *Scientific American* 223 (November 1970): 13-21.

66. Lewis, *The Nuclear Power Rebellion*, p. 255. See also "The Great Breeder Dispute," *Time* 98 (November 1, 1971):102, for a general discussion on the subject.

67. Cited in Lewis, *The Nuclear Power Rebellion*, pp. 255-56.

68. For more about the questions raised by the breeder reactor and the large-scale use of plutonium as fuel, see Alvin M. Weinberg, "Social Institutions and Nuclear Energy," *Science* 177 (July 7, 1972):27-34; John W. Gofman, "Time for a Moratorium" in *The Case for a Nuclear Moratorium* (Washington, D.C.: Environmental Foundation, 1972), pp. 8-55.; and Denis Hayes, *Nuclear Power: The Fifth Horseman* (Washington, D.C.: World Watch Institute, 1976). For a most informative and comprehensive treatment, including viable alternatives to the plutonium question, see Gustave J. Speth, Arthur R. Tamplin, and Thomas B. Cochran, "Plutonium Recycle: The Fateful Step," *Bulletin of the Atomic Scientists* 30 (November 1974): 15-22.

69. For an excellent discussion of the role played by the Union of Concerned Scientists in this matter, see Joel Primack and Frank von Hippel, *Advice and Dissent: Scientists in the Political Arena* (New York: Basic Books, 1974), pp. 208-35.

70. Ian A. Forbes, Daniel F. Ford, Henry W. Kendall, and John J. MacKenzie, "Nuclear Reactor Safety: An Evaluation of New Evidence," *Nuclear News* 9 (September 1971): 32-40.

71. Ibid., p. 37.

72. Ibid., pp. 37, 40.

73. Daniel F. Ford, Henry W. Kendall, John J. MacKenzie, "A Critique of the AEC's Interim Criteria for Emergency Core-Cooling Systems, *Nuclear News* 15 (January 1972): 28-35.

74. Ibid., p. 28.

75. Ibid.

76. Ibid.

77. Ibid., pp. 33-34.

78. One should add that Robert Gillette of *Science* magazine did much to generate public awareness in these matters in a series of illuminating

articles on nuclear reactor safety in 1972. See Gillette, "Nuclear Safety (I): The Roots of Dissent," *Science* 177 (September 1, 1972): 771-76; Gillette, "Nuclear Safety (II): The Years of Delay," *Science* 177 (September 8, 1972): 867-71; and Gillette, "Nuclear Safety" (III): Critics Charge Conflict of Interest," *Science* 177 (September 15, 1972): 970-75.

79. See Primack and von Hippel, *Advice and Dissent*, pp. 218-28.

80. Ibid., p. 228.

81. United States Congress, Hearings before the Joint Committee on Atomic Energy, *The Status of Nuclear Reactor Safety*, 93rd Congress, 1st Session, 1973 (Washington, D.C.: U.S. Government Printing Office, 1974), p. 6.

7
The Evolution of Opposition to Nuclear Power in the United States (III): The Ideological Cleavage

> Now, we have had a lot of gobbledegook from both sides of this question, a lot of verbiage that sometimes is hard for the average citizen to understand. I wish at some time somebody would come before this committee and tell the committee categorically a nuclear reactor is safe or it isn't safe so that the public will know exactly where it stands.
>
> -Senator John O. Pastore

INTRODUCTION

When the hearings on *The Status of Nuclear Reactor Safety* opened in January of 1973, the nuclear power controversy was fully developed. The hearings were staged by the Joint Committee on Atomic Energy under pressure to deal with public criticism and enhance understanding of nuclear power.[1] Coinciding with the safety hearings, the Joint Committee had requested in 1971 that the AEC "prepare a comprehensive report on nuclear reactor safety with principal emphasis on questions being raised with respect to the safety of light-water power reactors." In 1973, the AEC published this report, *The Safety of Nuclear Power Reactors and Related Facilities*,[2] and the Joint Committee scheduled the safety hearings to discuss the report and other matters related to reactor safety, especially, according to the Chairman of the Joint Committee, Representative Melvin Price of Illinois, "substantive issues involved with assessing safety, the underlying philosophy of safety," and "the operation of the safety review process."[3] Several of the most prominent and influencial pro- and anti-nuclear figures in the United States were invited to give testimony, and the hearings promised to be a major effort to establish a "public record" on the controversy over nuclear energy in America as it existed in the early 1970s.

As such, the safety hearings are an excellent source for uncovering the substantive arguments and issues involved in the dispute, as cited by pro- and anti-nuclear factions. By analyzing testimony given before the Joint Committee, the present chapter will attempt to show that the nuclear controversy had become extremely wide-ranging and complex, encompassing far more than a concern about the satisfactory operation of the plants. Rather, the essential conflict was now greatly expanded to include deep ideological differences over the direction and content of public policy concerning technological alternatives. There is reason to believe that while nuclear power may have represented the main nexus of concern, opposition also included anxiety about the alleged deleterious side-effects of high-technology in general, and of fears of a government-corporate monopoly and regulatory establishment that seemed responsible only to powerful, narrowly defined special interest groups. At the same time, it will be shown that proponents of nuclear power continued to hail its magnificent scientific and technical achievements, firmly advocating its use as the key to increasing the standard of living, and for aiding in social and economic development.

We should also point out that it is not our intent to determine which of these oversimplified views is "correct." Rather, our purpose is to show that by 1974 the conflict over nuclear energy was embedded in significant ideological differences between advocates and critics. The opposition to nuclear energy was not a straight technical issue; it was over *ideas* and systems of norms and values which defined the meaning, use, and significance of nuclear energy in society. It was also over how policy decisions ought to be made, and who should make them. In short, as the controversy expanded into the macropolitical sector, the stakes also expanded to include a myriad of political, ideological, and ethical issues.[4]

THE PRO-NUCLEAR IDEOLOGY

The hearings on *The Status of Nuclear Reactor Safety* were held in three "phases." Phase I of the hearings commenced on January 23, 1973, when the Joint Committee heard testimony from James R. Schlesinger, who was stepping down from his Chairmanship of the AEC to become Director of the Central Intelligence Agency. Phase II hearings received testimony from the Atomic Energy Commissioners, spokesmen from the Advisory Committee on Reactor Safeguards, members of the Atomic Safety Licensing Board Panel, and the AEC's principal staff on September 25, 26, 27, and on October 1, 1973. Phase III hearings were held on January 22, 23, 24, and 28, 1974 and heard testimony from representatives of the nuclear community, environmental groups, and the public at large.[5] Chairman Price indicated that the Joint Committee had received quite a large number of requests from persons desiring to testify during Phase III, and that the Joint Committee had "endeavored to organize the schedule in a manner which should result in the presentation of a wide cross section of views, representative of all sectors," (53-II). Thus, it looked as if the Joint Committee intended a major effort to evaluate the status of nuclear reactor safety and to provide an opportunity for interested parties to participate in the assessment.

The Peaceful Applications Plank

Throughout the hearings pro-nuclear witnesses from each of these groups advocated several ideological stands. Certainly the most fundamental were those stated under what might be called the "peaceful applications plank." As expressed by the proponents of nuclear energy, this plank contained several important sub-themes. Perhaps the most pervasive belief was that nuclear energy could ultimately benefit human welfare by increasing the standard of living and economic growth. For years it was believed that nuclear energy would revolutionize the nature of industrial society by providing virtually limitless energy,[6] which, some predicted, would greatly alter transportation systems,[7] transform the social order by reducing or eliminating manual labor,[8] and, as one observer put it, would promise "the greatest future ever spread before mankind with dazzling possibilities of life, liberty, and the pursuit of happiness."[9] Moreover, by 1973 and the beginning of the energy crisis, nuclear power was assumed crucial in the so-called programs of "energy independence by 1980," meaning, correspondingly, that it was a key element in balancing the trade deficit by stemming the dollar flow to oil exporting countries that had become acute by 1974.

Many of these and related themes continually surfaced in the hearings. A. Philip Bray, General Manager of the Boiling Water Projects Division of General Electric, perhaps the world's leading manufacturer of nuclear power plants, echoed several of them in the following comment to the members of the Joint Committee (444-II):

> These hearings on reactor safety come at a crucial point in our country's economic and social development. We are apparently moving from an era of relative energy abundance to an era of increasing scarcity, the duration of which will depend on future technological development and resource availability. We can and must be prudent in using our energy resources. But if we are to maintain our present standard of living as well as make it available to all segments of our society, increasing quantities of electric energy will be necessary during the coming decades.

Other witnesses representing the nuclear power industry also agreed with the General Electric statement, and there seemed to be fairly good consensus on the fact that the energy crisis and the goal of energy self-sufficiency required a full-scale effort at developing nuclear power. Lou Favert, Vice President of Babcock and Wilcox's Nuclear Divisions, which is a prominent manufacturer of nuclear power plant hardware and steam supply systems, told the Joint Committee that "in today's energy crisis Babcock and Wilcox has a parallel committment to insure that nuclear energy is utilized toward the vital national objective of self-sufficiency by 1980" (165-II). Favert implied that nuclear rather than some other form of energy ought to be the main element of a national energy policy aimed at self-sufficiency. However, Representative Chet Holifield of California, one of the original members of the Joint Committee when it was first established in 1946, best summarized the self-sufficiency argument in a discussion concerning the breeder reactor program (LMFBR). As he put it (170-71-II):

> I think the urgency for power is going to take care of a lot of things that seem most difficult.

> I think we do have on our side in this quest for a more efficient device such as we all believe the LMFBR will be, I think we have on our side a rapidly ascending cost of fossil fuels which I don't think the general public has comprehended yet.
>
> The studies that we have made have accented the almost unbearable fiscal burden that will rest upon the energy users in our country if this escalating quantity of imports from the Middle East continues...
>
> If we look back 2 or 3 years and see that the price has doubled, and if we anticipate another doubling, which is not fanciful at all, it will go to the fantastic amount of $45 billion outflow by 1980. This is a fiscal burden that this country can't stand...
>
> That is why I am so interested in getting this LMFBR on the line as fast as we can possibly do it. I am willing to make almost any sacrifice to get it going.

Holifield went on to say that the outflow of dollar deficit was $6.5 billion in 1972, and it would reach $22 billion by 1980. Consequently the rapid expansion of nuclear power, and especially deployment of fast-breeder reactors, had long been regarded by the Joint Committee as a solution to these fiscal problems.

Besides underscoring the importance of nuclear energy in helping the nation cope with the energy crisis and relieving the dependence on foreign suppliers, the continued expansion of nuclear power was also seen as a prime ingredient for maintaining the standard of living and promoting economic growth, perhaps one of the leading rationales behind the Atomic Energy Act of 1946.[10] Throughout the hearings, pro-nuclear witnesses assumed that increasing quantities of electricity and increasing the standard of living were casually related. The advocacy of this position was already noted in part in Bray's statement cited above. However, it was Representative Mike McCormack from the State of Washington, and a former employee at the AEC's Hanford research site, who put the matter into clear perspective (512-II):

> To assume that this country can continue to grow, to assume that we can have even a slight increase in population, to assume that we can maintain the standard of living that we want, to assume that we require the energy consuming environmental protection laws for stack gas emission from automobiles and electric energy production and everything else that we propose, and to assume that we can do this without additional production of significant amounts of energy is simply irrational.

McCormack further indicated that any energy policy which failed to consider significant growth "would have disastrous results for this country" (512-II). Thus, not only were increased standard of living, greater economic growth, and significantly expanded electricity generating potential important, but they were also reasons why *nuclear* power should be rapidly developed.

Finally, it should be mentioned that increasing growth and the standard of living were not the only elements of the peaceful applications plank. Several witnesses and Congressmen also emphasized that development of peaceful applications tended to shift the definition of nuclear energy from evil military applications to something that could benefit mankind. Senator John O. Pastore of Rhode Island, one of the senior members of the Joint Committee, best summarized this position in the following comment on the opening day of the hearings (6-7-I):

> Now I tell you very frankly, like yourself (speaking to Dr. Schlesinger), I am one who has a tremendous amount of confidence in the civilian uses of atomic energy. I have said time and again that if my job on this committee was only to make a bigger and better bomb, I would quit tomorrow; I am not interested, I am not interested. The only hope of the atom is in its service to mankind and not in its destruction.

Thus, besides the economic and development issues, the peaceful applications plank seems also to have been conceived as a bulwark against the military uses and interpretations of nuclear energy. Indeed, throughout the original legislative hearings in 1945-46, civilian control of atomic energy had been a major theme.[11]

In light of these facts, perhaps it is useful to end this section with a remark (cited in Chapter Two) made by James R. Newman, special council to the Senate's McMahon Committee. He could have made the following comment as easily in 1974 as he had in 1945:[12]

> The new force offers enormous possibilities for *improving public welfare*, for revamping our industrial methods, and for *increasing the standard of living*. Properly developed and harnessed, atomic energy can *achieve improvement in our lot* equalling or perhaps exceeding the tremendous accomplishments made possible through the use of electricity. (emphasis added)

The Faith in Science and Technology

While the peaceful applications plank was crucial for explaining the meaning and purpose of nuclear energy development in the United States since World War Two, the hearings were also pervaded with another ideological assumption. That is, all of these ambitious development schemes assumed that science and technology would be able to solve what David Lilienthal, the first Chairman of the AEC, had called "a whole mass of involved, difficult, scientific, technical, and industrial engineering problems."[13] This attitude was in part the result of the impressive War-time successes of science and technology, and most United States officials believed that with adequate resources and funding, the scientific-technological establishment could bring nuclear power to fruition in a short period of time. Certainly, in nearly every one of the Commission's annual reports which they are required by law to submit to Congress, the faith in science and technology to achieve the great promise of the peaceful atom was openly proclaimed,[14] particularly during the age of commercial acceptability.

By and large, the hearings were overwhelmed with this faith in science and technology, and one needs only look at the extent to which technical detail was marshalled by pro-nuclear witnesses to get some idea of its importance. For example, Atomic Energy Commission and industry witnesses framed their testimonies almost entirely in terms of highly complex scientific and technical data. In fact, over eighty percent of all testimony given by pro-nuclear witnesses was couched in terms of technical, facts-and-figures, or administrative expertise, as compared to some seventeen percent for anti-nuclear groups.[15] This suggests that pro-nuclear witnesses saw the use of technical expertise as a way of interpreting and resolving issues.

A good example of the highly technical data offered by pro-nuclear witnesses is seen in the testimony of William B. Cottrell, a nuclear engineer and Director of the Nuclear Safety Information Center at Oak Ridge National Laboratory. While his remarks were billed in the hearing transcript under the sub-title, "Safety Concerns Regarding the New ECCS (emergency core-cooling system) Criteria," the word "safety" did not appear in his subsequent comments even once (275-II):

> In particular, new criterion No. 1 reduces the maximum allowable temperature from 2,300° F, while new criterion No. 2 defines the maximum cladding oxidation that shall be permitted to occur. The two criteria combine to adequately limit embrittlement.
>
> The question of core flow blockage as results from fuel pin swelling is addressed only indirectly in new criterion No. 4 but is adequately covered later in the criteria in the discussion of evaluation models (sec. IB). There it is stated that clad swelling and rupture must be considered, and "shall be based upon applicable data in such a way that... (the effects) are not underestimated."

However, it was probably Representative Craig Hosmer of California, an ardent supporter of civilian nuclear power throughout his many years of tenure on the Joint Committee, who best articulated the faith in science and technology plank. In a discussion of the disposal of radioactive wastes with Dr. Henry Kendall, Professor of Physics at the Massachusetts Institute of Technology and representing the Union of Concerned Scientists, Representative Hosmer remarked (107-108-II):

> ...do you not think it possible that our scientific and other types during that hundred years can possibly devise some means to dispose of this stuff on a permanent basis?
>
> I think it could be, at least in my mind, a little unreasonable to expect man to have invented everything that is inventable at this

> particular moment before he can move ahead with any activity. After all, the period I talked about, a little over 25 years for this accumulation of waste, is not too unmanageable to store in a manageable fashion.
>
> It seems to me it should be reasonably safe for society to proceed in this area, and, if indeed by the end of a hundred years it turns out not to be a manageable problem why, then they can stop these nuclear programs. Meanwhile, possibly there is some benefit to society from the energy they produce that might be worth all this trouble.

Kendall replied that Hosmer's point suggested a legacy to future generations that "disturbed" him, but Hosmer rebutted his position by going on to say (108-II):

> Professor Kendall, I cannot share your pessimism on the ingenuity of man and his capability of coping with the problems presented to him in the world.
>
> I would believe that pessimism of yours would essentially cause people to stop every operation of any kind on the basis that something might happen some day that couldn't be coped with at some time in the future or might be a burden upon some members of some future society.

Hosmer's remarks plainly reflect the idea that with enough effort and time our, as he put it, "scientific and other types," would be able to devise a means of disposing radioactive wastes, perhaps the most difficult technical problem faced by the nuclear programs. This faith in the powers of science and technology is not simply lip-service on Hosmer's part, but reflects a deeply embedded belief in the utility of science for achieving practical goals. Furthermore, it is clear that the faith in science and technology plank fits together almost perfectly with the peaceful applications plank, for the civilian uses of nuclear energy--an awesome technical problem--would not have been possible with a value-orientation that held science and technology in low esteem. Thus, the two planks have combined to create a formidable ideology defining the meaning and use of nuclear energy in contemporary America, and are among the most important reasons why nearly seventy nuclear power plants generate significant quantities of electricity at the present time. The ideology of civilian nuclear power projected a dream about the benefits of the peaceful atom, and adherence to that ideology brought new reactors on-line in a relatively short period of time.

Impeaching the Opposition

The fervor of ideologies may influence behavior and perception such that one views his opponents' arguments as categorically "wrong" or "distorted." One's own position is the most believable and "correct," while opponents are seen as "misguided," and their arguments "falsified," "exaggerated," "sensationalized," or "irrational."[16] While impeaching the opposition in this fashion is a normal play in political debate, its pervasiveness and intensity in the reactor safety hearings suggests that it is probably also due to deeply held ideological beliefs.

James Schlesinger, for instance, charged that an article about nuclear hazards in the *Chicago Tribune* was "sensationalized," "exaggerated," and "distorted." In his words (36-I):

> ...the spokesman was talking about wiping out the entire population of the Midwest on the basis of calculations which nobody has ever been able to fathom. It does not demand explanation. This is just one of those sensational kinds of statements. It works in a process of reasoning from possible technical deficiencies in a prudent backup system, in the technical criteria, jumps to the fact that an accident has occured, and vastly exaggerates the consequences of that accident.
>
> Now, I do not believe that we can have full public understanding of these problems as long as we have this kind of distortion.

Although Schlesinger may have been correct in emphasizing the deficiencies of the *Tribune* statement, the entire thrust of his testimony intimated that the nuclear program's difficulties were due simply to inaccuracies in reporting and the penchant for sensationalizing. Moreover, he later characterized one of the AEC's own safety studies, *Theoretical Possibilities and Consequences of Major*

Accidents in Large Nuclear Powerplants (1957), the study to which critics most frequently refer, as based on "highly restrictive assumptions," and as "overly conservative." He didn't admit that on the basis of the study it is *theoretically* possible that the critics are correct, since a major accident could cause thousands of deaths and injuries, with billions of dollars of property damages.[17] Rather, Schlesinger implied that the solution to the nuclear program's ills was simply a matter of providing the critics with the "correct" information, so that "full public understanding" could be gained.

Impeaching the opposition also involved direct *ad hominem* attacks on the witnesses themselves, and, at times, even questioned the personal integrity of a witness. Perhaps most skillful in utilizing this technique was Representative Mike McCormack. Consider his attack on Dr. Henry Kendall, who had made some disparaging comments about the AEC's safety programs (113 ff.-II):

> Dr. Kendall, you are deliberately distorting the AEC position, and I think you know it when you say that. Three or four times in your statement today you have made reckless and irresponsible statements, and that is one of them...
>
> I think the credibility of the Union of Concerned Scientists would be substantially improved if such irresponsible remarks were not included in your statement...
>
> You said AEC policy is to keep the nuclear power program going at all costs. Now do you really believe that? Do you really believe that the AEC policy is to keep the nuclear program going at all costs, regardless of any hazard to human beings?

However, McCormack out-did himself on the final day of the hearings when he levelled the following indictment against Ralph Nader, who was testifying in behalf of the Center for Responsible Law and the Union of Concerned Scientists (502, ff.-II):

> Mr. Nader has made a number of very dramatic statements here, some of which I think are patently silly...
>
> When he says that the emergency core-cooling system is the most important safety feature in any nuclear power plant, I believe he is

> revealing his profound ignorance of the entire subject. I think the claim that environmental groups discovered the idea of the pollution of rivers absurd...
>
> Your conduct on this subject may be likened to fanatics talking to themselves around a circle to reinforce their own fanaticism...
>
> So the gentleman is just so much in error that it is impossible, as I say, to go through this and point out all the errors he makes...
>
> There seems to be several very serious flaws in your approach to this question of nuclear energy...

And finally, Representative Holifield told Nader that (508-II):

> You even said in your statement here today there was a critical mass of plutonium dumped into the ditches. Of course, that is an outright lie. There is no such thing as a critical mass of plutonium being released into any ditch anywhere... A critical mass you said. I say it is a lie.

Impeaching the opposition was not confined to AEC officials and members of the Joint Committee. To a considerable extent many witnesses used the tactic at some point in their testimonies, and the members of the Joint Committee were simply responding in kind. However, the most important consideration here is that impeaching the opposition strongly indicated the ideological nature of the debate. Each side viewed its own position and interpretation of the "facts" as the correct one, while the opposition was seen to be suffering from "distortion" and "errors" of interpretation, even reaching the point of depending upon "outright lies" to prove a point.

THE IDEOLOGY OF ANTI-NUCLEAR LEADERS

We turn now to the testimony of anti-nuclear witnesses. Just as for proponents of nuclear power, anti-nuclear spokesmen seemed influenced by their own ideological stance which interpreted the meaning and purpose of nuclear power. However, the ideology of anti-nuclear spokesmen dramatically conflicted in theme and substance with that of their counterparts, suggesting that much of the debate over nuclear energy can be traced to important ideological considerations.

What, then, was the substance of this ideology? By and large, opposition to nuclear energy seemed to be an arm of the environmental movement.[18] Throughout the United States and Western Europe environmental groups have played a growing role in opposing nuclear power installations. Allan Mazur estimates that more than two-thirds of the some thirty leaders of the United States anti-nuclear group, National Intervenors, had been environmental activists long before their anti-nuclear affairs began.[19] Furthermore, a poll by Louis Harris and Associates tells us that environmentalists oppose construction of nuclear power plants by more than a four-to-one margin, while other groups sampled favor construction of new units on the order of two-to-one.[20] Thus, the ideology of anti-nuclear spokesmen at the hearings is likely to reflect the same themes of the larger environmental movement at a number of key points.

The Legacy to Future Generations

Since conservation of the natural environment has always been the central ideological tenet of the environmental movement, it is not surprising that possible environmental liabilities of nuclear power --especially those which are thrust on future generations --were seen as prime issues of contention by nuclear opponents. In the hearings, it was argued that future generations would gain little benefit from presently operating plants, yet would suffer the burdens of the growing wastes from both civilian and military programs. Such wastes obviously would be radioactively "hot" for several thousands of years, even though the plants which produced them have useful lives of less than fifty years. Hence the question was raised whether power users in the next half-century had the moral right to impose such a burden onto millenia, a conclusion reiterated by the Sierra Club in 1975.[21]

Another theme which emerged throughout the hearings in connection with the legacy to the future argument, was concern about the hazards of the plutonium fuel cycle, a genuine fear considering the proponents' zeal for the development of fast-breeder reactors.[22] It was argued that the large-scale commitment to breeder reactors would require a restriction on civil liberties that might eventuate in a more centralized, totalitarian government. By 1976, this fear had grown to the point that the National Council of Churches--an earlier proponent of nuclear energy for its presumed role in economic development--reversed its position and proclaimed the use of breeder reactors and plutonium as "morally indefensible."[23] The hearings contain numerous examples of these essentially moral and ethical arguments which will illustrate the point.

For example, Mrs. Ann Carl, Research Director of the Lloyd Harbor Study Group, an active intervenor in nuclear power plant licensing cases for many years,[24] told the Joint Committee of her group's great concern with the consequences of the use of plutonium and breeder reactors, as well as their questions about the problems posed by the disposal of radioactive wastes. She said that "sabotage with the diversion of some materials becomes a very serious concern" (182-II), and that the problem would be compounded if the breeder reactor was pressed into service, because there would be the need "to criss-cross the country with truckloads of this highly toxic bomb potential" (182-II). She went on to say that only "with the rigid controls of a dictatorship would we be able to police this transportation and storage operation", and, "do we want to subject the nation to a dictatorship, for perpetuity, to insure perfect control of such fissionable material as plutonium?" (182-II).

Thus, Mrs. Carl was not concerned about the safety of nuclear reactors *per se*. Rather, she was afraid that a new kind of society might evolve to cope with the hazards of the plutonium fuel cycle, a society in which fundamental individual freedoms would be drastically curtailed in favor of a science fiction-like police state. The implication drawn by Mrs. Carl, of course, was that society would have to be operated in near tyrannical fashion, since no wars, uprisings, insurgence, or terrorism could be permitted.[25]

Mrs. Carl's position was corroborated by Franklin L. Gage, spokesman for the Citizens Association for Safe Energy and the Citizens Committee for the Protection of the Environment, both active citizens groups in New York. He told the Joint Committee that the use of nuclear fission was "probably the greatest single risk that any civilization has ever taken" (401-II), and that (404-II):

> The 100,000 megawatts of nuclear electricity projected for the United States before 1980 would generate as much long-lived radioactivity as the fissioning of about 100,000 Hiroshima size bombs each year, plus 60,000 pounds of radioactive plutonium-239 which has a radioactive half-life of 24,400 years and will almost surely reach the black market for use in private atomic bombs or other destructive devices by gangsters, terrorists, blackmailers, maniacs, and others.

In addition, Gage claimed that "more than 99.99 percent of that radioactivity must be kept isolated from the biosphere for at least the next 50 generations, since 00.01 percent leakage is the radioactive equivalent of 10 Hiroshima bombs per year" (404-II). And given the fact that "absolutely no one had made a case justifying any confidence whatsoever that such a high level of containment can or will be achieved," Gage concluded that "it is morally outrageous for one generation of humans to create a radioactive legacy which irreversibly mortgages the future of the next 50 generations in exchange for a very small amount of expensive, unreliable electric power today" (404-II). Safety, then, was not the *main* issue to Gage, but can in fact be taken as primarily symbolic, as an expression of diffuse latent beliefs about the social and moral implications of nuclear energy's irreversible effects on society and future generations.

Still another variant of the legacy to future generations ideology can be seen in opponents' interpretations of the "proliferation problem." The general argument used in the hearings ran something like this: If the United States "goes nuclear," then in the future the primary electricity generating technology it will be in a position to export to developing countries will also be nuclear. Considering the limited world supply of accessible uranium, breeder reactors must ultimately be deployed, meaning all countries with breeders will also possess plutonium, for which it is only a short step to constructing atomic bombs. Again, the opposition to nuclear energy was not based on safety and technical considerations alone, but was actually seen as a way of preventing "every little nation in the World (from) the business of making dangerous nuclear materials" (332-II), to use the words of Dr. David Inglis, Professor of

Physics at the University of Massachusetts, and representing Friends of the Earth.

However, Inglis' statement was actually part of a larger argument concerning the diversion of fissionable material and potential nuclear war.[26] As he expressed it to the Joint Committee (322-23-II):

> I feel that while there are great benefits to be had from the energy that we get out of it, the threat of nuclear war is something which I cannot forget. Some people, I think, get inured to the idea that we have been 30 years in the nuclear age without nuclear war so that they believe we are safe. I don't know how long we can last. I sometimes feel we are leading a charmed life, that sometime it will happen through some circumstance that we cannot foresee and that planning a plutonium economy in the future is going to help it happen.
>
> I won't try to give scenarios, but I think it is enough to give some brief ideas of my attitude toward the diversion problem. I think it is dangerous.
>
> It is one of the several reasons why I have serious doubt about the wisdom of going ahead with the program which you gentlemen are so ably promoting.

On the basis of these statements, it is possible to see that the issue of nuclear power in Inglis' opinion was not whether the reactors could be made to function without incident, but the more serious, if latent, problem of proliferation and possible nuclear war. Inglis ended his testimony with a plea to halt the nuclear program and a request to pour some $600 million into research on alternative technologies, for the frieghtening possibility of nuclear war was something he'd rather not think about.

Finally, the entire legacy ideology appeared grounded in a belief that acted as partial legitimation or support of earlier arguments. That is, nuclear opponents seemed generally skeptical of the abilities of science and technology, and openly expressed doubt that nuclear energy's technical problems could ever be solved. This stands in stark contrast to the views of nuclear proponents, and one needs only recall the discussion cited above between Professor Kendall and Representative Hosmer concerning the disposal of radioactive wastes to ascertain this fact. However, it was Ralph Nader who expressed the strongest doubt in the powers of science and technology when he remarked that nuclear power should be opposed because it required, he said, a degree of "technical perfection" that could not be achieved (495-II). Besides terming nuclear power as a severe case of "technological arrogance" (496-II), Nader went on to criticize what he called a "scientific certitude" that the problems with nuclear energy could be resolved. As he told the members of the Joint Committee (495-II):

> I must say that the credibility was attached to the sources of information should not have been so attached, that they reflected in part a scientific certitude that every technical problem yet unsolved dealing with nuclear power would somehow be solved, and that it was good to go full steam ahead because it would put the pressure on both the Government to fund and on the various scientific laboratories to solve these problems. This is really the most charitable description that can be made. There are less charitable descriptions of some other elements of the nuclear power establishment, economic, political, and otherwise, but the technical staff I think always had a kind of scientifically evangelistic belief that these problems would be solved and that nuclear power would present no risks of any significance whatsoever to present and future generations.

Thus, buttressed by this skepticism in science and technology, the legacy to future generations ideology actually contained several sub-themes--including the issue of radioactive waste disposal, the large-scale dependence upon plutonium, problems of sabotage and terrorism, and the proliferation issue--which seemed to symbolize uniquely the confrontation between pro- and anti-nuclear forces. Separately considered, any single sub-theme was bound to have little impact. But taken together as a system of beliefs, ideas, values, and interpretations--in short, as an ideology--these arguments combined to form a powerful nexus of concern which generated formidable opposition. It was left to Ralph Nader to put these sub-themes together in one succinct statement which best summarized the legacy to the future argument used by the anti-nuclear forces. As he told the Joint Committee in his closing comments (496-II):

> While many may not particularly care about what they do to the present generation, I think we have to consider this is not just a technical problem but a moral issue of the greatest gravity in terms of sending to future generations the kind of contaminated resources that major accidents could produce...the nuclear fission program is not worth the candle, whether for Americans or for the people overseas to whom these reactors are being promoted by corporations with Government support and in some cases with a subsidy.

Anti-Centralization and Political Accountability

The second ideological position that appeared in the hearings was a set of interrelated arguments, ideas, and beliefs we call the "anti-centralization and political accountability plank." The hearings revealed considerable evidence of a set of political and administrative concerns which seem to have blended with ecological concepts. The primary focus of these concerns was an outspoken opposition to political and administrative centralization of every kind, which, at the same time, displayed a clear preference for such ideas as the value of participatory politics, emphasis upon due process and political accountability, and a firm push for decentralized or so-called "low-technology" alternatives to nuclear power. Many of these same ideas characterize the ideology of the larger environmental movement.[27]

In using his opportunity to speak before the Joint Committee, Ralph Nader's central concerns were really non-technical in character and embraced several political and administrative questions. Thus he asks the members of the Joint Committee to "consider for a few minutes the responsibilities of the Joint Committee itself and how it has discharged those responsibilities..." (469-II). Nader claimed that the Joint Committee had performed "poorly" in its oversight function because the Committee represented a "concentration of power in a single legislative committee which means there is none of the valuable interaction and competition between separate House and Senate committees...

and the creative conflict that is necessary for a just pattern of policy-making" (470-II). Nader went on to describe the unique organizational character and authority of the Joint Committee and said that "its history will provide a classic illustration of why our founding fathers thought it so important to have a separation of powers and a system of checks and balances" (470-II). Clearly, Nader was concerned less with the safety question than with the "deficiencies" of the Congressional regulatory structure, which seemed to have centralized all decision-making in a single legislative committee.

As for the question of due process, Nader claimed that the AEC's hearing and licensing procedures all but denied due process to citizen groups and outside intervenors, and that current practices did not permit citizens to gain "full and effective participation in the licensing process" (479-II). Using the National Science Foundation-sponsored study of AEC procedures compiled by Ebbin and Kasper to support his remarks,[28] Nader charged the AEC and the Joint Committee with "collusion" against public groups in which utility companies were virtually assured a favorable ruling on their construction applications without the benefit of due process to dissenting groups. He offered the Joint Committee a summary of his views in the following remarks (480-II):

> The AEC's procedures pit the utilities, which have a huge economic stake, as well as a huge Federal subsidy in the outcome of the hearings and command tremendous resources, against consumer and environmental groups which are woefully underfunded and understaffed, and given no Federal subsidy, direct or indirect. The AEC procedures provide no mechanism for redressing the balance.
>
> The AEC has effectively denied citizen groups access to vitally needed information by supporting the utility companies and vendors' insistence in classifying documents as proprietary.

Taken together with his previous remarks about the Congressional regulatory structure of nuclear energy, Nader implied that a better system of regulation was both possible and desirable. As such, Nader's remarks extended far beyond the accident issue to include political values such as maximizing due process and political responsibility of governmental agents and imposing more pluralistic, less centralized administrative procedures on nuclear energy policy-making.

Nader's concern with accountability and appropriate procedure was shared, though expressed somewhat differently, by Henry Kendall. Kendall told the Joint Committee that the AEC had intentionally "withheld" and "suppressed" important documentary materials critical of the reactor safety program, thereby effectively circumventing citizens' rights of information and due process. Kendall said it took the threat of legal action before the Commission would disclose the information, all of which implied that the AEC had something to hide. As he repeated the charge to the Joint Committee in regard to the AEC's evaluation of reactor pressure vessels (115-II):

> We have documentation in the emergency core-cooling system hearings where Dr. Monroe Wexler, who is one of the AEC's leading experts on this subject, came to testify to the effect that the AEC's decisions that pressure vessel rupture was impossible was not sustainable, and that the matter should be reviewed in the light of his experience. The AEC refused to allow him to testify...

Kendall thus accused the Commission of "suppressing" critical safety documentation and said the nuclear program could not be "above suspicion" considering the overt lack of due process and political accountability displayed under the official mantle of AEC proceedings.

Finally, the value of decentralization was also applied to technological development and growth in general. Several nuclear opponents seemed to harbor a marked resistance to growing, increasingly centralized technology and technological change, and therefore advocated more diffuse, "low-technology" alternatives to nuclear power. In concert with recent proposals for small-scale technology,[29] anti-nuclear witnesses called for increased emphasis on conservation programs, the development of solar power, geothermal energy, windmills, and other decentralized forms of energy use. A good statement of this position is given by Franklin Gage. After calling for a "halt in the operation and construction of all nuclear fission powerplants in the United States," Gage went on to argue for (403-II):

> ...Conservation of all forms of energy, particularly inefficient electrical energy, to protect the environment and insure adequate supplies for essential functions of society now and in the future.
>
> ...Development and implementation of safe sources of clean energy, particularly solar-related technologies such as use of windpower, sea temperature gradients, organic materials, et cetera, for the production of clean, abundant fuels such as methane and hydrogen as well as electricity.

In contrast to nuclear proponents, Gage claimed that energy from low-technology alternatives was already cost-competitive, less complicated, and safer than nuclear energy, and that the nation ought to embark on a crash program to develop these decentralized solutions to the energy crisis. Gage so much distrusted the high-technology of nuclear power that he told the Joint Committee in his final comments that (410-II): "The time has long since passed for the Joint Committee to act on the unsafety of nuclear powerplants and to encourage development of safe, clean, abundant, domestic energy resources which will not endanger the lives of every American, living or as yet unborn." For those, like Gage, opposed to high-technology, nuclear energy was obviously an ideal target for attack.

To summarize the anti-centralization and political accountability plank, the beliefs and values expressed under this rubric actually ran hand-in-hand with increasing demands on the part of environmentalists for broader citizen participation in decisions about science and technology policy as a whole. Indeed, the nuclear power business, highly centralized and regulated largely from within the confines of Washington-based offices, makes individual citizens seem impotent in areas of technical decision-making that affect their interests. The statements cited above, however, indicate that some citizens were far from happy with this predicament, and were evidently unwilling to accept the rule of large, unwieldy administrative bureaucracies as a legitimate representative of their interests, or, for that matter, of the public interest as such.[30] Entwisel and Raun, writing for the Sierra Club, put it well: "...How does the development of fantastic, highly complicated technologies, such as nuclear fission, affect our culture, our 'good life'? Does our dependence on intricate and specialized machinery and the specialists who run them create a mystification of the source of power (both electrical and political)? Does this in turn make them inaccessible to individuals who are not bureaucrats of centralization?"[31]

Hence, the anti-centralization and political accountability plank's basic aim was to encourage citizen participation at grass-roots levels in an attempt to gain a more effective voice in crucial science and technology decisions--decisions, it should be added, which seemed to be made by irresponsible and impersonal government agencies more interested in their own goals than in protecting the public from the hazards of nuclear energy. This, at least, was the interpretation of the anti-centralization and political accountability plank espoused by nuclear opponents.

Impeaching the Opposition

The charges made by critics concerning the lack of due process and political accountability were strengthened by what we referred to above as "impeaching the opposition." That is, they attempted to demonstrate that the proponents of nuclear energy had been "misrepresenting" the facts, "lying," or had used other means of "distorting" the truth about nuclear energy. Analytically, impeaching the opposition isn't always easy to separate from some of the materials we have cited so far, in which the regulators had been charged with "suppressing" important information. Nevertheless, a number of personal *ad hominem* attacks were leveled against the members of the AEC and the Joint Committee.

As he had been throughout the hearings, Ralph Nader was the most outspoken critic of the regulators. Most of the other witnesses would probably agree with Nader's remarks, but it was Nader who made the strongest case. He attacked members of the AEC and the Joint Committee for their involvement in "collusion" and "conspiracy" against the public in which they had "suppressed" information "relating to atomic powerplant safety hazards" (477-II). He said the "conspiracy" between AEC officials and members of the Joint Committee dates to at least the period of 1964-1965 when a secret study on the consequences of major accidents was undertaken," and that key members of the Joint Committee and the AEC "did not want to make the results of the study public" (477-II). Nader also said that AEC officials had opposed expanded safety programs "in an effort to shield the nuclear industry from inspections that will disclose the shoddy work they are doing in construction, maintaining, and operating these complex nuclear machines" (477-II). Finally, he made a sweeping charge against the Joint Committee and some of its senior members (478-II):

> The AEC and the JCAE subsequently decided to use the ultimate subterfuge: none of the results would be made public. The AEC would issue no technical report presenting the results of the study and the Joint Committee would hold no hearings on the results of the study.
>
> Many people have spoken of the AEC's involvement in a coverup of reactor hazards. But the AEC has not acted alone in trying to prevent the public from knowing about these very great hazards. They have acted in concert with this committee which is supposed to be a watchdog but instead is a Siamese twin. Indeed, far from being a passive partner, this Joint Committee through such veteran members as Representatives Holifield and Hosmer have condemned, bullied, or ridiculed citizens who tried to convey facts and concerns about nuclear power hazards and risks.

Besides Nader's formidable barrage, Mrs. Ann Carl of the Lloyd Harbor Study Group alleged that AEC officials never discussed what she called "serious gaps in the knowledge" (178-II) about the reliability of emergency core-cooling systems (ECCS), and yet the Commissioners still issued industry guidelines. She claimed that dissent within the AEC regarding the ECCS deficiencies was "suppressed in the manner of Watergate" (181-II), and that the AEC's own critics of the criteria "were not allowed to discuss their concerns with the press." Among the critics, she said, "Rosen was 'promoted' out of his responsibility for the ECCS, Colman was transferred to Korea, and Rittenhouse's grants began to fade" (181-II).

As in the case of nuclear proponents, both Carl and Nader tried to impeach the opposition in order to destroy their credibility. To be sure, the primary reason for impeaching the opposition in this fashion was not simply to demonstrate their lack of truthfulness, but also, to enhance the legitimacy of anti-nuclear witnesses' own arguments. The object of course was to suggest the righteousness of the anti-nuclear position and the legitimacy of its own motives, for they had interpreted the situation in terms of their own well-motivated intentions. The opposition, therefore, had by definition misrepresented and subverted the facts; indeed, as far as the nuclear opponents were concerned, it had simply concocted definitions of the situation that were little more than self-serving.

SUMMARY AND CONCLUSIONS

On the basis of the above analysis, it is clear that proponents and opponents of nuclear energy at the reactor safety hearings subscribed to conflicting ideologies which defined the meaning, purpose, and significance of nuclear energy within society. For the proponents, nuclear energy seemed to comprise a veritable technological revolution that promised a great bounty for mankind in the form of abundant, cheap electrical energy which would raise the standard of living, promote economic growth, and solve the problems of the energy crisis with the eventual deployment of breeder reactors. Indeed, when in 1945 Robert Hutchins called nuclear energy the greatest single invention since the discovery of fire, he expressed confidence that nuclear energy promised to revolutionize the very foundations of industrial society.[32] Together with a strong belief in the powers of science and technology to help realize these ends, the optimistic belief in the great worth of the peaceful atom has been a central guiding force in the history of nuclear energy development in the United States ever since.

By contrast, in the minds of the opponents of nuclear energy, there seemed little question that the atom symbolized a national committment to technocracy and greater technical complexity, to the expansion of centralized, impersonal decision-making, and to increased growth and unchecked consumption of finite natural resources. And considering the moral and ethical problems posed by radioactive wastes, proliferation, diversion, and other difficulties, the atom would require, they argued, a new society based on greater restriction of individual freedom, civil liberties, and other principles of democratic government. Far from the rosy picture of cheap power and rising standard of living painted by the proponents, the opposing forces viewed nuclear energy as the scourge of mankind and the environment. A summary of these conflicting ideologies is shown in Table 7.1.

Now even though this analysis represents a limited sample of hearings and testimony, there is still considerable evidence that conflicting ideologies of nuclear power appear to have surfaced at the center of the debate. This is significant for several reasons. To begin with, the hearings revealed that conflict over nuclear power by 1974 had been greatly expanded and interpreted by partisans to cover all manner of concerns, and ranged far beyond any simplistic formulae or technological panaceas. While it is true that the ability of the plants to function without accidents still formed the centerpiece of the debate, also at stake were a host of social, political, moral, and other issues about the regulation and use of technology in a democratic society. As a result, the partisans were engaged in an ideological confrontation concerning the costs, benefits, and impact of nuclear technology in particular and technological change in general. The expansion of issues in this fashion is one of the things that happens when increasing numbers of interest groups from the macropolitical sector become involved in the debate.

Second, our analysis of the hearings shows that even for scientific and technical questions, non-cognitive, evaluative factors cannot be dismissed just because a given technicology can be made to "work." Indeed, may of the ideas, beliefs, and values expressed by ideologies revealed in the hearings reflected non-cognitive or affective factors that clearly transcended the scope of rational analysis: It was not simply scare talk or hysteria that persons or groups *felt* threatened or alienated by high-technology and its centralized regulatory decision-making machinery; or *feared* for their progeny about the kind of society that might evolve because of major political decisions made in the present century. Certainly, Senator Pastore was sincere when he said that he would quit his job if it simply meant devising bigger and

TABLE 7.1
Major Tenets of Pro- and Anti-Nuclear Ideologies at the Hearings

Pro-Nuclear Witnesses	Anti-Nuclear Witnesses
The Peaceful Applications Plank	The Legacy to Future Generations Plank
-The use of nuclear energy promotes the standard of living.	-The use of nuclear energy is morally indefensible.
-The use of nuclear energy increases economic growth.	-The use of nuclear energy will lead to a totalitarian police state.
-The use of nuclear energy promotes fiscal well-being.	-The use of nuclear energy will promote sabotage and diversion, resulting in restrictions of individual freedoms.
-The use of nuclear energy provides unlimited energy.	-The use of nuclear energy will result in proliferation and eventual war.
-The use of nuclear energy will solve the energy crisis.	-Science and technology cannot solve all the problems associated with nuclear energy.
-The use of peaceful nuclear energy will deemphasize military applications.	
Faith in Science and Technology Plank	Anti-Centralization and Political Accountability Plank
-Political and value issues are amenable to scientific and technical solutions.	-Nuclear energy decision-making should be decentralized.
	-Nuclear energy decision-making lacks due process.

-Science and technology can solve all practical problems associated with nuclear energy.

Impeaching the Opposition

-Opposition misrepresents or distorts the facts.

-Opposition uses exaggeration and scare talk.

-Opposition employs personal, *ad hominem* attacks.

-Opposition has no credibility.

-Nuclear regulators should be made more politically responsible.

-Regulatory procedings should be more responsive to citizen groups and public participation expanded.

-Decentralized, low-technology alternatives preferable to nuclear energy.

Impeaching the Opposition

-Opposition distorts and suppresses the facts.

-Opposition employs personal, *ad hominem* attacks.

-Opposition involved in collusion and conspiracy against the public.

-Opposition has no credibility.

better bombs. He remained on the job, he said, because of the *hope* of the atom's service to mankind. Thus, because science and technology cannot tell us *what is important*, we must look to political and ideological conflict as ways of promoting acceptable action, and as a means of pursuing and clarifying our goals.

Finally, the increasingly ideological nature of the nuclear power debate in America suggests that the controversy is not likely to subside easily, for ideologies can neither be "proved" nor "disproved," nor do people let go of them easily. Rather, when issues reach the stage of ideological conflict, the confrontation is likely to deepen and polarize as the sides become more entrenched in their positions. Additional "safety studies," tightening of regulatory standards, construction of more large-scale back-up safety systems, or other technological "fixes" will probably not assuage the conflict in the near future. Instead, what is needed at this stage is the opportunity for directed and sustained political and ideological negotiation and compromise. This will give us an important way to modify and sharpen our values, and thereby allow more informed decision-making on future energy strategies--nuclear or otherwise.

NOTES

1. United States Congress, Hearings before the Joint Committee on Atomic Energy, *The Status of Nuclear Reactor Safety*, 93rd Congress, 1st Session, 1973, Part 1 (Washington, D.C.: U.S. Government Printing Office, 1974).

2. United States Atomic Energy Commission, *The Safety of Nuclear Power Reactors and Related Facilities* (Washington, D.C.: United States Atomic Energy Commission, 1973).

3. United States Congress, Hearings before the Joint Committee on Atomic Energy, *The Status of Nuclear Reactor Safety* 93rd Congress, 2nd Session 1974, Part 2 (Washington, D.C.: U.S. Government Printing Office, 1974), pp. 53-54.

4. It is not our intention to refine the concept "ideology." Rather, we employ a relatively straightforward definition of the term to mean systems of ideas, beliefs, and values which both emotionally steer and cognitively orient individuals and groups of people. As such, ideologies may allow for the rationalization of aggressiveness and prepare for conflict. Because ideologies also legitimize interests, they may channel emotions and thereby also material and human energies and resources. For a good discussion of the concept see the reviews by Edward Shils, "The Concept and Function of Ideology," *International Encyclopedia of the Social Sciences*, V. 7 (New York: MacMillan, 1968), pp. 66-76; Clifford Geertz, "Ideology as a Cultural System," in Geertz, *The Interpretation of Cultures* (New York: Basic Books, 1973), pp. 204-233; and Talcott Parsons, "An Approach to the Sociology of Knowledge," in *Transactions of the Fourth World Congress of Sociology*, IV (Louvain: International Sociological Association, 1959), pp. 25-49.

5. Joint Committee on Atomic Energy, *The Status of Nuclear Reactor Safety*, Part 2, p. 53. Hereinafter, references to these hearings are found in parentheses with page numbers followed by Roman Numerals indicating either Parts 1 or 2.

6. For a summary discussion, see Chapter Two above.

7. William F. Ogburn, "Sociology and the Atom," *American Journal of Sociology* 51 (January

1946): 267-75.

8. F. Gross, "On Peacetime Uses of Atomic Energy," *American Sociological Review* 16 (February 1951): 100-02. See also Leslie A. White, "Energy and the Evolution of Culture," *American Anthropologist* 45 (July-September 1943): 335-56.

9. C. E. Merriam, "On the Agenda of Physics and Politics," *American Journal of Sociology* 53 (November 1947): 167-73.

10. See Public Law 585, "The Atomic Energy Act of 1946," in *United States Statutes at Large, 1946* V. 60, Part 1 (Washington, D.C.: U.S. Government Printing Office, 1947), p. 757. For a related discussion see Byron S. Miller, "A Law is Passed--The Atomic Energy Act of 1946," *University of Chicago Law Review* 15 (Summer 1948): 799 ff.

11. United States Congress, Hearings Before the Special Committee on Atomic Energy, 79th Congress, 2nd Session, 1946, *A Bill for the Development and Control of Atomic Energy* (Washington, D.C. U.S. Government Printing Office, 1946). See also Chapter Two above.

12. Cited in Richard G. Hewlett and Oscar E. Anderson, *The New World, 1939/1946: Volume One of the History of the United States Atomic Energy Commission* (University Park: Pennsylvania State University Press, 1962), p. 482.

13. Cited in Oliver Townsend, American Assembly, "The Atomic Power Program in the United States," in *Atoms for Power: United States Policy in Atomic Energy Development* (New York: American Assembly, 1957), p. 51.

14. See, for example, United States Atomic Energy Commission, *Eighteenth Semi-Annual Report, 1954* Washington, D.C.: U.S. Government Printing Office, 1954). See also Chapters Three and Four above.

15. See Steven L. Del Sesto, *Science, Politics, and the Technical Controversy: The Case of Civilian Nuclear Power in the United States, 1946-1974* (Providence: Unpublished Doctoral Dissertation, Brown University, 1978), pp. 248-303.

16. For a discussion of how impeaching the opposition is tied to ideology, see Shils, "The Concept and Function of Ideology."

17. United States Atomic Energy Commission, *Theoretical Possibilities and Consequences of Major Accidents in Large Nuclear Power Plants*, Wash-740 (Washington, D.C.: U.S. Government Printing Office, 1957).

18. See Dorothy Nelkin and Susan Fallows,

"The Evolution of the Nuclear Debate: The Role of Public Participation," *Annual Reviews of Energy* 3 (1978): 275-312.

19. Allan Mazur, "Opposition to Technological Innovation," *Minerva* 13 (Spring 1975): 68.

20. Louis Harris and Associates for Ebasco Services, Inc., *A Survey of Public and Leadership Attitudes Toward Nuclear Power Development in the United States* (New York: Ebasco Services, 1965).

21. *The Sierra Club and Nuclear Power* (San Francisco: The Sierra Club, 1975), p. 6. See also Barry Commoner, "The Myth of Omnipotence: The Hidden Costs of Nuclear Power," *Environment* 11 (March 1969): 8-13, 26-28.

22. See Nixon's energy message to Congress in the discussion of the breeder controversy found in Chapter Five above. See also John G. Yevick, "Breeder Reactors," in Leonard A. Sagan, (ed.), *Human and Ecologic Effects of Nuclear Power Plants* (Springfield, Illinois Charles C. Thomas, 1974) p. 245.

23. See the review by Philip M. Boffey, "Plutonium: Its Morality Questioned by the National Council of Churches," *Science* 192 (April 23, 1976): 359.

24. Ann Carl, "The Lloyd Harbor Study Group Intervention--A Response," *Bulletin of the Atomic Scientists* 28 (June, 1972): 31-36.

25. A relevant discussion is to be found in Alvin M. Weinberg, "Social Institutions and Nuclear Energy," *Science* 177 (July 7, 1972): 27-34.

26. See Mason Willrich and Theodore Taylor *Nuclear Theft: Risks and Safeguards* (Cambridge, Mass.: Ballinger, 1974).

27. Nelkin and Fallows, "The Evolution of the Nuclear Debate."

28. Steven Ebbin and Raphael Kasper, *Citizen Groups and the Nuclear Power Controversy: The Uses of Scientific and Technological Information* (Cambridge, Mass.: MIT Press, 1974).

29. See E.F. Schumacher, *Small is Beautiful: Economics as if People Mattered* (New York: Harper and Row, 1973).

30. See Friends of the Earth, Friends Committee on National Legislation, "Energy and Nuclear Policy Statement" (Washington, D.C.: Friends of the Earth, 1976).

31. Andrea Entwistel and Steve Raun, "The Good Life and Nuclear Energy" *Yodeler* 38 (1976): 16.

32. Special Committee on Atomic Energy, *A*

Bill for the Development and Control of Atomic Energy, p. 102.

8
Summary and Conclusions

> It seems useful to point out that the nuclear question may only be part of a larger problem of long-term resource management and the management of technology. It is hard to know how we got to this point at this time. Looking back to twenty years ago it seems almost inconceivable that we should have reached the point where the giving up of the nuclear option is a distinct possibility. In part, the opposition to nuclear power appears to be a product of long resentment of arrogance and high-handedness on the part of some members of the nuclear establishment; in part it may be more broadly antiscientific in nature, with nuclear power as the symbol of science in general. Certainly it seems to reflect a disenchantment with the highly touted benefits of technology which many took for granted for so long.
>
> -Arthur W. Murphy

INTRODUCTION

When the hearings on *The Status of Nuclear Reactor Safety* terminated in 1974, the opposition to nuclear energy was here to stay. On the one side, proponents were claiming a victory for the commercialization of nuclear power. In the other camp, meanwhile, critics argued that nuclear power was a threat to human life and the environment and should be halted immediately. This book has attempted to view the process of commercialization accompanied by growing controversy in terms of three broad dimensions or themes: (1) the problems inherent in federal regulation of nuclear power; (2) the limits of the regulatory subsystem's procedures and the gradual entrance of more diverse interest groups (the macropolitical sector) into the political arena; and (3) the shift of the debate from essentially scientific and technical issues to political and ideological questions. At this point, we summarize the main findings of the study in terms of these dimensions.

FEDERAL REGULATION AND THE COMMERCIALIZATION OF NUCLEAR POWER

From the start, federal regulation of nuclear power was unique. Significantly, the basic regulatory machinery, as well as the goals and major policies, of nuclear energy utilization were first set forth in statute by the Atomic Energy Act of 1946. The Act spelled out the prime elements of the atom's regulatory subsystem by creating the Atomic Energy Commission and the Joint Committee on Atomic Energy. The Act also stipulated the AEC and the Joint Committee's responsibilities to develop the peaceful applications of nuclear energy. There was little question that the Act had stated these responsibilities in no uncertain terms; it established a *legal mandate* for developing the peaceful atom, clearly re-emphasized in 1954 with the revision of the Atomic Energy Act. By promulgating these requirements in statute, the United States Government had embarked upon a boldly innovative legislative strategy by setting up regulatory agencies and policies *before* rather than *after* experimental programs were in operation and operating experience had been accumulated.

Moreover, the Atomic Energy Acts set an important requirement on *how* nuclear energy development should proceed. They called for developmental programs to be conducted in terms of the "free enterprise system." The Acts could have retained the war-time policy of nuclear energy development as a strict government monopoly. Yet its framers were convinced that if development could be turned over to private business and industry, as part of civilian control, then perhaps the military uses of nuclear energy could be steadily downplayed. If one adds to this the basic failure of international control, as well as the growing possibility of a terrifying acceleration of the nuclear arms race, the framers of the 1946 Act were under heavy pressure to somehow remove nuclear energy development to the private sector, thereby hoping to mitigate the military emphasis of atomic energy at the same time.

In the meantime, the government's efforts to involve private business and industry in nuclear energy development met with substantial difficulty. Much of this difficulty resulted from the peculiar circumstances of nuclear energy research under the Manhattan Project. The bomb project had erected an entirely new relationship between government and technological innovation, since the highly classified nature of esoteric scientific and technical information required that the government enter into a kind of "partnership" with private industry. There was little question that the government and industry would have to establish some type of sharing, almost symbiotic, relationship to achieve the dictates of the 1946 Act. At the very least, the government would have to provide considerable research and development and financial assistance if it wanted to bring a reluctant industry into the then uncertain nuclear energy business. And this, of course, is exactly what happened with the AEC-sponsored Power Reactor Demonstration Programs of the 1950s and 1960s.

This basic anomoly between government and industry *vis-a-vis* nuclear technology has been a complicating factor ever since. Because the government, which, in the form of the AEC and the Joint Committee, was also the regulator of nuclear energy, critics could easily charge conflict-of-interest with respect to the government-industry partnership. Even though it is not always clear that such conflict-of-interest was necessarily detrimental, it is true that the regulatory agencies involved in such an arrangement came in time to be more closely identified with the regulated activity than with the public they were supposed to serve. This problem is not unique to nuclear energy, but tends to characterize federal regulation of any activity.[1]

Consequently, the government-industry partnership led to a domination of the nuclear energy business in which regulatory strategies tended to become overly promotional. In the process of achieving commercialization, the AEC and the Joint Committee therefore created procedures which left themselves open to charges of lack of external credibility, and of showing undue favoritism to a relatively small interest group who stood to gain a great deal from favorable government actions regulating their businesses. Favoritism charges could easily be leveled at the AEC despite the fact that their procedures had the advantage of efficiency and economy. Thus in their push for commercialization, the AEC and the Joint Committee unwittingly contributed to their own undoing, for with every commercial success the critics were almost lying in wait for their opportunity to charge the regulatory subsystem with a promotional bias.

Yet even if the regulators had been able to overcome the institutional problems created by the partnership between government and industry in the commercialization process, they nevertheless would eventually encounter problems of another sort. That is, it was not as if huge reservoirs of experience and know-how were available for dealing with technological innovations whose effects were as pervasive, wide-spread, and dangerous as those of nuclear energy. By and large, the regulators' chief problem was methodological, particularly the question of how to handle the uncertainties of risks posed by nuclear power.

The problems of uncertainties of risks were heightened from the very beginning by the statutory mandates calling for rapid development. The pressures generated by these mandates led to various attempts to rapidly deploy new applications with less operating experience than is usually available, and in a state of higher uncertainty than otherwise would be permitted. The leapfrog effect spoken of earlier suggested that industry and the utilities hoped to "learn as they went along," as it were. Under these circumstances regulators were left with the thorny problems of deciding how much uncertainty would be acceptable? How would anyone know what this amount should be? Who should bear the burden of proof? How much deficiency should be accepted in available data bases? And how much reliance should be placed on the predictive judgement of experts? Perhaps the most frequent example of this problem which surfaced in the hearings analyzed in the previous chapter concerned the loss-of-fluid accident and subsequent core-meltdown, where huge amounts of lethal radioactivity would almost certainly breech reactor containment. But since the core-meltdown had never occured, no one could say for sure exactly what the effects would be.[2] Underscoring these points of course was the serious reactor accident at Three Mile Island, Pennsylvania in March of 1979. In this accident, utility and government experts had great difficulty controlling a run-away reactor because they did not know what the sequence of events would be. They encountered a host of unforeseen conditions for which no previous data existed, and a near all-out evacuation was almost called for. This accident highlighted the lack of experience and uncertainty related to the operation of nuclear power reactors.

Thus, regulators were faced with a novel problem in estimating the risk parameters of nuclear power in the absence of actuarial data. Without experience, there was basically no way to objectify risk factors, not mention that nuclear power presented *collective* rather than individual risks--something with which regulators had little previous experience.[3]

This situation led to problems of combining separate assessments of empirical gains and risks to develop an overall portrayal of the differential impacts associated with nuclear energy development. Not only did the regulators face substantial difficulties in defining the term "risk" and establishing some basic criteria of measurement and evaluation of such risks, but the "costs" and "benefits," differentially borne by various publics, were largely undefined. The entire matter was grounded in the fact that there were, and are not, any highly developed analytical and theoretical schemes for identifying either social impacts or the indicators of change in which second, third, and even fourth order effects could be identified and measured.[4] What was, and still is, needed is an exhaustive and universally accepted list of indicators, and the working out of more clearly quantifiable relationships between technological applications, impacts, and processes of change.[5] In sum, the conceptual and methodological procedures used by most regulatory agencies, including the now defunct AEC, were not entirely adequate for such complex technologies and left something to be desired.[6] These and other partly unprecedented and unusual methodological problems of assessing nuclear technology, then, have contributed to the profound dilemmas confronting nuclear regulators and should not be underestimated as sources of difficulty in the present controversy.

THE LIMITS OF SUBSYSTEM PROCEDURES AND THE EXPANDING POLITICAL ARENA

A second theme used to help explain the paradox between the so-called successful commercialization of nuclear power and the growing controversy was seen in the limits of the AEC licensing and regulation procedures which contained a strong promotional bias. Focusing on the AEC hearing procedures, Chapter Five demonstrated that public participation in the licensing process was so ritualistic that citizens left the experience with bitter feelings toward the AEC, their procedures, and the safety of nuclear plants. Rather than instilling additional confidence in the nuclear power program, the public hearing resulted in alienation and the augmentation of conflict. Even though a number of difficulties with public participation resulted from its novelty and the fundamental lack of institutionalized guidelines for accomodating such practices within the normal political machinery, other problems existed from the outset and are summarized below.

Schematically, one may present the major components of nuclear energy regulation in summary form by means of Figure 8.1.* In the interest of simplicity, regulatory efforts could occur at any one or more of the three distinct, but overlapping, "stages" of product development. First, regulation could occur at the *conceptualization stage*, whereby an attempt was made to forecast the results of various developments, to determine their likely and unlikely consequences, and to choose among competing policy decisions which set the specific goals and direction of developmental efforts. Second, regulatory activities could occur at the *implementation stage* in which serious cost-benefit analyses of alternative policies could be conducted, where the extent of investment in different product developments could be negotiated, and where contradictory evidence could be ironed out. Finally, regulatory efforts could focus on the *operation stage*. Here, operating experience and system performance could be monitored, and both equipment and facilities could be periodically inspected under actual operating conditions. At this stage, detection of all important positive and negative effects is sought, and regulatory agencies are embued with sufficient authority to correct for any deficiencies or undesired side-effects that come to

*see page 223

light. In addition, the initial policy choices and goals of development could be reexamined, such that the actual, empirical conditions of operation could be compared to previously projected ideals.[7]

Now as Figure 8.1 attempts to show, the regulatory subsystem of nuclear energy had direct input at all three stages, while public groups and additional subsystems ordinarily were more directly involved at the operation stage. The input of public groups at the initial conceptualization and implementation stages, as shown in Figure One, *occured primarily through the regulatory subsystem's own procedures and forums* which were constructed for the smooth and efficient operation of the regulatory subsystem. In other words, at conceptualization and implementation stages regulatory proceedings for nuclear energy, as they stood in 1974, were mainly responsive to the regulatory subsystem and its requirements, and outside input was thus shaped, if not entirely predisposed, by the inherent nature of subsystem proceedings. As a result, the regulatory process was not nearly as pluralistic as it might have been at many crucial decision points, and was almost entirely dominated by the AEC, the Joint Committee on Atomic Energy, and the nuclear power industry.[8] This of course left the status of public participation and political accountability in serious question.

In addition to these points it was argued that the public participation procedures seemed to ignore that many of the issues raised by interveners concerned matters that were primarily non-technical in character. Yet the assumption behind the hearings seemed to be that somehow, with properly designed administrative procedures, scientific "truth" could be achieved. Such an assumption appeared, to use Whitehead's dictum, to "misplace concreteness."[9] That is, the hearings attempted to reduce very complex social and political issues--i.e., whether the costs and risks of nuclear power were worth certain benefits, how much risk should the public tolerate, and whether nuclear power was better than existing alternatives--to scientific and technical problems, assuming the operation of scientific method would eventually arrive at the "best" or "right" interpretation of "the facts." This was even further compounded when it is considered that such procedures appeared to ignore the role of economics and other social sciences in helping to determine the relevant facts and materials on which policy decisions are routinely based. Thus, it was concluded that public participation could never have been effective in view of these facts, and that the very structure of the public hearing promoted rather than relieved conflict.

No doubt realizing the regulatory subsystem's procedures did not allow meaningful input, the early 1960s saw citizen groups shifting to other political arenas, and the subsequent expansion of conflict into what we have termed the macropolitical sector. Throughout the 1960s, additional interest groups, local, state, and national officials, increasing numbers of scientists, and other government agencies entered the controversy. Particularly important was the enactment of the National Environmental Policy Act of 1969, which brought the courts into the controversy and gave interveners the political and legal clout they were lacking. This probably marked the first real step in transcending the limits of the regulatory subsystem's procedures and breaking the closed political loop which represented nuclear energy policy-making in America up to about 1970.

Yet perhaps most important in extending the debate further into the macropolitical sector was the increasing involvement and polarization of scientists. More than ever before, scientists and technical experts began taking sides, each suggesting that his opponents were wrong or operating on the basis of misleading data. This served to consolidate and strengthen pro- and anti-nuclear factions, sway moderates to one side or the other, and whet the interest of individuals and groups that were not previously involved. Indeed, when the experts began to disagree this left the public in a greater state of confusion and uncertainty, resulting in increased political action.

FROM SCIENTIFIC ISSUES TO POLITICAL AND IDEOLOGICAL DEBATE

Finally, as the controversy expanded to include more and more groups from the macropolitical sector, the substantive issues in the debate also tended to expand into other arenas. Scientific and technical questions, formerly the focal point of concern, became rallying points around which additional, non-technical issues could be raised. Starting from such issues as whether the reactors were in fact safe, critics easily moved to questions of whether the government had the legal or moral right to impose nuclear power on the public. Similarly, the proponents started with the same question and moved to advocating the use of nuclear energy as the answer to economic development and the energy crisis. The hearings analyzed in the previous chapter indicate that the nuclear debate has moved in this direction. Each side attempted to legitimize their position by including it within larger ideological systems that provided significance and meaning concerning the place of nuclear energy in particular and technological change in general.

Considering this shift from scientific and technical issues to political and ideological questions, it must be concluded that the nuclear debate is likely to be with us for a long time to come. Although the so-called closed political loop of nuclear energy policy was broken with the dissolution of the AEC and the Joint Committee on Atomic Energy in 1974 and 1977, respectively, additional conflict resolution will result only by further opening the nuclear question to significant and widespread political debate at all levels of government. Local, state, and national policymakers will have to participate, and the national commitment to civilian nuclear power will have to be reconsidered to account for the changing political climate and attitudes of the American people in both the near and long-term future. Very possibly, the nuclear program might even have to be phased out altogether or severely curtailed from the optimistic projections of only a few years ago.[10] In any case, it will be for the people who must live with nuclear energy, influencing policy through normal political channels, to make the ultimate decision on what should be done with nuclear energy in the years ahead. It is no longer acceptable that these decisions will be made by a relatively small scientific-technical-political elite which has formed the regulatory subsystem of the atom and devised nuclear policy for years. In an immediate sense, this seems to be the central message of the nuclear power controversy in the United States in the late 1970s.

Yet on a more general level, the nuclear controversy reminds us that while society cannot cease to demand scientific knowledge of the highest possible objectivity and empirical accuracy, it is another matter altogether to allow the application of such knowledge--by means of technological imperatives--to predispose or direct fundamental policy choices that affect different groups in society in different ways. Indeed, the very point of the nuclear debate is whether technology in the end will serve mankind, or mankind will serve technology.

FIGURE 8.1

The Regulation of Nuclear Energy

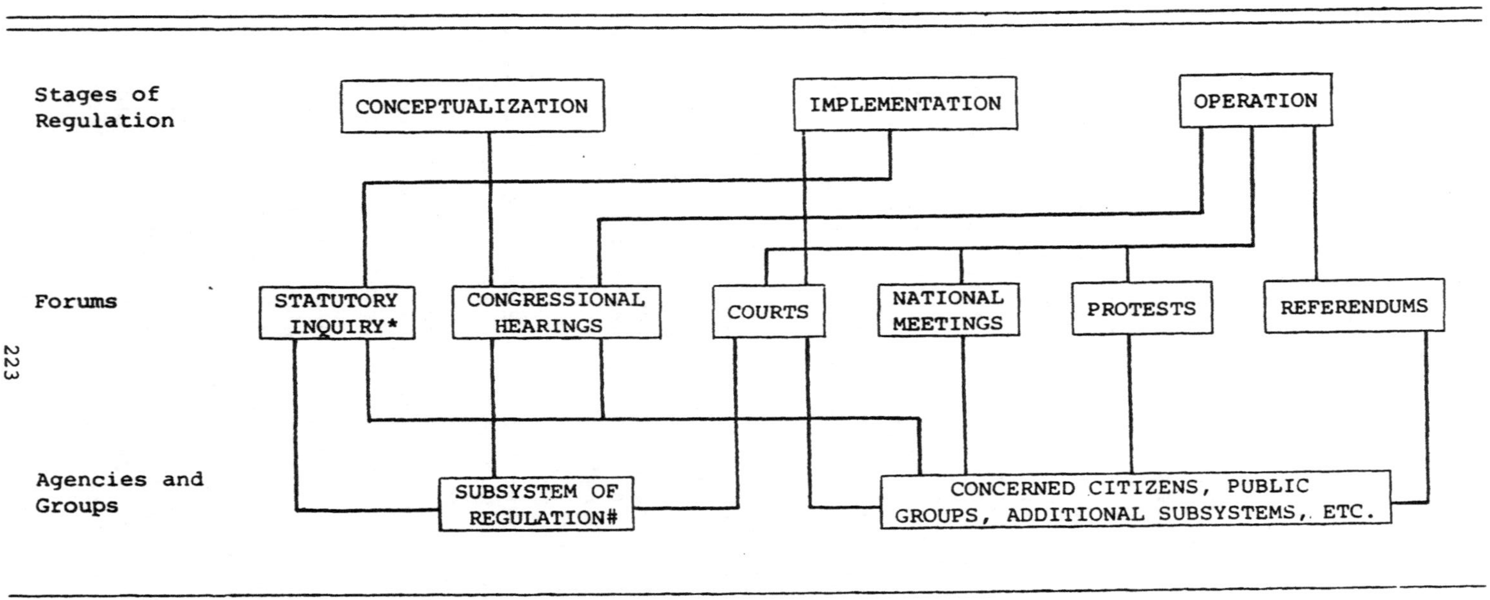

*Construction Permit Hearing and Operating License Hearing.

#The Atomic Energy Commission, the Joint Committee on Atomic Energy, and the nuclear power industry.

NOTES

1. See Marver Bernstein, *Regulating Business by Independent Commission* (Princeton: Princeton University Press, 1955); Henry J. Friendly, *The Federal Administrative Agencies* (Cambridge, Mass.: Harvard University Press, 1962); Allyn D. Strickland, *Regulation: A Case Approach* (New York: McGraw-Hill, 1976); and William G. Shepard and Thomas G. Gies (eds.), *Regulation in Further Perspective* (Cambridge, Mass.: Ballinger, 1974).

2. For a good discussion of the problems posed by these and other related issues, see Joel Primack (ed.), "Nuclear Reactor Safety," *Bulletin of the Atomic Scientists* 31 (September 1975): 15-41.

3. Louis Slesin, "Nuclear Power as a Low Probability Catastrophe," *Issues: The Brown Review* 7 (December 1976): 9.

4. Mark A. Shields, "Social Impact Assessment: An Expository Analysis," *Environment and Behavior* 7 (September 1975):280-82; R. P. Mack, "Criteria for Evaluation of Social Impacts of Flood Management Alternatives," in C. P. Wolf (ed.), *Social Impact Assessment* (Milwaukee: Environmental Design Research Association, 1974), pp. 175-95; and Louis H. Mayo, "Contextual Approach to Technology Assessment: Implications for 'One Factor Fix' Solutions to Complex Social Problems," in Program of Policy Studies in Science and Technology, *Readings in Technology Assessment* (Washington, D.C.: The George Washington University, 1975), p. 15.

5. Vary T. Coates, "Technology and Public Policy: The Process of Technology Assessment in the Federal Government," in Program of Policy Studies in Science and Technology, *Readings in Technology Assessment*, p. 10.

6. National Academy of Sciences, *Technology: Processes of Assessment and Choice* (Washington, D.C.: U.S. Government Printing Office, 1969), pp. 43 ff.

7. For a related discussion, see Council for Science and Society, *Superstar Technologies: The Problem of Monitoring Technologies in those Instances where Technical Competence is Monopolized by a Small Number of Institutions Committed to the Same Interest* (London: Barry Rose, Ltd., 1976).

8. See Coates, "Technology and Public Policy," pp. 42-44; and National Academy of Sciences, *Technology: Processes of Assessment and*

Choice, pp. 123-35.

9. Alfred N. Whitehead, *Science and the Modern World* (New York: MacMillan, 1946).

10. It should be pointed out that even if the nuclear program in America was halted completely, the nuclear debate would not suddenly vanish. To be sure, many of the problems of the nuclear fuel cycle, exclusive of power generation, would still have to be solved, and it is not at all clear that the conflict over what are acceptable solutions would be insignificant. I am indebted to Michael Pollak for suggesting this point to me.

Bibliography

Adelman, Morris A. "Is the Oil Shortage Real?" *Foreign Policy* 9 (Winter 1972-73): 69-107.
Adelman, Morris A. *The World Petroleum Market.* Baltimore: Johns Hopkins University Press, 1972.
Allardice, Corbin and Edward R. Trapnell. *The Atomic Energy Commission* New York: Praeger Publishers 1974 .
Allen, Wendy. *Nuclear Reactors for Generating Electricity: U.S. Development From 1946 to 1963*, Rand Report R-2116-NSF Santa Monica, Calif.: Rand Corporation, 1977 .
American Assembly, *Atoms for Power: United States Policy in Atomic Energy Development.* New York: American Assembly, 1957 .
Anderson, Clinton P. "The Atom--Everybody's Business or Nobody's Business?" *State Government* 29 (December 1956): 243-47.
Benveniste, Guy. *The Politics of Expertise* Berkeley: Glendessary Press, 1972.
Berstein, Marver. *Regulating Business by Independent Commission* Princeton: Princeton University Press, 1955.
Blair, John M. *The Control of Oil.* New York: Pantheon, 1976.
Boffey, Philip M. "Ernest J. Sternglass: Controversial Prophet of Doom," *Science* 166 (October 10, 1969): 195-200.
Boffey, Philip M. "Plutonium: Its Morality Questioned by the National Council of Churches," *Science* 192 (April 23, 1976): 356-59.
Boffey, Philip M. "Radioactive Pollution: Minnesota Finds AEC Standards Too Lax," *Science* 163 (March 7, 1969): 1043-44.
Bupp, Irvin C. and Jean-Claude Derian, *Light Water: How the Nuclear Dream Dissolved.* New York: Basic Books, 1978.
Capron, Willaim G. (ed.). *Technological Change in Regulated Industries.* Washington, D.C.: The Brookings Institution, 1971.
Carl, Ann. "The Lloyd Harbor Study Group Intervention--A Response," *Bulletin of The Atomic Scientists* 28 (June 1972): 31-36.
Clark, Ian D. "Expert Advice in the Controversy About Supersonic Transport in the United States" *Minerva* 12 (October 1974): 416-32.
Coates, Vary T. "Technology and Public Policy: The Process of Technology Assessment in the Federal Government," in Program of Policy

Sciences in Science and Technology, *Readings in Technology Assessment*. Washington, D.C.: The George Washington University, 1975.

Council for Science and Society. *Superstar Technologies: The Problem of Monitoring Technologies in Those Instances Where Technical Competence is Monopolized by a Small Number of Institutions Committed to the Same Interest*. London: Barry Rose, Ltd., 1976.

"Cooling it in Minnesota," *Environment* 11 (May 1969): 21-25.

Commoner, Barry. "The Myth of Omnipotence: The Hidden Costs of Nuclear Power," *Environment* 11 (March 1969): 8-13, 26-28.

Curtis, Richard and Elizabeth Hogan. *Perils of the Peaceful Atom*. Garden City: Doubleday and Company, 1969.

Dawson, Frank G. *Nuclear Power: Development and Management of a Technology*. Seattle: University of Washington Press, 1976.

Dean, Gordon. *Report on the Atom*. New York: Knopf, 1953.

Del Sesto, Steven L. *Science, Politics, and the Technical Controversy: The Case of Civilian Nuclear Power in The United States, 1946-1974*. Providence: Unpublished Doctoral Dissertation, Brown University, 1978.

Doty, Paul A. "Can Investigations Improve Scientific Advice? The Case of the ABM," *Minerva* 10 (April 1972): 280-94.

Eads, George and Richard R. Nelson, "Governmental Support of Advanced Civilian Technology: Power Reactors and the Supersonic Transport," *Public Policy* 19 (Summer 1971): 405-27.

Ebbin, Steven and Raphael Kasper. *Citizen Groups and The Nuclear Power Controversy: Uses of Scientific and Technological Information*. Cambridge, Mass.: MIT Press, 1974.

Einstein, Albert. "The Einstein Letter," in Morton Grodzins and Eugene Rabinowitz (eds.), *Scientists in National and World Affairs*. New York: Basic Books, 1963.

Entwistel, Andrea and Steve Raun. "The Good Life and Nuclear Energy," *Yodeler* 38 (1976): 6-10.

Forbes, Ian A., Daniel F. Ford, Henry W. Kendall, and John J. MacKenzie, "Nuclear Reactor Safety: An Evaluation of New Evidence," *Nuclear News* 9 (September 1971): 32-40.

Ford, Daniel F. and Henry W. Kendall. "Nuclear Misinformation," *Environment* 17 (July-August 1975): 17-20, 25-27.

Ford, Daniel F., Henry W. Kendall, and John J. MacKenzie. "A Critique of the AEC's Interim Criteria for Emergency Core-Cooling Systems," *Nuclear News* 15 (January 1972): 28-35.

Freeman, J. Leiper. *The Political Process: Executive-Bureau-Legislative Committee Relations* New York: Doubleday, 1955.

Friendly, Henry. *The Federal Administrative Agencies*. Cambridge, Mass.: Harvard University Press, 1962.

Friends of the Earth, Friends Committee on National Legislation, "Energy and Nuclear Policy Statement." Washington, D.C.: Friends of the Earth, 1976.

Geertz, Clifford. *The Interpretation of Cultures*. New York: Basic Books, 1973. Especially "Ideology as a Cultural System."

General Electric Company, *1966 Annual Report*. New York: General Electric Company, 1967.

Gillette, Robert. "Nuclear Safety (I): The Roots of Dissent," *Science* 177 (September 1, 1972): 771-76.

Gillette, Robert. "Nuclear Safety (II): The Years of Delay," *Science* 177 (September 8, 1972): 867-71.

Gillette, Robert. "Nuclear Safety (III): Critics Charge Conflict of Interest," *Science* 177 (September 15, 1972): 970-75.

Gofman, John W. "Time for a Moratorium," in *The Case For a Nuclear Moratorium*. Washington, D.C.: Environmental Foundation, 1972.

Gofman, John W. and Arthur R. Tamplin. *Poisoned Power*. Emmanus, Pa.: Rodale Press, 1971.

Goodman, Leo. "Atomic Science Fatalities," Report Prepared for Energy and National Resources, United Automobile Workers, 1968.

Gordzins Morton and Eugene Rabinwitz (eds.). *Scientists in National and World Affairs*. New York: Basic Books, 1963.

Green, Harold P. "Nuclear Power Licensing and Regulation," *The Annals* 400 (March 1972): 116-26.

Green, Harold P. "Nuclear Safety and the Public Interest," *Nuclear News* 15 (September 1972): 75-78.

Green, Harold P. "Nuclear Technology and the Fabric of Government," *The George Washington Law Review* 33 (October 1964): 121-61.

Green, Harold P. "'Reasonable Assurance' of 'No Undue Risk'," *Scientist and Citizen* 10 (June-July 1968): 128-40.

Green, Harold P. "The Risk-Benefit Calculus in Nuclear Power Licensing," in Harry Foreman (ed.), *Nuclear Power and the Public*. Minneapolis: University of Minnesota Press, 1970.
Green, Harold P. "The Risk-Benefit Calculus in Safety Determinations," *The George Washington Law Review* 43 (March 1975): 791-807.
Green, Harold P. "Safety Determinations in Nuclear Power Licensing: A Critical View," *Notre Dame Lawyer* 43 (March 1968): 633-56.
Green, Harold P. "The Strange Case of Nuclear Power," *Federal Bar Journal* 17 (April-June 1957): 100-28.
Green, Harold P. and Alan Rosenthal. *Government of The Atom: The Integration of Powers*. New York: Atherton Press, 1963.
Green, Harold P. and Alan Rosenthal, *The Joint Committee on Atomic Energy: A Study in the Fusion of Government Power*. Washington, D.C.: George Washington University, 1961.
Gross, F. "On the Peacetime Uses of Atomic Energy," *American Sociological Review* 16 (February 1951) 100-02.
Groves, Leslie R. *Now It Can Be Told: The Story of The Manhattan Project*. New York: Harper and Brothers, 1962.
Hafstad, Lawrence R. "Reactor Program of the AEC," *Bulletin of the Atomic Scientists* 7 (April 1951): 109-14.
Harris, Louis and Associates for Ebasco Services, Inc., *A Survey of Public and Leadership Attitudes Toward Nuclear Power Development in The United States*. New York: Ebasco Services, Inc., 1965.
Hayes, Denis. *Nuclear Power: The Fifth Horseman* Washington, D.C.: World Watch Institute, 1976.
Hedgepath, Joel W. "Bodega Head--A Partisan View," *Bulletin of the Atomic Scientists* 21 (March 1965): 2-7.
Heinmann, Fritz F. "How Can We Get the Nuclear Job Done?" in Arthur W. Murphy (ed.), *The Nuclear Power Controversy*. Englewood Cliffs: Prentice-Hall, 1976.
Hewlett, Richard G. and Oscar E. Anderson, Jr. *The New World, 1939/1946: Volume One of The History of The United States Atomic Energy Commission*. University Park: Pennsylvania State University Press, 1962.
Hewlett, Richard G. and Francis Duncan. *Atomic Shield, 1947/1952: Volume Two of The History of The United States Atomic Energy Commission.*

University Park: Pennsylvania State University, 1969.
Hewlett, Richard G. and Francis Duncan. *Nuclear Navy, 1946-1962.* Chicago: University of Chicago Press, 1974.
Hogerton, John F. "The Arrival of Nuclear Power," *Scientific American* 218 (February 1968): 21-31.
Holden, Constance. "Nuclear Waste: Kansans Riled by AEC Plans for Atom Dump," *Science* 172 (April 16, 1971): 249-50.
Holdren, John and Phillip Herrara. *Energy.* San Francisco: Sierra Club, 1971.
Holifield, Chet. "Who Should Judge the Atom?" *Saturday Review,* August 3, 1957.
Huntington, Samuel P. "The Maramus of the ICC: The Commission, The Railroads, and the Public Interest," *Yale Law Journal* 62 (December 1952): 171-225.
Keating, Thomas W. "Politics, Energy, and the Environment: The Role of Technology Assessment," *American Behavioral Scientist* 19 (September-October 1975): 37-74.
Kingsley, Sidney G. "The Licensing of Nuclear Power Reactors in the United States," *Atomic Energy Law Journal* 7 (Fall 1965): 309-52.
Knowles, Ruth Sheldon. *America's Oil Famine.* New York: Coward, McCann, and Geoghegan, 1975.
Lambright, W. Henry. *Governing Science and Technology.* New York: Oxford University Press, 1976.
Lambright, W. Henry. *Shooting Down the Nuclear Plane.* Indianapolis: Bobbs-Merrill, 1967.
Lawrence, Samuel A. *The Battery Additive Controversy.* Montgomery, Alabama: University of Alabama Press, 1962.
Lewis, Richard S. *The Nuclear Power Rebellion: Citizens vs. The Atomic Industrial Establishment.* New York: Viking Press, 1972.
Lewis, Richard S. "The Radioactive Saltmine." *Bulletin of The Atomic Scientists* 27 (June 1971): 27-34.
Like, I. "Multi-Media Confrontation--The Environmentalists' Strategy for a 'No-Win' Agency Proceeding," in United States Congress, Hearings before the Joint Committee on Atomic Energy, *AEC Licensing Procedure and Related Legislation,* 92nd Congress, 1st Session, 1971. Washington, D.C.: U.S. Government Printing Office, 1972.
Lilienthal, David. "Free the Atom," *Collier's* 125 (June 1950): 13-15, 54-58.

Lilienthal, David. "Private Industry and the Public Atom," *Bulletin of the Atomic Scientists* 5 (January 1949): 6-8.
Little, Arthur D., Inc. *Competition in the Nuclear Power Supply Industry*. Report to the United States Atomic Energy Commission and the United States Department of Justice. Washington, D.C.: U.S. Government Printing Office, 1968.
Lowrance, William W. *Of Acceptable Risk: Science and The Determination of Safety*. Los Altos, Calif.: William Kaufmann, 1976.
Mack, R.P. "Criteria for Evaluation of Social Impacts of Flood Management Alternatives," in C.P. Wolf (ed.). *Social Impact Assessment*. Milwaukee: Environmental Design and Research Association, 1974.
Mayo, Louis H. "Contextual Approach to Technology Assessment: Implications for 'One Factor Fix' Solutions to Complex Social Problems," in Program of Policy Studies in Science and Technology, *Readings in Technology Assessment* Washington, D.C.: The George Washington University, 1975.
Mazur, Allan. "Disputes Between Experts," *Minerva* 11 (April 1973): 243-62.
Mazur, Allan. "Opposition to Technological Innovation," *Minerva* 13 (Spring 1975): 58-81.
McKinney, Robert. "Impact of the Peaceful Uses of Atomic Energy," *State Government* 29 (December 1956): 248-52.
Merriam, C.E. "On the Agenda of Physics and Politics," *American Journal of Sociology* 53 (November 1947): 167-73.
Metzger, H. Peter. *The Atomic Establishment*. New York: Simon and Schuster, 1972.
Miller, Byron S. "A Law is Passed--The Atomic Energy Act of 1946," *University of Chicago Law Review* 15 (Summer 1948): 799-821.
Mullenbach, Phillip. *Civilian Nuclear Power*. New York: The Twentieth Century Fund, 1963.
Murphy, Arthur W. "Atomic Safety and Licensing Boards: An Experiment in Administrative Decision Making on Safety Questions." *Law and Contemporary Problems* 33 (Summer 1968): 566-89.
Murphy, Arthur W. "Nuclear Power Plant Regulation," in Arthur W. Murphy (ed.), *The Nuclear Power Controversy*. Englewood Cliffs: Prentice-Hall, 1976.
Murphy, Arthur W. (ed.). *The Nuclear Power Controversy*. Englewood Cliffs: Prentice-Hall 1976.

Nader, Claire, M. *American Natural Scientists In The Policy Process: Three Atomic Energy Issues and Their Foreign Policy Implications.* New York: Unpublished Doctoral Dissertation, Columbia University, 1964.

National Academy of Sciences. *Technology: Processes of Assessment and Choice.* Washington D.C.: U.S. Government Printing Office, 1969.

National Academy of Sciences--National Research Council, Publication No. 519. *The Disposal of Radioactive Waste On Land.* Washington, D.C.: National Academy of Sciences--National Research Council, 1957.

Nehrt, Lee C. *International Marketing of Nuclear Power Plants.* Bloomington: Indiana University Press, 1966.

Nelkin, Dorothy. "The Political Impact of Technical Expertise," *Social Studies of Science* 5 (January 1975): 34-54.

Nelkin, Dorothy and Susan Fallows. "The Evolution of the Nuclear Debate: The Role of Public Participation," *Annual Reviews of Energy* 3 (1978): 275-312.

Newman, James R. "The Atomic Energy Industry," *Yale Law Journal* 60 (December 1951): 1263-1394.

Newman, James R. and Byron S. Miller. *The Control of Atomic Energy; A Study of Its Social, Economic, and Political Implications.* New York: McGraw-Hill, 1948.

Niehoff, Richard O. "Organization and Administration of the United States Atomic Energy Commission," *Public Administration Review* 8 (Spring 1948): 91-102.

Niss, James F. and M. T. Pledge (eds.). *Competition in Regulated Industries: Essays on Economic Issues.* Macomb, Illinois: Center for Business and Economic Research, Western Illinois University, 1975.

Nucleonics Week, October 18, 1971.

Novick, Sheldon. *The Careless Atom.* Boston: Houghton-Mifflin Co., 1969.

Ogburn, William F. "Sociology and the Atom." *American Journal of Sociology* 51 (January 1946): 267-75.

Oppenheimer, J. Robert. "International Control of Atomic Energy," in Morton Gordzins and Eugene Rabinowitz (eds.), *Scientists in National and World Affairs.* New York: Basic Books, 1963.

Orlans, Harold. *Contracting For Atoms.* Washington, D.C.: The Brookings Institution, 1967.

Palfrey, John Gorham. "Atomic Energy: A New Experiment in Government-Industry Relations," *Columbia Law Review* 56 (March 1956): 367-92.
Parsons, Talcott. "An Approach to the Sociology of Knowledge," in *Transactions of the Fourth World Congress of Sociology, IV*. Louvain: International Sociological Association, 1959.
Perry, Robert, et.al. *Development and Commercialization of the Light Water Reactor, 1946-1976*. Rand Report R-2180-NSF. Santa Monica, Calif.: Rand Corporation, 1977.
President's Office of Science and Technology, *Report on Considerations Affecting Steam Power Plant Site Selection*. Washington, D.C.: U.S. Government Printing Office, 1968.
Primack, Joel (ed.). "Nuclear Reactor Safety," *Bulletin of The Atomic Scientists* 31 (September 1975): 15-41.
Primack, Joel and Frank von Hippel. *Advice and Dissent: Scientists in The Political Arena*. New York: Basic Books, 1974.
Program of Policy Studies in Science and Technology, *Readings in Technology Assessment*. Washington D.C.: The George Washington University, 1975.
Public Law 585. "The Atomic Energy Act of 1946," in *United States Statutes At Large 1946*, V. 60, Part 1. Washington, D.C.: U.S. Government Printing Office, 1947.
Public Law 703. "The Atomic Energy Act of 1954," *United States Statutes at Large 1954*, V. 68, Part 1. Washington, D.C.: U.S. Government Printing Office, 1955.
Public Law 85-256. "An Amendment to the Atomic Energy Act of 1954," in *United States Statutes At Large 1957*, V. 77. Washington,D.C.: U.S. Government Printing Office, 1958.
Public Law 87-615. "An Act to Amend the Atomic Energy Act of 1954," in *United States Statutes At Large 1962*, V. 76. Washington, D.C.: U.S. Government Printing Office, 1963.
Public Law 89-210. "An Act to Amend the Atomic Energy Act of 1954," in *United States Statutes At Large 1965*, V. 79. Washington, D.C.: U.S. Government Printing Office, 1966.
Public Law 91-190. "National Environmental Policy Act of 1969," in *United States Statutes At Large 1969*, V. 82. Washington, D.C.: U.S. Government Printing Office, 1970.
Redford, Emmette S. *Democracy and The Administrative State*. New York: Oxford University Press, 1969.

"Report of the AEC Industrial Advisory Group." *Bulletin of The Atomic Scientists* 5 (February 1949): 51-55.
Ridenour, Louis. "Pilot Lights of the Apocalypse," in Morton Gordzins and Eugene Rabinowitz (eds.), *Scientists in National and World Affairs*. New York: Basic Books, 1963.
Rolph, Elizabeth. *Regulation of Nuclear Power: The Case of The Light Water Reactor*. Rand Report R-2104-NSF. Santa Monica, Calif.: Rand Corporation, 1977.
Sagan, Leonard A. (ed.). *Human and Ecologic Effects of Nuclear Power Plants*. Springfield, Illinois: Charles C. Thomas, 1974.
Sailor, Vance L. "The Role of the Lloyd Harbor Study Group in the Shoreham Hearings," *Bulletin of The Atomic Scientists* 28 (June 1972): 25-31.
Saint-Amand, Pierre. "Geological and Seismic Study of Bodega Head,"Northern California Association to Preserve Bodega Head and Harbor, 1963.
Salomon, Leon I. (ed.). *The Independent Federal Regulatory Agencies*. New York: H. Wilson Co., 1959.
Schumacher, E.F. *Small Is Beautiful: Economics As If People Mattered*. New York: Harper and Row, 1973.
"Scientists Question Reactor Effects: A Study of the Monticello Generating Plant in Minnesota," *Scientist and Citizen* 10 (August 1968): 154-57.
Seaborg, Glenn T. Letter to President Kennedy, November 20, 1962. Reprinted in United States Atomic Energy Commission, *Civilian Nuclear Power A Report To The President--1962*. Washington, D.C.: U.S. Government Printing Office, 1962.
Seaborg, Glenn T. and Justin L. Bloom. "Fast Breeder Reactors," *Scientific American* 223 (November 1970): 13-21.
Shepard, William G. and Thomas G. Gies (eds.). *Regulation in Further Perspective*. Cambridge, Mass.: Ballinger, 1974.
Shields, Mark A. "Social Impact Studies: An Expository Analysis," *Environment and Behavior* 7 (September 1975): 280-82.
Shils, Edward. "The Concept and Function of Ideology." *International Encyclopedia of The Social Sciences*, V. 7. New York: MacMillan, 1968.
The Sierra Club and Nuclear Power. San Francisco: The Sierra Club, 1975.

Slesin, Louis. "Nuclear Power as a Low Probability Catastrophe," *Issues: The Brown Review* 7 (December 1976): 7-9.
Smith, Alice Kimball. *A Peril and A Hope.* Chicago: University of Chicago Press, 1965.
Smith, L.D. "Evolution of Opposition to the Peaceful Uses of Nuclear Energy," *Nuclear Engineering International* 17 (June 1972): 461-68.
Smyth, Henry D. *Atomic Energy For Military Purposes: The Official Report on The Development of the Atomic Bomb Under the Auspices of The United States Government, 1940-1945.* Princeton: Princeton University Press, 1945.
Speth, Gustave B., Arthur R. Tamplin, and Thomas B. Cochran. "Plutonium Recycle: The Fateful Step," *Bulletin of The Atomic Scientists* 30 (November 1974): 15-22.
Steiner, Arthur. "Scientists, Statesman, and Politicians: The Compelling Influences on American Atomic Energy Policy, 1945-1946." *Minerva* 12 (October 1974): 469-509.
Strickland, Allyn D. *Regulation: A Case Approach.* New York: McGraw-Hill, 1976.
Strickland, Donald. *Scientists In Politics.* Lafayette: Purdue University Press, 1968.
The Case For A Nuclear Moratorium. Washington, D.C.: Environmental Foundation, 1972.
"The Great Breeder Dispute." *Time* 98 (November 1, 1971): 102.
"The Jersey Central Report." *Atomic Industrial Forum Memo* 11 (March 1964): 3.
Thomas, Morgan. *Atomic Energy and Congress.* Ann Arbor: University of Michigan Press, 1956.
Townsend, Oliver. "The Atomic Power Program in the United States," in American Assembly, *Atoms For Power: United States Policy In Atomic Energy Development.* New York: American Assembly, 1957.
United States Atomic Energy Commission. *AEC Considers Amendments To Regulations and Revised Policy Statement on Reactor Licensing Procedures.* Washington, D.C.: U.S. Government Printing Office, 1967.
United States Atomic Energy Commission. *Annual Report To Congress 1960.* Washington, D.C.: U.S. Government Printing Office, 1961.
United States Atomic Energy Commission. *Annual Report To Congress 1961.* Washington, D.C.: U.S. Government Printing Office, 1962.

United States Atomic Energy Commission. *Annual Report To Congress 1963.* Washington, D.C.: U.S. Government Printing Office, 1964.
United States Atomic Energy Commission. *Annual Report To Congress 1965.* Washington, D.C.: U.S. Government Printing Office, 1966.
United States Atomic Energy Commission. *Annual Report to Congress 1968.* Washington, D.C.: U.S. Government Printing Office, 1969.
United States Atomic Energy Commission. *Annual Report To Congress 1972-1974.* Washington, D.C.: U.S. Government Printing Office, 1975.
United States Atomic Energy Commission. *Civilian Nuclear Power: A Report To The President--1962.* Washington, D.C.: U.S. Government Printing Office, 1962.
United States Atomic Energy Commission. *Civilian Nuclear Power: The 1967 Supplement To The 1962 Report To The President.* Washington, D.C.: U.S. Government Printing Office, 1967.
United States Atomic Energy Commission. *Civilian Power Reactor Program, Part IV, 1959.* Washington, D.C.: U.S. Government Printing Office, 1959.
United States Atomic Energy Commission, Directorate of Regulatory Standards. *Guide To The Preparation of Environmental Reports For Nuclear Power Plants 1972.* Washington, D.C.: U.S. Government Printing Office, 1972.
United States Atomic Energy Commission, Division of Operational Safety. *Operational Accidents and Radiation Experience Within The United Staes Atomic Energy Commission, 1943-1967.* Washington D.C.: United States Atomic Energy Commission, 1968.
United States Atomic Energy Commission. *Eighteenth Semi-Annual Report 1954.* Washington, D.C.: U.S. Government Printing Office, 1954.
United States Atomic Energy Commission. *Major Activities In The Atomic Energy Programs, January-June 1953.* Washington, D.C.: U.S. Government Printing Office, 1953.
United States Atomic Energy Commission. *Major Activities In The Atomic Energy Programs, January-December 1961.* Washington, D.C.: U.S. Government Printing Office, 1962.
United States Atomic Energy Commission. *Major Activities In The Atomic Energy Programs, January-December 1962.* Washington, D.C.: U.S. Government Printing Office, 1963.
United States Atomic Energy Commission. *Research On Power From Fusion and Other Major Activities*

In The Atomic Energy Programs, January-June 1958. Washington, D.C.: U.S. Government Printing Office, 1958.
United States Atomic Energy Commission. *Semi-Annual Report To Congress, July-December 1946.* Washington, D.C.: U.S. Government Printing Office, 1947.
United States Atomic Energy Commission. *Semi-Annual Report To Congress, July-December 1948.* Washington, D.C.: U.S. Government Printing Office, 1949.
United States Atomic Energy Commission. *Semi-Annual Report To Congress, July-December 1952.* Washington, D.C.: U.S. Government Printing Office, 1953.
United States Atomic Energy Commission. *Step-By-Step Procedure In Licensing Nuclear Power Reactors.* Washington, D.C.: U.S. Government Printing Office, 1972.
United States Atomic Energy Commission. *Studies In Workmen's Compensation and Radiation Injury, V.5.* Washington, D.C.: United States Atomic Energy Commission, 1969.
United States Atomic Energy Commission. *The Safety of Nuclear Power Reactors and Related Facilities* Washington, D.C.: U.S. Government Printing Office, 1973.
United States Atomic Energy Commission. *Theoretical Possibilities and Consequences of Major Accidents In Large Nuclear Power Plants, Wash-740.* Washington, D.C.: U.S. Government Printing Office, 1958.
United States Atomic Energy Commission, *Twentieth Semi-Annual Report 1956.* Washington, D.C.: U.S. Government Printing Office, 1956.
United States Congress, Hearings before the Joint Committee on Atomic Energy. *AEC Licensing Procedure and Related Legislation.* 92nd Congress, 1st Session, 1971. Washington, D.C.: U.S. Government Printing Office, 1972.
United States Congress, Hearings before the Joint Committee on Atomic Energy. *Atomic Power and Private Enterprise,* 82nd Congress, 2nd Session, 1952. Washington, D.C.: U.S. Government Printing Office, 1952.
United States Congress, Hearings before the Joint Committee on Atomic Energy, *Civilian Atomic Power Acceleration Program,* 84th Congress, 2nd Session, 1956, Parts 1 and 2. Washington, D.C.: U.S. Government Printing Office, 1956.

United States Congress, Hearings before the Joint Committee on Atomic Energy. *Cooperative Power Reactor Demonstration Program, 1963*, 88th Congress, 1st Session, 1963. Washington, D.C.: U.S. Government Printing Office, 1963.

United States Congress, Hearings before the Joint Committee on Atomic Energy, *Development, Growth, and State of The Atomic Energy Industry*, 86th Congress, 1st Session, 1959. Washington, D.C.: U.S. Government Printing Office, 1959.

United States Congress, Hearings before the Joint Committee on Atomic Energy. *Licensing and Regulation of Nuclear Reactors*, 90th Congress, 1st Session, 1967. Washington, D.C.: U.S. Government Printing Office, 1967.

United States Congress, Hearings before the Joint Committee on Atomic Energy, *Nuclear Power Economics 1962 Through 1967*, 90th Congress, 2nd Session, 1968. Washington, D.C.: U.S. Government Printing Office, 1968.

United States Congress, Hearings before the Joint Committee on Atomic Energy, *Nuclear Power Plant Siting and Licensing*, 93rd Congress, 2nd Session, 1974. Washington, D.C.: U.S. Government Printing Office, 1974.

United States Congress, Hearings before the Joint Committee on Atomic Energy, *Private Ownership of Special Nuclear Materials*, 88th Congress, 1st Session, 1963. Washington, D.C.: U.S. Government Printing Office, 1964.

United States Congress, Hearings before the Joint Committee on Atomic Energy, *Report of The Panel on The Impact of The Peaceful Uses Of Atomic Energy*, 84th Congress, 2nd Session, 1956, V.1 Washington, D.C.: U.S. Government Printing Office.

United States Congress, Hearings before the Joint Committee on Atomic Energy, *The Status Of Nuclear Reactor Safety* 93rd Congress, 1st Session, 1973. Washington, D.C.: U.S. Government Printing Office, 1974.

United States Congress, Hearings before the Joint Committee on Atomic Energy, *The Status Of Nuclear Reactor Safety*, 93rd Congress, 2nd Session, 1974. Washington, D.C.: U.S. Government Printing Office, 1974.

United States Congress, Hearings before the Special Committee on Atomic Energy, *A Bill For The Development and Control of Atomic Energy*, 79th Congress, 2nd Session, 1946. Washington, D.C.: U.S. Government Printing Office, 1947.

United States Congress, House, *The Congressional Record*, 88th Congress, 2nd Session, 1964. Washington, D.C.: U.S. Government Printing Office, 1964.
United States Congress, House of Representatives, *Legislative History of The Atomic Energy Act of 1954*, 83rd Congress, 2nd Session, 1954, House Document No. 328. Washington, D.C.: U.S. Government Printing Office, 1954.
United States Congress, Joint Committee on Atomic Energy, *A Study of AEC Licensing Procedures and Organization in Licensing Reactor Facilities*, 85th Congress, 1st Session, 1957. Washington, D.C.: U.S. Government Printing Office, 1957.
United States Congress, Joint Committee on Atomic Energy, *Current Membership of The Joint Committee on Atomic Energy*, 92nd Congress, 2nd Session, 1973. Washington, D.C.: U.S. Printing Office, Joint Committee Print, 1973.
United States Congress, Joint Committee on Atomic Energy, *Five-Year Power Reactor Development Program Proposed By The Atomic Energy Commission*, Joint Committee Print, March 1954.
Weinberg, Alvin M. "Social Institutions and Nuclear Energy," *Science* 177 (July 7, 1972): 27-34.
Weinberg, Alvin and Gale Young, "The Nuclear Energy Revolution, 1966," *Proceedings Of The National Academy of Sciences* 57 (January 1967): 1-15.
White, Leslie A. "Energy and the Evolution of Culture," *American Anthropologist* 45 (July-September 1943): 335-56.
Whitehead, Alfred North. *Science and The Modern World*. New York: MacMillan, 1946.
Willrich, Mason and Theodore Taylor. *Nuclear Theft: Risks and Safeguards*. Cambridge, Mass.: Ballinger, 1974.
Wolf, C.P. (ed.). *Social Impact Assessment*. Milwaukee: Environmental Design Research Association, 1974.
Yevick, John G. "Breeder Reactors," in Leonard A. Sagan (ed.), *Human and Ecologic Effects of Nuclear Power Plants*. Springfield, Illinois: Charles C. Thomas, 1974.
Zinn, Walter H., Frank K. Pittman, and John F. Hogerton. *Nuclear Power U.S.A.* New York: McGraw-Hill, 1964.

Index

For Product Safety Concerns and Information please contact our EU representative GPSR@taylorandfrancis.com Taylor & Francis Verlag GmbH, Kaufingerstraße 24, 80331 München, Germany

Batch number: 10726013

Printed by Printforce, the Netherlands